1044-6494

Ashlan(

ASHLAND TH

CONTENTS

Journal articles are indexed in *Elenchus of Biblica, New Testament Abstracts, Old Testament Abstracts, Religious and Theological Abstracts,* and *Religion Index One*; reviews are indexed in *Index to Book Reviews in Religion.* The latter two indices, published by ATLA, 820 Church Street, Evanston, Illinois 60201, are also available online through BRS Information Technologies, DIALOG Information Services and Wilsonline. Views of contributors are their own and do not necessarily express those endorsed by Ashland Theological Seminary.

VOLUME XXXIII
Published and copyright held by Ashland Theological Seminary, Ashland, Ohio, 44805.
Printed in the USA.

Editor's Introduction

Humans are a visual creatures. Our eyes are among the main portals for information and stimuli, as both teachers and television producers know. The Bible shows an awareness of the importance of the eye, with the prophets using visual metaphors such as plumb-lines and holes in house walls, and Jesus using visual images such as white fields and shepherdless sheep. We at Ashland Theological Seminary have been visually impacted over the past year, in one case with images of international import, and in another by those which, while more local, will also have international import.

The world was stunned by the stark images of planes deliberately crashing on September 11th. These events left a permanent change on the visible landscape of New York, a scar on our memory of the city. There has also been a significant landscape change at Ashland Theological Seminary, but in this case it is for the good. This fall saw the opening of a beautiful and functional new building which houses both the Sandberg Leadership Center and the Smetzer Counseling Center. The latter will be a place of education but also of healing as students partake in the healing of people from the community who can come to the Center for care. As they enter they will be visually impacted by a statue of Jesus which was crafted by an ATS graduate, Louise Waller. Jesus is seated holding in one hand a newborn baby, with the other hand and arm reaching out, providing a support for any who would care to literally sit in his lap. In this seat, the visitor will see Jesus looking at them with an expression of love as he enfolds them in his lap. This is what the Center hopes to provide, the loving compassion of Christ to those who are wounded and in pain. This mission is spelled out here by the Director of the Midwest Counseling Center.

The Leadership Center has both a local and a global vision to model and teach leadership with integrity to those involved in all spheres of influence. Its Director presents a sample of the activities sponsored by the Center. Much more is planned, and information on both of these centers can be obtained by contacting ATS. While not directly deriving from the Leadership Center, we also include a look at one style of leadership which will face all involved in ministry.

This year has also seen the phenomenal sales of several Christian books. The name of Jabez has become better known than ever before. We present a different perspective on that faithful biblical character. Four other characters are also presented, representing different aspects of ministry, at least one of which will no doubt strike a chord with each of our readers. This chapel talk needs to be heard by all of us as we seek to serve our Lord.

Last but not least, we have books, books, and more books. There are lengthier articles on such things as the current theological controversy of the openness of God- what does he know and when does he know it, as well as recent literature on the prophets and on spiritual formation. With our regular book review section and a new section of shorter book notes, we hope that there are books which will interest everyone.

Baruch hashem hamevorach.
David W. Baker

"Four Friends"
Paul Overland*

Recently I met four friends. They proved remarkably wise. Suggestions they offered were borne out of their experiences in ministry, in the hope that my ministry might be richer. Their advice deeply moved me. Perhaps it will you, as well.

Before proceeding, I must admit that these insights are not my own. They come from someone else's sermon. By now it must be "public domain", since it was first preached in approximately 627 B.C. That places us at the opening days of Jeremiah's ministry, just a bit ahead of the closing days of the Southern kingdom of Israel. Jeremiah will personally witness the demise of Jerusalem in 586 B.C. Listen, then, with both mind and imagination to what may have been Jeremiah's inaugural sermon (Jer. 2.1-9).

1 The word of the Lord came to me: 2 "Go proclaim in the hearing of Jerusalem: 'I remember the devotion of your youth,
At once as these words open to us it is as if someone were leafing thoughtfully through a cherished album. God is the one opening the album - a very personal album. In fact, albums don't come with more deeply-cherished memories than these. Picture scenes from the next leaf.
I remember...how as a bride you loved me and followed me through the desert, through a land not sown.

3 Israel was holy to the Lord, The first fruits of his harvest; All who devoured her were held guilty, And disaster overtook them,'" declares the Lord.
At this point God shuts the album. He has something very, very sobering to say to his people.

4 Hear the word of the Lord, O house of Jacob, all you clans of the house of Israel.

5 This is what the Lord says: "What fault did your fathers find in me, that they strayed so far from me?

Was there a divine pause after this question? Did God wait for a reply? Perhaps so. The people answered nothing. So he went on.

---

* Paul Overland (Ph.D., Brandeis) is Assistant Professor of Old Testament at ATS. This is a slightly edited transcript of an ATS chapel sermon delivered 10/26/01.

They followed worthless idols, And became worthless themselves.

Do not these few words convey an enormous truth? What I follow, that I become, for good or ill.

6 They did not ask, 'Where is the Lord, who brought us up out of Egypt and led us through the barren wilderness, through a land of deserts and rifts, a land of drought and darkness, a land where no one travels and no one lives?'

7 I brought you into a fertile land to eat its fruit and rich produce. But you came and defiled my land And made my inheritance detestable.

Now we meet our four friends.

8 (First) *The priests did not ask, 'Where is the Lord?'*

(Second) *Those who deal with the law did not know me;*

(Third) *The leaders rebelled against me.*

(Finally) *The prophets prophesied by Baal, Following worthless idols.*

9 Therefore I bring charges against you again," declares the Lord. "And I will bring charges against your children's children.

The passage continues to unfold, reading very much like a court case. God probes: "By walking away from our relationship your fathers lodged an implicit complaint against me. Tell me: Was it I who let them down? Did I offend them? Was I an abusive husband? What went wrong?"

A hollow silence echoes in response. Then God proceeds to present His case. "The actual fault," he explains, "is not with me, but with you." That fault confronts us like a banner emblazoned across the courtroom wall: "*They did not ask, 'Where is the Lord...who led us through the barren wilderness, through...a land where no one travels? (v. 6)*'" After arriving in Canaan, Israel should easily have realized that they owed their transit through the severe Sinai Peninsula to nothing less than God's miraculous leadership and provision.

God led them with a towering cloud by day and a column of fire by night. One Jewish commentator suggests that the pillar fundamentally consisted of fire symbolizing God's presence. During the night the fire blazed through a cloud which encased it, a bright contrast against the night sky. During the day, however, sunlight made the fire less obvious and caused the encasing cloud to become more evident. Whether day or night, the fiery pillar reminded them of God's immediate presence. His presence is illuminating. His presence is powerful.

As the Presence moved, the people packed up and moved. But when the Presence stayed, the people stayed. So there was keen connection linking the people with the presence of God as he led them *through the barren wilderness, through...a land where no one travels.*

Some 900 years later in Jeremiah's day, it was a callous insensitivity to this Presence which comprised Israel's fundamental flaw. No one missed God's presence. No one thought to inquire, "Where is the Lord?" And we could, I suppose, stop the lesson there. But Jeremiah keeps preaching.

Beyond this fundamental flaw of failing to inquire after the presence of God, the four friends expose four particular fissures, cracks in the foundation of Israel's spiritual life which led to her eventual downfall. One of them speaks especially to me, for I am very like him. Perhaps one of the four will speak to you.

The first friend to introduce himself to us is a priest. What uniquely characterized the ministry of a priest in the Old Testament? Fundamentally, the priest was charged by God through ceremony to bring men and women into the presence of God. We associate their ministry with ceremony, since they executed prescribed liturgies. They were the ones who knew which sacrifices must be offered for what offenses. They knew when and how much should be burned on the bronze altar, what may be eaten, and that by whom. Festivals were their domain as well--prescribed events recurring with caledrical circularity. So you may think of the priests as men charged by God through ceremony to bring men and women into his presence. For, you see, of anyone they served closest to that place which of all places in the entire cosmos was thought to be *where God resided*-- the Holy of Holies. In addition, one of these priests dared annually to actually enter that space. In the fall of the year, at Yom Kippur, he cautiously crossed the threshold to effect atonement.

Priests were, then, men charged by God through ceremony to bring others into God's very presence. They were charged to clear out roadblocks of sin so that commoners may draw close to God. And so my friend "Kohen", the priest would say to me, "If ever such a ministry is entrusted to me-- if at any point in my ministry, God may entrust me with the privilege of escorting people into his presence, whether it is leading a worship liturgy, a conducting a baptism, or officiating a wedding, then take my advice: do not venture into the service without sincerely inquiring, 'Where is the Lord?'"

What shall I do if in response to that question, I sense that the Lord is not present? Move. Search out where the column of fire has gone, and move after it.

The second friend belongs to those who deal with the law: "Law-handlers". Some versions translate "judge". But in reality, the Hebrew at this point does not use *shophet*, judge, but rather "those who handle the law." "Handle" (*tapas*) is an interesting word. It was used in battle to describe a victor's the control over vanquished peoples. POW's are "handled," captured. Sometimes *tapas* is simply translated "capture". But here it characterizes how the professionals were treating biblical law.

A puppy is the newest member of our family. When go out we attach a leash to her collar-- you might say we are "puppy handlers." We are clearly in control. Or at least that is the illusion she allows us to entertain!

Transfer the leash-and-collar image to "law handlers", and I suspect we will have grasped Jeremiah's point. God's law, his Torah, had become their puppy. They could lead, manipulate it as they wished. They represented the professionals, the law was their subject.

Of the four friends, this "law handler" speaks most clearly to me. I, too, am a law handler by profession. I even have alphabet soup after my name to prove it. So Friend #2 asks me, "Overland, you know so much about the Bible. It reminds me of my back in the 7th century B.C. Don't you make it too. I knew so much about the Torah, but there was a piece of knowledge even more vital, which I overlooked. I did not know God! (v. 8b)."

As I read Jeremiah's words it's rather like a sonic boom echoing within. I'm paid to *know*. However, as I prepare for lecture, the first item which routinely must appear on my checklist is this: to know *God*. Then knowledge about literary structure, authorship, historical background, word studies will take their place. But first know God. So the law handler speaks to me.

The third friend introduces himself as a "leader" (v. 8c). The word back of "leader" is shepherd. Many versions appropriately render it "leader" since it is clear we are not talking about care of animals of the four-legged variety, but the two-legged variety. What distinguishes the leader from the priest and law handler? By the way: all four of these roles are *good roles*. They are God-ordained roles, to be regarded with honor. However, they are susceptible to spiritual diseases, maladies which our friends would inoculate us against.

Back to the shepherd: what distinguishes this role? The shepherd stands out as one charged with caring for other people. More than scrutiny of scripture, more than guiding people into God's presence, the shepherd cares for the daily needs and concerns of a cluster of people. Through a modern lens we may picture administrators, committee chairs, and counselors caring for people and their problems.

So I turn to the 7th century leader and ask, "What can go wrong in the ministry of a shepherd?" His response cuts to the heart of leadership. "I lost

4

sight of the fact that my power over people was an entrustment. I was all the while accountable to an over-shepherd for how I used my power. But instead of standing accountable, I *rebelled* (v. 8c). With the best of intentions I pursued my godly agenda. As my agenda substituted for God's, I continued to pursue it, even though it set me at cross-purposes against God. Don't make that mistake!"

Another fisherman-turned-shepherd put leadership in perspective some 600 years later. He wrote, *Be shepherds of God's flock that is under your care, serving as overseers -- not because you must, but because you are willing, as God wants you to be; not greedy for money, but eager to serve; not lording it over those entrusted to you, but being examples of the flock. And when the Chief Shepherd appears, you will receive the crown of glory that will never fade away* (1 Pet. 5.2-4). So the third friend urges me always to bear in mind that I care for these people *for him*. It is *his agenda*, not mine, I must pursue.

The fourth friend calls himself a prophet. What exactly was a prophet? Among many definitions, each with their merit, it helps me to picture the prophet as a man (and sometimes a woman) who claimed divine authorization as he agitated God's people. They sought to awaken God's people from moral and spiritual slumber, a slumber which if left unattended would lead to destruction. One Jewish writer, Abraham Heschel, observes that had Israel not slumbered, there would have been no need for the prophets. They would have been splendidly unemployed. But, alas, Israel often drifted, so our Bible is rich with their arresting agitations.

If I find myself from time to time entrusted with a message of warning, sent to awaken God's people, I may be able to learn a bit of wisdom from this fourth friend. He warns me, "Beware of becoming so enamored with your message that you failed to check the source. The cause may seem right, but unless you are careful, you will start preaching sermons inspired from a faulted source: too late we discovered that we *prophesied by Baal* and were *following worthless idols* (v. 8d)."

We need agitators today. I need friends who will confront me: "Overland, you're asleep on this issue or that. You're pretending everything all is well, but it's not!" However, it's possible for me to become agitated for an important cause (spiritual, social), yet failing to ensure that my script comes from God. Failing that checkpoint, I'm just a cannon firing in all directions, damaging the flock. Sometimes the error will be a surplus of truth with a deficit of love. Or the error will be caving in to the wishes of the people, assuring "Peace, peace" when there will be no peace.

As we met these four friends, did you find yourself identifying with any one of them? Be grateful for the role entrusted to you. Each is honorable. Then take a page from our friends' notebook. Am I a priest? Then in all my ceremonial routines, routinely I must ask, "Where is the Lord?" So simple a question! So profound a probe! Is the Lord not near? Then move.

Am I a law handler, knowing much about the content of this inspired book? Above all I must purpose to know its author, else I know nothing.

Am I a leader? Then I must seek the chief-shepherd's favor, always aware that it is for him that I care for them.

Am I a prophet? May I always check the source of my sermons, stirring others to action with messages that spring from divine authorization, not of my private musing.

The four friends offer profound counsel. Aided by their discoveries may we fulfill our ministry with even greater effectiveness.

JABEZ: A MAN NAMED PAIN: AN INTEGRATIVE .
HERMENEUTICAL EXERCISE
by Elaine Heath*

Hermeneutics, the Bible and Barth
A kind of holy unrest is brewing in biblical scholarship today. Camps are mingling, walls are coming down, the old labels aren't working so well anymore.[1] The causes are many: ecumenism, spiritual hunger, a renewed respect for the genuine wisdom of the ancients, a growing humility toward the limitations of the scientific method. Whatever the cause, it is no longer enough to speak only of the historical setting of the text, the original audience, authorship, or date. Nor is it enough to read the Bible with a fideistic literalism, or as an esoteric analogue in which nothing means what it says because everything means something else. It is not enough to analyze the Bible as if it were merely another book, for to do so is to ignore the claims the Bible makes of itself.[2] What then is a responsible hermeneutic of scripture?

The current struggle in biblical hermeneutics reflects the struggle in Christian theology. The stuggle is, to borrow William Thompson's words, to put back into biblical studies and Christian theology the "soul" which has been demythologized nigh unto death.[3] That soul is the very Spirit of Christ.

The struggle is not new. It emerged in this century most vigorously in the work of Karl Barth, whose response to Protestant liberalism and fundamentalism was neoorthodoxy—a return to the best of the old while reaching out for the best of the new.[4] For Barth, the centrality of Christ is the foundation for biblical hermeneutics. In many ways he is a man for our time, as we struggle to hear what the Bible says.

The Bible audaciously claims to be the written word of God for the people of God. Both Old and New Testaments are the written means through which the Holy Spirit reveals Jesus Christ to the church.[5] This is the central conviction of Barth. While Barth welcomes the tools of historical-critical scholarship, literary criticism and typological reading, and so on, his overall concern is that readers submit themselves to the claims made by the Word of God encountered in the text.[6] All tools of scholarship are to serve the reader in that task.

The essay that follows is an exercise in (primarily) Barthian hermeneutics. It combines scholarly exegesis and hermeneutics in a way that exalts Jesus Christ and submits the author to the claims of Jesus Christ made

---

*Elaine A. Heath (M.Div, ATS) is a PhD candidate in theology at Duquesne University and pastor of the United Methodist Church in McDonald, OH.

through the text. I have deliberately avoided pedantic labels for each hermeneutical movement to notify the reader that "we will now incorporate Ricoeur's second naiveté" or "here is an example of Tracy's conversation model" and so on. Instead I have endeavored to combine naturally and conversationally the fruits of historical-critical research with those of literary criticism and hermeneutics, drawing from the insights of psychology, spirituality and the wisdom of the saints. Footnotes are plentiful enough for the reader who wishes to catalogue and list such things. In this particular essay to have made such notations within the text would have seemed akin to a composer interrupting the performance of her overture every few measures to explain to the audience precisely how she was influenced by this musician or that poet in each section of music. My goal is to integrate and orchestrate a diverse array of voices concerning the text, in order to better hear what the Holy Spirit is saying through the text, so that my reader may also hear. This is a Barthian approach.[7]

Part Two of the essay is developed in four progressions which are named after the four steps of *lectio divina*.[8] This has been done to emphasize the foundational role of "listening" prayer in a responsible interpretation of the Bible.[9] First we encounter the text itself, nakedly, unhurriedly. The text should be read several times before consulting secondary sources so that it can speak for itself before others speak about it. This step is *lectio*.

Then we begin to listen in earnest not only to the text but also to the voices of others who converse with the text. For the Holy Spirit speaks to us in concert. Questions arise for the reader in the process of listening and speaking, which lead to an awareness of particular words, images, or themes from the text that seem to stand out.[10] This second step is *oratio*.

Meditatio comes next. In it there is a "descent from the mind into the heart," as our Eastern Orthodox friends would say, of the particular word, phrase or theme that has been heard. There the conversation grows more intimate, more fecund, more *theological*, perhaps less verbal. All that has been heard in the text and in the conversation must percolate in the heart, fueled with Spirit fire. When this truly happens, the text begets a Word that is "living and active, sharper than any two-edged sword, piercing until it divides soul from spirit, joints from marrow; it is able to judge the thoughts and intentions of the heart."[11] The word of life that has been spoken must now be internalized and lived out. This is *contemplatio*, the overflowing fullness of prayer. As Barth would say, in this part we submit ourselves and our lives to the Word's decision about us.[12] Unless Bible study leads to obedience to the Word, it is fruitless. *Contemplatio* is the final obedience, the glad surrender of oneself to the transforming Word. It is worship.

Like Barth, my conviction is that the Holy Spirit speaks in concert through all these voices—the biblical text, scholars, saints,[13] reasoned reflection and our own life experiences—if we will only listen. The Bible, when taken in isolation from the other voices, becomes dry and lifeless, or worse, an instrument for unbridled eisegesis. The other voices without the Bible are like a compass without the needle. If, on the other hand we approach the text on our knees, listening with all our might to the Holy Spirit speaking in community, the compass leads us home. The text that I have chosen seems particularly apt for this endeavor, for it seems as dead and dry as ever a text could be, at first reading. It is an old, forgotten passage, buried in a lengthy genealogy, left out of the lectionaries and unmentioned in the hymns. I stumbled across it several years ago while methodically reading through 1 Chronicles, a practice I learned from Betty, the pastor who taught me to "pray the scriptures." She was childlike enough to believe that every word of the Bible trembles with incipient life for those who have ears to hear. This brief text has become a "living word" for me, which continues to form my spirituality and to fuel my passion for God. I hear it speak fresh wisdom with each new reading. Barth would be pleased. So would Betty.

I invite the reader, on that note, to approach these humble musings in the spirit in which they were written, with a kind of holy listening and a playful heart. Perhaps you, too, will be found and "read" by the Word. Who knows what might happen next?

Part Two

Lectio

Jabez was honored more than his brothers; and his mother named him Jabez, saying, "Because I bore him in pain." Jabez called on the God of Israel, saying, "Oh that you would bless me and enlarge my border, and that your hand might be with me, and that you would keep me from hurt and harm!" And God granted what he asked (1 Chronicles 4:9-10 NRSV)

Meditatio

In these two brief verses we find the summary of a man's entire life: an epitaph. This memorial of Jabez's life is carefully woven into a lengthy genealogy. The epitaph is a narrative containing both a prayer of supplication and at least the suggestion of a curse. Thus we find in this short text no fewer than four genres. The primary literary forms of Chronicles are genealogies, lists, sermons or speeches, prayers, and a curious "unnamed genre" that is a somewhat midrashic narrative plus interpretation.[14] What we have in 4:9-10, then, is actually a literary microcosm of 1 Chronicles as a whole.

While much could be said concerning the nature and function of genealogies in the OT, for our purposes it is enough to note that the Chronicler[15] probably intended to survey "all Israel" in order to emphasize the continuity of God's presence among God's people through all times, even during national catastrophes such as the Exile.[16] The first nine chapters of 1 Chronicles traces the chosen people of God from Adam and Eve to the Exile under Nebuchadnezzar. It is necessary to the writer for the audience to connect themselves with generations of past Hebrews, particularly the line of Judah, for their sense of identity has been compromised by captivity.[17] While Jabez is located in the genealogy of the tribe of Judah his precise relationship within the lineage is unclear.[18] The purpose for his inclusion will be readily apparent in light of the author's themes and method.

The post-exilic Chronicler, writing during the late fifth century B.C., is a court historian who writes from a priestly perspective. Both political and religious motives prompt him to write. In focusing on Judah the Chronicler wishes to highlight the positive aspects of the Davidic monarchy. Particular weight is given to the eschatalogical hopes associated with the Davidic line.[19] Concerned with preserving the hope of Israel which is to come through David's line, the author exalts those who call on the Lord and submit their lives to his sovereignty. He uses them to demonstrate the connection between faithfulness to God and the fulfillment of Israel's hope.

The temple cultus, priests and Levites, the doctrine of retribution and the condition of the human heart are primary theological themes in Chronicles. Kings are described in terms of their relationship to the temple and to God.[20] With their theology kings rise and fall, taking Levites, priests, and Israel with them. Second Chronicles concludes with the decree of Cyrus which permits the exiles to return to Jerusalem to rebuild the temple.

While a number of theories have been proposed, the most probable original audience for Chronicles was "the author's own community and its purpose was to assure them of the value of their life, even under foreign rule: they as a community are sustaining the worship of God, which is the primary function of Israel, indeed, the chief purpose of the world's creation."[21] The remnant has come home to carry out its mission of living as the people of God. Will Israel learn from its past? That is the author's question.

Along with other epitaphs[22] in Chronicles, the mini-narrative of Jabez serves the author's purpose. Most of the Chronicler's theological themes are found in this story. Jabez is from the line of Judah. He is an honorable man

10

despite the limitations of his life. Like Israelite children born in exile, Jabez is born under a curse. The saving grace that lifts him from the curse is his trust in God, which prompts him to seek a blessing. God rewards Jabez for his faith. His story of hope and redemption could become the story of any Israelite who calls on the name of the Lord. It could become the story of all Israel.

What is most striking about Jabez' story is that his name is represented as a kind of curse placed on him by his mother.[23] With a bitter word-play Jabez' mother names him after her suffering. (The Hebrew word for pain is "atseb.")[24] We know nothing else about Jabez' mother except that she suffers. For the ancient Hebrew reader it is understood that a negative spiritual force is released upon Jabez in his mother's naming of him. "For the Hebrew just as a word was not a mere sound on the lips but an agent sent forth, so the spoken curse was an active agent for hurt. Behind the word stands the soul that created it."[25]

While the text itself does not say how Jabez experienced the curse, the implication is that his pain caused him to cry out to God for deliverance. It seems clear that Jabez would not pray for God to bless and protect him from pain and suffering (the curse of his name) if he was not threatened in some way by pain. Neither would he pray for his borders to "be enlarged" if he was not in some way confined. Was his confinement geographic, emotional, spiritual, relational? We cannot be certain, but there are hints in the text.

Notice the nuanced phrase: "he was more honored than his brothers." Was Jabez, like Joseph, the target of his brothers' abuse? Was he a younger brother like David, honored yet rejected, anointed but hunted down? The text does not tell us. What it does suggest is that he was favorably singled out from his brothers by the community. Sibling rivalry and resentment from the less-favored brethren is a *lietmotif* in OT narratives: Cain and Abel, Isaac and Ishmael, Jacob and Esau, the list goes on. Could it be that his brothers were part of Jabez' pain?

Even though he is born under a curse, Jabez is exemplary in his faith. He turns to God who has the power to uncurse. Jabez cries out to be delivered from pain. Instead of allowing his suffering to make him "curse God and die," he lets it lead him closer to God.[26] Furthermore he asks for a blessing, the kind of blessing his mother did not give him, the kind that a good mother gives. Jabez' prayer is the most important thing he does. It is the essence of who he is. It is the secret to his liberation from the curse. God's word to Jabez is "Yes."

Oratio

Jabez stands as a testimony to God's grace for all who are born under a curse, under an "evil word." Jabez is incarnate hope for those whose identity is defined by their parents' pain. His story is about the power of prayer, the power of the word of blessing, the mighty "Yes!" of God. To Jabez, God reveals himself as Redeemer, the one who becomes Healer, Protector and Life-giver. God becomes the mother Jabez never had, speaking the blessing Jabez needs. Jabez discovers that evil that is passed "from generation to generation"[27] is no match for the redeeming, blessing Word of God. A new life is possible for anyone.

Let us come alongside Jabez on his journey, and eat of Jabez' bread. For many of us, in the words of the old spiritual, "feel like a motherless child." God is omnipotent, omniscient, omnipresent and omniman. The ball and chain of woundedness, that peculiar shame of being which was handed on to us, will not be broken by the Warrior or the Judge. The key to our unshackling is the blessed face of Mother, the ferocious protection, the sweet kiss of Mother love.

"Can a woman forget her nursing child, or show no compassion for the child of her womb?" God asks his people.[28] Yes, Jabez answers. A mother can do such a thing. "Even these may forget," God answers, "yet I will not forget you...I have inscribed you on the palms of my hands. Your walls are continually before me."[29] Jabez looks at the scarred, outstretched hands of Mother God, reaching inside the walls, deeper than the pain, the memories, the everything. "As a mother comforts her child, so I will comfort you," whispers Jesus,[30] bending low to lift his child to his breast.

"For this is that property in God which opposes good to evil," writes Julian. "So Jesus Christ, who opposes good to evil, is our true Mother. We have our being from him, where the foundation of motherhood begins, with all the sweet protection of love which endlessly follows."[31] For every Jabez among us Jesus offers words of blessing: "This is my body, which is given for you."[32] "I came that you may have life," Jesus insists, "and have it abundantly."[33]

Mother Jesus is our "Pelican," the one who feeds us with herself for she is the one who bore us, who nurses us, and who leads us in the way of life:

Pie pelicane, Jesu Domine, me immundum munda tuo sanguine, cuius una stilla salvum facere, totum mundum quit ab omni scelere.[34]

The Word Become Flesh is the Word of uncursing to all who will receive. Christ is God's glad "Yes!" to deliver us from destruction and to transform our suffering into joy. For it is Jesus' deepest joy to bless us:

Christ redeemed us from the curse of the law by becoming a

curse for us—for it is written, "Cursed is everyone who hangs on a tree"—in order that in Christ Jesus the blessing of Abraham might come to the Gentiles, so that we might receive the promise of the Spirit through faith.[35]

Jabez is all of us, we who are born laboring under the first mother's pain, we who are the seed of Adam. Jabez is creation, groaning beneath the weight of multiplied sin. Jabez is the universe crying for release. Thanks be to God for the mighty Word of hope:

All creation anticipates the day when it will join God's children in glorious freedom from death and decay. For we know that all creation has been groaning as in the pains of childbirth right up to the present time. And even we Christians, although we have the Holy Spirit within us as a foretaste of future glory, also groan to be released from pain and suffering. We, too, wait anxiously for that day when God will give us our full rights as his children, including the new bodies he has promised us.[36]

Jabez is beauty for ashes, the oil of joy for mourning, a garment of praise for a spirit of heaviness.[37] He is promise.

Contemplatio

Not for myself alone, beloved Word Incarnate, do I lift my life in trembling gratitude for all that you have done to lift me from the pit of evil, from generations and generations of violence and shame, from selfhoods forged in Mama's pain. Not for myself alone do I weep these tears of joy. Your Word is alive, sharper than a scythe, sharp-honed wisdom won from living into wholeness, the freedom of the Word. Your Word swells large within me, sweet frankincense and myrrh, a living Word of blessing which you speak to all the world.

Endnotes
[1]A new kind of "conversation" is emerging that is decidedly postmodern in its acceptance of the ambiguities both in scripture and in biblical hermeneutics. David Tracy, *Plurality and Ambiguity* (Chicago: University of Chicago Press, 1987), ix.

[2]2 Tim 3:16-17; 2 Peter 1:19-21.

13

[3]William M. Thompson, *The Struggle for Theology's Soul* (New York: Crossroad, 1996), 1-32.

[4]Of course, Barth himself did not like to be pigeonholed within neo-orthodoxy.

[5]Karl Barth, *The Doctrine of the Word of God*, vol. 2, *Church Dogmatics* (Edinburgh: T.&T. Clark, 1056), 882-883.

[6]Ibid., 702, 723-727.

[7]Mark I. Wallace, *The Second Naiveté: Barth, Recoeur, and the New Yale Theology*, Studies in American Biblical Hermeneutics Series, vol. 6 (Macon, GA: Mercer University Press, 1990), 1-26.

[8]*Lectio divina* is commonly

[9]Barth, 697ff.

[10]The reader brings to the text his or her experiences, knowledge, questions, opinions, limitations, fears, hopes, all the conscious and unconscious material of life. Thus the questions and issues are dynamic, growing and changing with the reader's growth. For a fine introduction to a psychological hermeneutic of the Bible that draws from Jungian analysis, Barth and others see Wayne G. Rollins, *Jung and the Bible* (Atlanta: John Knox Press, 1983). Rollins speaks particularly of Barth on pp. 86, 98, 106, 115.

[11]Hebrews 4:12, NRSV.

[12]Barth, 702-703.

[13]I speak not only of canonized saints and "official sages" but also of the saints in the local church-the lovers of Jesus who know God intimately and who serve as companions on the journey.

[14]Roddy Braun, *1 Chronicles*, Word Biblical Commentary Series, vol. 14 (Waco: Word Books, 1982), xxiv.

[15]Tradition says the author was Ezra, but parts of the text suggest a much later writing, perhaps around 400 B.C. 1 and 2 Chronicles are one book, the final book in the Hebrew Bible.

[16]Braun, 3.

[17]cf. Ezra and Nehemiah.

[18]Jabez story is an example of the combination of local tribal history with a more formal genealogy (ibid., 4-5). The only other biblical mention of Jabez is 1 Chron 2:55, which names Jabez as the city occupied by the descendants of Hur (through Salma's line).

[19]Braun, xxxii-xv.

[20]1 Chron 10:1-29:30 follows the reign of David, while 2 Chron 1:1-9:31 is a commentary on the reign of Solomon, followed by 10:1-36:23 which details the remainder of the kings up to the captivity.

[21]David Cliines, "Secondary History," in *Harper's Bible Commentary* [CD-ROM} (New York: Harper and Row, Publishers, Inc. 1988; Oak Harbor, WA: Logos Research Systems, 1997).

[22]1 Chron 2:3, for example, remembers Er the son of Judah as a wicked man whom the Lord killed.

[23]J.A. Motyer, "Curse," and A. Van Selms, "Balaam," *New Bible Dictionary* 2ⁿᵈ ed [CD-ROM] (Wheaton: Tyndale, 1982; Oak Harbor, WA: Logos Research Systems, 1997).

[24]We find a similar phenomenon in Hosea, where the prophet is commanded by Yahweh to name his children "Jezreel" (God Plants), "Loruhama" (Not Loved" and "Lo-ammi" (Not My People). Recall the naming of Jacob (Deceiver) and how he lived his name. The theme of the power of naming runs throughout the Bible.

[25] A. Van Selms, "Balaam," *New Bible Dictionary* 2ⁿᵈ ed [CD-ROM] (Wheaton: Tyndale, 1982; Oak Harbor, WA: Logos Research Systems, 1997).

[26]Job 2:9.

[27]Ex 34:7.

[28]Is 49:15a, NRSV.

[29]Is 49:15b-16, NRSV.

[30]Is 66:13, NRSV.

[31]Julian of Norwich, *Showings*, Classics of Western Spirituality Series, trans. Edmund College and James Walsh (New York: Paulist, 1978), 295.

[32]Luke 22:19, NRSV.

[33]John 10:10, NRSV.

[34]"Deign, O Jesus, Pelican of heaven, me, a sinner, in Thy Blood to lave, to a single dro p of which is given all the world from all its sin to save." Stanza 6 of the 13th century Eucharistic hymn by Thomas Aquinas, "Adoro Te Devote," *Jubilate Deo*, Casa Musicale Edizione (Bergamo, Italy: Carrara, 1980).

[35]Gal 3:13-14, NRSV.

[36]Romans 8:20-23, NLT.

[37]Isaiah 61:3.

For His Glory:
Mission And Vision of the Smetzer Counseling Center of the Ashland
Theological Seminary

by Michael Reuschling

The purpose of man is to glorify God and enjoy his company forever.
(Westminster Catechism)

It wasn't so many years ago that reading the Psalms was much more
of a duty than a delight for me. It wasn't that many years ago that the thought
of praying, let alone "praying without ceasing," lead to more thoughts of
drudgery than delight. And if you had told me, not that many years ago, that I
would be spending hours alone with God, just enjoying His company, I would
have politely dismissed you, at best, and harshly criticized you (at least in my
mind) for not really knowing me at all, at worst. Yet all of these, enjoyment of
God's words (and Word), delight in talking to and hearing from God, resting
with great contentment in His presence, all of these have become my ongoing
experience and blessing. God has faithfully been showing me His great love
for me and for others through His kind and gentle and loving treatment of me.
He has been answering my prayer that He transform me into the image and
likeness of His Son, no matter what the "cost" might be. He has taken me at my
word and honored my surrender of my all to Him. May He be praised forever
for His great love toward us as His people!

In this and other areas, I have been reminded many times of the words
of a Salvation Army officer quoted years ago on the Paul Harvey radio
program. The officer was asked at Christmas-time what he thought of telling
children tales of flying reindeer and the like, of filling their heads with such
fantastic stories. His response was, "Flying reindeer? When I think of what
God has done with this black heart of mine, flying reindeer is child's play!"
And so it is for me and for many of us. The closest I have witnessed to
miracles is in what God has done with this "black heart" of mine. Who I once
was, and who I once feared I was (that one who would someday be found out
and exposed), have been largely left behind, by the grace of God, and I come
to see these "self-images" as the lies they were and are, as contrasted with His
truth of who I am because of Him. I have come to see that God's words in
Romans 14:4, *Who are you to judge someone else's servant? To his own master
he stands or falls. And he will stand, for the Lord is able to make him stand*

Michael Reuschling (MA, ATS; PhD, University of Akron) is Associate professor of
Pastoral Counseling and Director of the Midwest Counseling Center at ATS.

(NIV), words that I was mostly able to apply to my treatment of others, also apply to my treatment of myself since God tells me *"You are not your own; you were bought at a price.* (1 Cor. 6:19-20, NIV). In these and countless other ways, He extends his love and kindness to me which, in turn, makes me want to extend them to others and lead them to Him.

Lest this turn into the random ramblings of a raving Reuschling, my point is that God has been glorifying Himself to me and in me in the ways described above. After so many years of trying to *"work out (my own) salvation with fear and trembling"* (Phil. 2:12, NIV), only under my own power and cleverness, only to fail time after time (after time), and after so many years of evidencing only paltry and measly spiritual "fruit" (hardly worth eating and precious little to nourish self or others), God's unfailing love has rescued me from a spiritual desert and set my feet more firmly in His kingdom. Whether it is more remarkable or simply more understandable that this has taken place in a "mental health professional," in someone with lots of degrees and lots of titles and lots of clinical experience, I will leave to the reader to decide. Suffice it to say that all of these degrees and titles and experiences did precious little to contribute to my enjoyment of God or my glorifying Him.

So we come to the mission and vision of the Smetzer Counseling Center of Ashland Theological Seminary. What is it that the Lord would have us to do in this place and in this ministry? The mission statement of the Smetzer Counseling Center states,

> *The Smetzer Counseling Center of Ashland Theological Seminary exists to glorify our great and gracious God! We strive to bring His comfort to a hurting and heavy-laden world through training exceptional Christian counselors, obedient to the Master's command to "Go and do likewise."*

We believe that the Smetzer Counseling Center is, first and foremost, a gift from God. A gift to those of us privileged to work there, a gift to the students who will be trained there, a gift to Ashland Theological Seminary, and, finally, a gift to those "hurting and heavy-laden" ones who will receive God's comfort through this ministry. This author saw a need for a training laboratory for counseling students upon first being hired at ATS in the Fall of 1997. At that time, the Seminary president, Dr. Fred Finks, and the Pastoral Counseling department chair, Dr. John Shultz, graciously agreed to make available money and space for a modest lab for student training. In what seemed like very short order, it was announced that Mrs. Smetzer had donated one million dollars for the creation of a counseling lab to train Christian counselors and minister to the community! It was as if God was saying, "Yes, you do need a training center, but I've got something much better in mind!" This began the dream and vision of what God might do and would have ATS to do in and through this ministry.

First, and foremost, the mission and vision of the center is to glorify God. Throughout my twenty-plus year career in mental health, I have had the opportunity, and occasionally the privilege, of working in a variety of settings. These have included private practices, group practices, community mental health agencies, non-profit mental health and family service agencies, for-profit corporations providing mental health care, and in-patient psychiatric settings, among others. While many of the mission statements of these organizations contained lofty sentiments and aspirational language, the reality of day-to-day operations usually betrayed the stated mission. The "actual mission statement" of some of these organizations could, more honestly, have been stated as "Circle the wagons" (in an agency where an "us (staff) versus them (clients)" mentality was prominent), "Go for the gold" (in a for-profit corporation much more interested in earthly treasure than in any other kind), or "Divide and conquer" (in an organization headed by an insecure and even paranoid leader intent upon maintaining his position and power). Day-to-day reality has a way of eroding even the loftiest of ideals until mission statements are only resurrected in annual reports and fund-raising efforts. In many of the organizations mentioned, any glory sought was usually self-glory.

"First, and foremost, the mission and vision of the center is to glorify God." How will God be glorified in this ministry and place? He will not be glorified by the self-effort, clinical cleverness, professional degrees, nor licenses of those ministering therein. My experience and the experience of many of my colleagues speak to the ultimate emptiness of such "resources." Rather, He will be glorified by those of us ministering in the Center fixing our eyes on Jesus as *"the author and perfecter of our faith"* and by considering Him, so that we do not *"grow weary and lose heart"* (Heb. 12:2-3, NIV), so that we do not elevate self, and so that we are not sidetracked in the "weeds" of our clients' woes (Matt. 13:3-23, NIV). It is God who will glorify Himself in his setting, to and in and through those devoted to His glorification. Our "job" will be to earnestly and faithfully seek Him in our own lives and in the lives of our clients, intent upon pleasing Him and, in return, being rewarded by Him, especially through the privilege of being participants in a glorious endeavor (Heb. 11:6, NIV). Those of ministering in the Center must be devoted to Him, first and foremost, or we will be devoted to self or to others at the expense of glorifying Him.

Personally, one of my primary motives for involvement in the Center is to see what God will do in a place devoted to His glorification. Having spent most of my professional career seeking self-glorification (no matter how lofty my sentiments and rationalizations), I now desire to see Him glorified and clients truly comforted. While it was my privilege to work in and to lead many fine organizations, with many dedicated and gifted professionals, most of this time and energy was driven by motives other than His glorification. I have also seen the baser side of professional mental healthcare, with its petty territoriality (sometimes at the client's expense), its rampant bureaucracies, and its all-too-frequent clinical impotence. For once in my career, more importantly, in my Christian journey, I want to see what God will do in a place and ministry devoted to His glorification. If He, in His sovereignty, decides to do nothing in the Smetzer Counseling Center, then to Him be all glory! However, I have this sneaking suspicion (more accurately, this eager expectation) of what He will do in this place.

Those of us who will minister in the Smetzer Counseling Center must *"strive to bring His comfort to a hurting and heavy-laden world..."* The best definition of Christian counseling I have ever found is contained in Paul's letter to the Corinthians (2 Cor. 1:3-4, NIV) which says *Praise be to the God and Father of our Lord Jesus Christ, the Father of compassion and the God of all comfort, who comforts us in all our troubles, so that we can comfort those in any trouble with the comfort we ourselves have received from God.* It is because of God's comfort to each of us in the troubles we face, that we learn more about His great and unfailing love for us. In this way we are greatly comforted. His comfort is manifested in a myriad of ways, not the least of which are the kind and gentle encouragers He sends our way at such times. As we grow in His love, as we realize more and more in the depth of our heart how much He loves us, we are then enabled and empowered to love Him and others more ably and healthily. *We love because he first loved us* (1 John 4:19, NIV) and so loving, we are commanded to *love each other deeply, because love covers over a multitude of sin.* (1 Peter 4:8, NIV). Perhaps we will best glorify God and bring comfort to others by showing clients God's great love for us all. I have often remarked that the mental health professions are a "growth industry," as there seems to be no shortage of pain, quite the contrary, there seem to be increasing levels of anxiety and other forms of distress. Ultimately, the only true and lasting comfort will be found from the great Physician and not from clinical cleverness nor from the greatest human compassion.

Who will God use to provide such comfort to a "hurting and heavy-laden world?" Those "exceptional Christian counselors" who will be *"obedient to the Master's command to 'Go and do likewise.'"* Academic excellence has been a core value of Ashland Theological Seminary since its inception, whether explicitly stated or implicitly practiced. Such excellence has been evident in the training of countless godly men and women for a variety of ministries, including pastoral counseling. While academic excellence will be critical in providing needed comfort, thereby glorifying God, it must take a back seat to the more essential core values of Scripture, spiritual formation, and community, or, another of ATS' "core values," servant leadership. It is only by acknowledging one Master (and that He is not "me") and by being obedient to Him that true comfort will be provided and true freedom occur. The Smetzer Counseling Center will strive to equip exceptional Christian counselors, "shepherds" of their respective "flocks," who will demonstrate "technical and clinical proficiency" energized and enlightened by a vibrant and vital faith. The mental health world and profession does not need more "proficient clinicians," the world needs the Life and the Light and the Truth and the Power. These are the type of "exceptional Christian counselors" the Center aspires to train and disciple.

When it's all said and done, when we all stand before His throne at the final judgement, may we all hear the Lord's words from Mat. 25:23 spoken to us, *Well done, good and faithful servant! You have been faithful with a few things; I will put you in charge of many things. Come and share your master's happiness!* It is toward this end, toward these words, and toward honor of the Word that we press on. May God find us faithful.

ETS Studies

The ETS Studies series, a joint venture between Baker Book House and the Evangelical Theological Society, publishes works in the areas of biblical studies and theology that are judged to make a significant contribution to evangelical scholarship. The general editor of the series is Dr. David W. Baker of Ashland Theological Seminary.

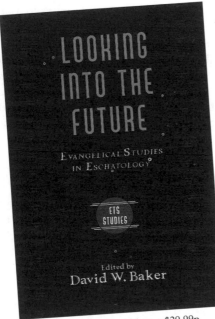

0-8010-2279-7 • 384 pp. • $29.99p

THIS LATEST ADDITION to the ETS Studies series presents a collection of essays from leading evangelical scholars probing eschatological issues in theology, biblical studies, and ethics, demonstrating the breadth and maturity of current evangelical thought. Contributors include: Bruce Waltke, Darrell L. Bock, Hans F. Bayer, Fred P. Hall, Robert L. Thomas, Clark H. Pinnock, John Sanders, Guenther Haas, John Warwick Montgomery, and James A. Borland.

ALSO IN THE SERIES

The Gods of the Nations
Studies in Ancient Near Eastern National Theology, 2d ed.
Daniel I. Block
Foreword by Alan R. Millard
0-8010-2201-0 • 176 pp. • $19.99p

Listening to the Text
Oral Patterning in Paul's Letters
John D. Harvey
Foreword by Richard N. Longenecker
0-8010-2200-2 • 384 pp. • $24.99p

Baker Academic

Subscribe to Baker Academic's electronic newsletter (E-Notes) at
www.bakerbooks.com/academic

Leadership Character: A Matter of Trust
Richard Parrott*

Leadership is the process of influencing others to reach a common goal. Influence is the *sine qua non* of leadership. Without influence, leadership does not exist. Leaders develop a pattern of behavior used to influence others. This pattern includes the way a leader responds and relates to others in order to influence them toward the accomplishment of the groups goals.

Character is the *"aggregate of qualities that distinguish one person from another"* (American Heritage Dictionary). If you speak of a person as displaying "strange character," you mean they exhibit a pattern of behavior that distinguishes them from their normal pattern. If the pattern is consistently different, you may refer to them as "quite a character." If you break your normal pattern of relating and responding, you may say, "I was out of character."

When you speak of a person as having "moral character," they exhibit a pattern or quality of behavior that distinguishes them from an immoral person. Much leadership talk on character is aimed at "moral character." Moral character makes you a good person. However, it takes more than being a good person to provide good leadership.

A person of "leadership character" has a quality or pattern of behavior that distinguishes them from people who are not leaders. Leaders display patterns of relating and responding that influence the actions of others. Leadership character is the habit or pattern of behavior that provides good leadership.

If you habitually say one thing and follow through on it, if you habitually stand up for the greater good of the organization, if you habitually reconsider a decision when the situation has changed, if you habitually learn from others, then you are providing a pattern of good leadership – you display leadership character.

However, if you habitually say one thing but do another, if you habitually back down under pressure, if you habitually push ahead with your original plans even when the situation has changed, if you habitually refuse to learn from others, then you are providing a pattern of poor leadership – you lack leadership character.

---

* Richard Parrott (Ph.D., Oregon State University), is Executive Director of the Sandberg Leadership Center and of the Doctor of Ministry Program at ATS.

* What is the pattern of behaving and relating that provides good leadership?
* What is the spiritual foundation of good leadership character?
* How is good leadership character developed?

These are the questions discussed at a Roundtable Convocation held at The Sandberg Leadership Center on the campus of Ashland Theological Seminary, October 25-27, 2001. There were 25 participants representing business, government, nonprofit organizations, academics, and the church. Four keynote speakers set the direction for the discussion. A brief excerpt from each address is presented in this article.

Lovett H. Weems, Jr.
President of Saint Paul School of Theology
in Kansas City, Missouri.

A leader who consistently demonstrates quality of character is reciprocated with followers who place trust in their leader. Trust is *"firm reliance on the integrity or ability of a person"* (American Heritage Dictionary). Lovett Weems reflects the significance of trust in the leader in this personal story.

Seminary presidents spend much time raising money. Years ago I heard the statistic that large gifts tend to come after a dozen or so visits, often by the president. I was close to that statistical average with a woman in her nineties. She had ample resources, no family, close ties to the church, interest in our school, yet had never given a single gift. I scheduled yet another visit with her by scheduling a flight with a lengthy layover in her city so I could take her to dinner, as was our usual pattern.

When I arrived at her home, she was not dressed to go out. She indicated that she was not feeling well and perhaps we could visit for a few minutes and then I could head back to the airport. We talked briefly in her living room. Then, as we were standing at the door as I was leaving, she said simply, "I trust you." I knew then that we would receive a major gift. She left half of her estate to the seminary for student scholarships.

24

That was the day I learned that the term "development" was no mere euphemism for "fund raising." It became abundantly clear to me that people give out of trust and that trust grows out of relationships and experience that engender such trust.

The level of trust that exists within an organization and toward leaders is crucial to the effectiveness of leadership. When trust is limited, it is difficult for progress to take place. Conversely, in places where a high level of trust has been developed, remarkable change can be accomplished with a minimum of acrimony and delay.

A leader's trust is won very slowly, but it can be lost quickly. Once lost, this trust is very difficult to regain in that leadership setting. People may give us a leadership position through election or employment. However, the credibility needed to lead must be worked out among the people with whom we serve. It is trust from those with whom the leader works most closely that gives a leader the essential element of credibility.

Valerie K. Brown, CPA

Executive Director and founder of the Church Financial Management and Leadership Institute, Assistant Professor of Management at the Samuel D. Proctor School of Theology.

Leaders need support structures that protect and validate the trust placed upon them. Valerie Brown shared a wonderful, biblical illustration focusing on financial trust. Read the story and consider the question, "How can a leader build systems and structures that protect and validate trust such as 'being honest' and 'keeping promises'?"

Trust is lifted up as the paramount character trait for leaders in the church, yet we find violations of trust every day. The Bible teaches us that we are our brothers' keepers. We find in the Word of God in the book of Ezra an example of how the church can become the "brothers' keeper" of the financial officers by instituting checks and balances. In Ezra 8:24-26 we find these words:

> "I appointed twelve leaders of the priests...to be in charge of transporting the silver, the gold, the gold bowls, and the other items that the king, his council, his leaders, and the people had presented for the temple of God. I weighted the treasure as I gave it to them and found the totals to be..."

This passage was written during the rebuilding of the Temple. People and leaders gave money to the priests for the rebuilding of the Temple. The people surely "trusted" the priest and other workers in the Temple, yet they still counted what was given to the priest prior to giving it to them. The priests were required to transport all that was given back to Jerusalem. Later, after the journey to Jerusalem, we find in Ezra 8:33:

> "On the 4th day after our arrival the silver, gold, and other valuables were weighed at the Temple...everything was accounted for by number and weight and was officially recorded."

The priests were held 'accountable' and there were checks and balances put in place to ensure that the priests were not even tempted to misappropriate or steal any items entrusted in their care.

It is wise for a leader to build personal systems of accountability rather then wait for followers to rise up and demand such a structure. What is your personal accountability system for maintaining your trustworthiness?

Bill Perkins
Founder and president of the Million Mighty Men, author of
Awaken the Leader Within and was one of three
contributors to the *Leadership Bible.*

Integrity is the character quality of a leader that, over time, fosters
genuine trust in leaders. Bill Perkins describes integrity and shares a story of
testing.

Integrity is the foundation upon which the character of a
leader will stand or fall. Whether you're leading a company,
a church, a family, a battalion or an athletic team—those you
lead want to know they can trust you.

The word *integrity* speaks of someone who is "whole or
complete" and has the same root word as does the word
integrated. A leader of integrity has taken the principals that
govern his life, internalized them, and integrated them into
every area of his life. A leader of integrity isn't like a
weathervane that changes direction with every shift of the
social winds. He's like a compass that is internally
magnetized so it always points north regardless of what's
happening around it. He is honest at work *and* at home. He
keeps promises *even* if it means a financial loss. He speaks
well of his clients in their presence *and* behind their back.
He doesn't treat his wife with respect in public and belittle
her behind closed doors. A leader of integrity doesn't switch
masks to win the favor of the audience he's playing for.

Because leaders of integrity don't pretend to be something
they're not, with them, what you see is what you get,
literally. And it's not that leaders of integrity are
perfect—they aren't. But they're aware of their weaknesses
and don't lead others to believe they have no personal flaws.
When my friend admitted he cared for people but had a hot
temper, his statement demonstrated integrity.

It's a fact of life that you never know when your integrity
will be tested. That's a lesson learned by an ambitious nurse
who was being considered to lead the nursing team at a
prestigious hospital. The chief of surgery had just completed

27

an operation in which she was assisting when he snapped off his surgical gloves and told her to close the incision. "But doctor, you've only removed eleven sponges. We used twelve." "I removed them all," the doctor declared. "Now close the incision." "No!" the nurse objected. "We used twelve sponges and there are only eleven on the table." "I'll take full responsibility," the surgeon said sternly. "Suture." "You can't do that," the nurse insisted. "What about the patient?" The surgeon smiled, lifted his foot, and showed the nurse the twelfth sponge, which he had hidden under his shoe. Smiling, he said, "You'll do. The nursing team is yours to lead."

The nurse passed the integrity test. She held to the highest standard of patient care and put it into practice—even when a promotion was at stake.

Everyday you'll face similar tests. They'll be unannounced. Some will be subtle and others will be in your face. Whether you know it or not those you lead will be watching you. They'll observe how you handle those unexpected character tests. As you allow the wisdom of Jesus to awaken the leader within you, your integrity will grow. As it does, those you lead will trust you more. As their trust grows so will their eagerness to follow you.

Paul Blease
Director of Advanced Training at
Salomon Smith Barney in New York.

A loss of integrity comes from an inward "disconnect" as described by Paul Blease as he shares the story of the kind of conversations he has with some of the highest producers in the world of finance.

If you have ever been around extraordinary achievers, there is an edge, volatility, intensity, sometimes it comes out as intensity, sometimes as volatility. When it gets pathological, I get involved. I have found that all of our top producers have a high level of confidence. Confidence is based on the task: I can do it! When you feel confident, you feel confident about your capacity to do something. It is a task orientation. However, there is another element that comes into play: Self-esteem. Self-esteem asks, "Am I worthy?" I have found that if there is a disconnect between confidence and self-esteem, volatility will emerge.

I work with people that have confidence bordering on arrogance coupled with low self-esteem. They can do the job, but they lack a sense of worthiness. This comes out in one-on-one conversations. It almost always stems from how they were raised. They are trying to prove someone wrong; oftentimes, fathers, sometimes other people.

One individual invited me to his home after a day of working with his management team. He indicated he had some individual issues that "I need to talk to you about". In the 5-hour conversation that followed, the disconnect between confidence in the job and personal work in the soul emerged. On one hand, there was this businessperson that was Machiavellian on the other side was this born-again Christian who had a wonderful family, wonderful church life and all the great stuff in life. This was a disconnect from his childhood, where he learned the classic, "I'll show you" type of behavior in response to a very autocratic, demanding father where nothing was ever good enough."

Everything in this man's life was designed to win favor, and, in our culture, you win favor through tangible accomplishments. This drives your confidence level very high but does nothing for your self-esteem. Self-esteem is, "Am I worthy in spite of…and without an reference to my performance." Brought up to be measured on his performance, he said that he had always been afraid that if he let down his guard, he would loose his edge and would cease to perform to his current level. He said, "This is what drives me."

I asked him if he understood that that is not what drives him. What drives him is how he is wired, "You are a type 'A' personality. You will achieve at this point, based on habit, based on who you have become. Why you achieve will change if you bring this person that you are at home and in church into your business life. You'll still achieve, but the reason for the accomplishment will change. Rather than to prove your dad and everybody else wrong, it will be to fulfill and fuse who you are with what you do. Your mission will change. The 'why' will change. Your sense of fulfillment will dramatically improve. Your stress level will dramatically decrease. You live in a constant state of stress. Every time you fail to achieve marginally, your self-esteem is again hammered. It is a no-win scenario."

What you see in the volatility issue is a lack of maturity. A person will stop growing, emotionally, at some point in childhood. As an adult you put a façade over the child. You dress for success and you are more articulate. You have possessions. You look like an adult. But you are really a child saying, "I hope no one figures this thing out."

One of the problems is that when you have a high level of confidence, bordering on arrogance, people figure you can take it. They come at you head on. Then, you blow up. No one sees that low self-esteem beneath the façade unless they really know the person and they really love them.

The question I always get from people is, "How do I create high self esteem?" I cannot use the word "Christ" in a business setting so I use, "it's a spiritual element." It is a "spiritual connection." But, in this setting I have an audience that I can speak plain—it is called "grace." "Grace" says, "I love you, period!" That is the conversation I have with some of our largest producers in the Salomon Smith Barney organization.

* * * * *

The task of leadership has not changed. Leaders move/influence people to work together toward the accomplishment of mission. What has changed is the situation of leadership. The leaders power to move/influence others no longer rests primarily in a position of having, but in a relationship of trust. Let me summarize the lessons:

* The purpose of good leadership character is to engender trusting relationships so that leaders and followers can work together in healthy ways to accomplish the mission of the organization.

* Leaders must take responsibility to develop systems, structures and supports that protect and verify the trust that is placed upon them.

* The character pattern of integrity—speak the truth, keep your promise, and be authentic—will, over time and consistency, foster genuine trusting relationships.

* Integrity is born out of an awareness of our own inward disconnects (brokenness) and the embrace of the grace of Christ that reconnects (heals) us as whole persons.

If you want to learn how to get people to trust you, begin by learning how you can trust God.

> "Trust in the Lord with all your heart and lean not on your own understanding; in all your ways acknowledge him, and he will make your paths straight." Proverbs 3:5-6 (NIV)

This article is based on excerpts from the new publication "Leadership Character". This book contains the writings and reflections of the 25 participants of a Round Table Convocation on leadership character held October 25-27, 2001 at The Sandberg Leadership Center, Ashland Theological Seminary, 910 Center Street, Ashland OH 44805. Copies of the book may be purchased for $10 from The Sandberg Leadership Center. Email leadon@ashland.edu.

For Such a Time as This:
A Situational Model of Leadership
by William D. Dobbs*

Leadership is the challenge of the hour. Leadership in the church in the 21st century demands responsiveness to change. Situations change. Ministry opportunities change. Persons who would provide leadership in the context of change can benefit greatly from knowledge of how other leaders have dealt with change. For those of us in the religious community, we often begin with biblical leaders and then look to more contemporary models. The current model of choice seems to be Servant leadership, but I believe there are other models that are equally valid. I propose to reflect on the leadership of Moses as a different model of leadership. We will examine other biblical examples to see how they relate to the model and then discuss this model in light of current leadership theory.

Moses as the Archetype

The first thing we discover as we read the book of Exodus is that there is a crisis affecting God's chosen ones who had come to Egypt with Jacob. This is the first criterion of Situational leadership. Some crisis must arise which causes those who know God's name to cry out for God's deliverance. This cry for deliverance is, I believe, the second criteria. It implies a realization that self-sufficiency doesn't work, repentance, and a willingness to renew the covenant. In Egypt, the sons of Israel and their descendants "groaned under their slavery, and cried out. Out of the slavery their cry for help rose up to God. God heard their groaning, and God remembered his covenant with Abraham, Isaac, and Jacob" (Exodus 2:23c-24 NRSV).

Even as the Israelites were crying for deliverance, God took notice of their plight and began to prepare a leader for them. From Moses' birth, God was preparing him for the task of leadership that lay ahead. The infancy narrative and the early career of Moses all contribute to making Moses the kind of person who could speak to Pharaoh and survive the wilderness for 40 years. This is not to suggest that God's power and presence did not play an integral part in Moses' ministry post "burning-bush." It is meant to state that God's gift of life experiences is the third criteria for a Situational leader.

All of which brings us to the call of Moses and three more criteria for a Situational leader. We begin with the Divine-human encounter. "The angel of the Lord appeared to Moses" (Ex. 3:2 NRSV). In Moses' case, this angelic appearance came in the form of a bush that was burning, but not consumed by

---

* William Dobbs (M.Div.Garrett Evangelical Theological Seminary) is pastor of First United Methodist Church, Holland, MI, and a D.Min. student at ATS.

the flame. As Moses turned aside to see why the bush was not burned up, he experienced the miraculous authentication of God's call. To which, Moses responded, "Here I am" (Ex. 3:4 NRSV). This personal response to God's call then becomes the sixth criteria for a Situational leader.

A seventh criterion for a Situational leader also becomes visible in Moses' call experience: the leader's willingness to step outside the box of conventional thinking. We see that in Moses' turning aside to look at the burning bush. We see that in his appearances before Pharaoh. And we see that in his wilderness trials with the stiff-necked and stubborn people he had led to freedom through the sea. Moses is not bound by the things that "have always been done that way." And, in the end, Moses is not bound by the image he has of himself. He does try to keep the shackles of impossibility firmly in place, but God will have none of that and, in the end, Moses was indeed able to get beyond his own vision of himself. So there are two subsets of this criterion: 1) the ability to see reality in new ways, and 2) the ability to see oneself with new eyes.

Following Moses acceptance of God's call we find the next three criteria of the biblical model. In verse seven, we discover God giving Moses a vision for his life, his ministry. He would be the one whom God used to lead God's people to freedom. This vision would require Moses' being willing to go where God led, to be faithful to God when the going got rough, and to trust God when he could not see the way clearly. In addition to a vision, God also gave Moses a promise that God would be with him. Moses would not be alone. He could go wherever he was led, even into Pharaoh's palace, secure in the knowledge that God was with him and God's power was in him. He was not promised a journey without difficulties. He was promised that God would give him whatever he needed to do God's will   His was the confidence of a Paul who was "sure that nothing in all creation could separate him from God's love" (Romans 8:38-39 NRSV). God gave him others as well, to walk beside him in the journey: Aaron, Hur, Jethro, Joshua and Miriam all served to strengthen Moses in his leadership role. Some gave him advice, some gave him a supporting arm, and some joined him in song but all were instruments of God in Moses' life. And finally, there is a spiritual relationship or intimacy between God and the human leader God has called "for just such a time as this" (Esther 4:14 NRSV).

In summary, then, we find 10 criteria for a Situational leader in the biblical account of Moses:

1) Presence of a Crisis
2) Cry for deliverance
3) Gift of life's experiences
4) The Divine-Human encounter

5) Divine authentication of the call
6) Human response to God's call
7) Willingness to step outside the box.
8) Vision.
9) Promise or Assurance.
10) Spiritual Relationship or Intimacy.

To this list, we need to add an eleventh criterion that would be true for every model. There needs to be the authentication of the "fruit of the Spirit" (Galatians 5:22 NRSV). In any authentic biblical leadership model, we can look backward in time and see the evidence of God's handiwork. Unlike Abimelech (Judges 9ff.) who gave no evidence of God's Spirit in his leadership and quickly lost his power and his life, biblical leaders demonstrate the ability to stay the course and give evidence of God's continued affirmation. In the Moses model of Situational leadership, God's authentication is visible in the continual demonstrations of God's power from the court of Pharaoh to the top of Mount Sinai. God authenticated Moses' leadership in the sight of the people. Moses' was God's leader for that moment and those people.

Other Examples of the Situational Leadership model.

Many of the leaders named in the Hebrew Scriptures demonstrated some of the criteria but not necessarily all. For example, Judges 6 and following tell the story of Gideon. The Israelites were being oppressed by the Midianites, who were confiscating the food necessary for the survival of the people. They had done what was evil and finally came to their senses and cried out to the Lord. God appeared to Gideon while he was at work and called him to a divine task or vision. God authenticated that call and confirmed that God would be with Gideon (v.16). While we do not know much about Gideon's life experiences that prepared him for God's call, except that he was the son of Joash the Abiezrite, we do know that he "did as the Lord told him" (v.27). Gideon demonstrated an ongoing relationship with God. And there is the evidence of the fruit as Gideon and his small band of 300 prevailed over "the Midianites and the Amalekites and all the people of the east" (7:12 NRSV).

Or again, the story of Jephthah the Gileadite illustrates some of the criteria for a Situational leader. Consider: "the people did what was evil in the sight of the Lord" (Judges 10:6 NRSV) and then repented and "put away the foreign gods from among them and worshiped the Lord" (v.16). While the call of Jephthah came from the elders of Gilead, the authentication came from God as Jephthah proved victorious. Jephthah demonstrated a trust in God and a relationship with God that culminated in his faithful keeping of his vow even at the cost of his daughter's life.

I believe that Deborah fits the pattern, even though God is not named in the usual way. Certainly she came forward in response to a call at a crisis moment for the Hebrew people. The Israelites had again done "what was evil in the sight of the Lord" and they had "cried out to the Lord for help" (Judges: 4:2ff). And her prophecy of God's word for Barak, son of Abinoam, was authenticated by victory. This victory came because God sent the rain (Judges 5:4-5).

Or consider Queen Esther. Again, the name of God does not appear, but can there be any doubt that she was prepared by her life experiences and called by God's servant "for such a time as this" (Esther 4:14 NRSV). The *Additions to the Book of Esther* in the Apocryphal Books does name God as the source of her leadership. However, the Esther account by itself leaves little doubt God is the power behind the scenes and the One who authenticates her leadership.

As we come forward in time to the period of the new covenant, we would have to alter the criteria in order to name Situational leaders from the followers of the Way. There is not a sense that the people recognized their sinfulness or their arrogance, repented of their actions, and cried out to God for deliverance. It is possible to find those, like Stephen in Acts 6, who respond to a call authenticated by God's Spirit and come forward for a specific time or situation. However, they do not give evidence of leading a group of God's people or acting of God's behalf to save the people, with the singular exception of the man from Nazareth. Let us look more closely at Jesus.

It may have been an intentional design to validate Jesus in Jewish eyes by the synoptic writers, but no other account of a New Testament personality so closely parallels the account of Moses life. Beginning with the God-protected infancy narratives, the life stories of these two leaders offer many similarities. For Moses and Jesus, there are angelic appearances, divine authentications of a divine call, personal responses, and God-given visions for each one's message and ministry. And there can be no denying that Jesus' appearance in history came as a response to the sinfulness of the people. An interesting note in Luke's gospel is that Jesus also came into the public sphere at a time when the people were responding to a message of repentance proclaimed by the Baptizer. There is the image of both men calling the people to think "outside the box" of the ways the people had always done things as covenant people. Finally, there is that sense of conversational intimacy with God that so marked the leadership of these two central figures in the salvation history of God's people. To see these parallels is not new, of course. And there are many in the literature who would name Jesus as a Servant leader. I would like to suggest, however, that reading the gospels with an Old Testament filter allows one to posit that Jesus is also the chief example of a Situational leader in the New Testament. Truly, Jesus was a leader for such a time as his.

Situational Leadership in Contemporary Leadership Models.
From looking at Moses and Jesus as Situational leaders, I would like to move forward in time to reflect on a contemporary model and then suggest several principles of Situational leadership that would be available to the reader. The thinking in this portion of the article has been influenced by the work of Robert Quinn: *Change the World*, and the trio of Jim Herrington, Mike Bonem and James Furr: *Leading Congregational Change, a Practical Guide for the Transformational Journey.*

An examination of Martin Luther King Jr.'s life reveals several similarities to the criteria we have already established: First, King was prepared by his life circumstances for the moment of his call. His birth, his early education, his formal training and his natural gifts of intellect and personality all conspired to prepare him for a public ministry which could bridge the gap and speak to both the "palace of Pharaoh" and the people of his birth. King could speak with eloquence in the language of those who held the power, and King could speak to the hearts of those in bondage. Secondly, there was a "burning bush" moment in King's life. Rosa Parks would not take her usual place in the back of the bus and King turned aside from his pastoral work to play a pivotal role in leading the successful Montgomery boycott. I would suggest that God called Martin in those days and Martin stepped forward, all without fully knowing where the journey would lead. Further, I would suggest that God had given King a vision of the possible future into which he would lead his people. God even allowed King to echo Moses' words and feelings at having been to the "mountain top" to see a future he would never enter. And, by King's own words, God strengthened him in those moments when his own people murmured against him:

> The words I spoke to God that midnight are still vivid in my memory. "I am here taking a stand for what I believe is right. But now I am afraid. The people are looking to me for leadership, and if I stand before them without strength and courage, they too will falter..." And almost at once my fears began to pass from me. My uncertainty disappeared. I was ready to face anything. The outer situation remained the same, but God had given me inner calm... I knew now that God is able to give us the interior resources to face the storms and problems of life. [1]

There is also evidence of the fruit of King's leadership. Even he was allowed to see some of the changes that his leadership brought forth. He got to experience some victories as well as the struggle. And there is something else...

another criteria which has become evident by looking backward from King through Jesus to Moses. Each of these Situational leaders was able to commit themselves totally to something that would take them away from their usual places of comfort and familiarity. They would each commit themselves to a vision that ultimately claimed their lives. It was not death or martyrdom that they sought, however. They simply gave themselves over to the power of the vision and the leadership of God. Finally, like the other leaders we have mentioned, M.L. King had a deep and intimate relationship with God. He had a consciousness of being where God intended him to be.

We have looked briefly at several persons in history, ancient and modern, as we have considered Situational leadership. Is there anything we can apply to ourselves in all this? Are we Situational leaders? Do we even want to be? What contemporary leadership principles carry over from the biblical models?

I do not believe we choose to be Situational leaders. I do believe that we can choose to respond to God's call, and, depending on the circumstances, may be seen to have been a Situational leader. I believe that God is already at work in us, by the means of grace, to equip us for leadership. I do not mean to suggest that each one of us will be a Moses or Martin Luther King, but I am convinced that God is preparing us for our moment to respond to God's call. Family of origin, early childhood experiences, life lessons and opportunities for learning, successes and failures all contribute to making us who we are at a given moment in time. Some of us will not recognize God's handiwork; some of us will not know God's name. Some of us will not know the situation to which we are being called. We will not have heard the cries of the people. But there will come a moment (or moments) when we will have an opportunity to "turn aside and see this thing" which God is doing outside the ordinary of our experience. It will require us to make a commitment to leave the comfort of our cultural "safe place" and follow the leading of our God-given vision and be true to our God-shaped values. Many us will not be able to leave our flocks or family business or even our holy work. Some of us will be so preoccupied with self that we will not even see the burning bushes or hear the voice from the wilderness. But for those who do, their lives will never be the same. They will be invited into a closer relationship with God that will strengthen them for the difficult moments and days ahead. And they will see the evidence of God's hand upon their witness. People will be influenced. Lives will be changed. The Kingdom will come closer and God will be glorified.

Endnotes

1 Quinn, Robert E. *Change the World: How Ordinary People Can Accomplish Extraordinary Results.* 2000. Jossey-Bass Inc. P. 56

REFERENCE LIST

Block, Peter. 1993. *Stewardship: Choosing Service Over Self-Interest.* San Francisco, CA: Berrett-Koehler Publishers, Inc.

Clinton, J. Robert. 1988. *The Making of a Leader.* Colorado Springs, CO: NavPress

Fisher, David. 1996. *The 21st-Century Pastor.* Grand Rapids, MI: Zondervan

Goldsmith, Malcolm. 1997. *Knowing Me - Knowing God: Exploring Your Spirituality with Myers-Briggs.* Nashville, TN: Abingdon

Herrington, Jim, Bonem, Mike, Furr, James H. 2000. *Leading Congregational Change: A Practical Guide for the Transformational Journey.* San Francisco, CA: Jossey-Bass Publishers

Interpreter's Dictionary of the Bible. 1962. Nashville, TN: Abingdon. s.v "Moses" by R.F. Johnson

Malphurs, Aubrey. 1996. *Values-Driven Leadership: Discovering and Developing Your Core Values for Ministry.* Grand Rapids, MI: Baker Book House

Markham, Donna J. 1998. *Spiritlinking Leadership: Working Through Resistance to Achieve Organizational Change.* Mahwah, NJ: Paulist Press

McKim, Donald K. 1994. *The Bible in Theology and Preaching: How Preachers Use Scripture.* Nashville, TN: Abingdon

Metzger, Bruce M., Coogan, Michael D., eds. 1993. *The Oxford Companion to the Bible.* New York, NY: Oxford University Press

Mulholland, M. Robert. 1985. *Shaped by the Word: The Power of Scripture in Spiritual Formation.* Nashville, TN: Upper Room

New Interpreter's Bible. 1994. Nashville, TN: Abingdon

Quinn, Robert E. 2000. *Change the World: How Ordinary People Can Accomplish Extraordinary Results.* San Francisco, CA: Jossey-Bass Publishers

A Tale of Two Providences
John Sanders*

This is a review of three books on divine providence: *Still Sovereign: Contemporary Perspectives on Election, Foreknowledge, and Grace*, eds. Thomas R. Schreiner and Bruce A. Ware. Baker Books (Grand Rapids, Mich., 1995, 2000), 356 pages. *God of the Possible: A Biblical Introduction to the Open View of God*, Gregory A. Boyd. Baker Books (Grand Rapids, Mich. 2000), 175 pages. *God's Lesser Glory: The Diminished God of Open Theism*, Bruce A. Ware. Crossway Books (Wheaton, Ill. 2000), 240 pages.

Debate on the doctrine of divine providence has been heating up in recent years. A spate of books, journal articles and conference papers has appeared for and against "freewill theism" in general and the openness of God model in particular. Throughout this essay I will interact the broader topic while concentrating on these books. These three books tell the stories of two different views of divine providence: two from a strong Calvinistic (meticulous providence) perspective and one from an openness/Arminian (general providence) perspective.

Still Sovereign

The thirteen essays in *Still Sovereign* attempt to present a case for Calvinism and rebut many of the arguments found in two volumes edited by Clark Pinnock which sought to defend Arminianism.[1] The book was first published in two volumes in 1995, but in 2000 a number of essays were omitted in order to republish it in a single volume. The editors, Schreiner and Ware, are to be commended for producing a fine collection of essays that are, for the most part, well researched and well written. The book is divided into three parts: biblical analysis (nearly two-thirds of the book), theological issues and pastoral reflections (very brief).

The purpose of the book is to "defend the classical view of God's sovereignty" from the corrosive acids of our culture that exalts the human over the divine. Arminian theology, they claim, is pushed around by cultural forces and exalts the human over the divine such that the divine glory is stolen away from God and given to humanity because, for Arminians, humans are the "ultimate determiners of salvation." (pp. 11, 49, 101, 237, 286 and 323). "The doctrines of grace are questioned" today (p.18). The "plain teaching" of scripture is distorted by Arminians who, as "rationalistic" logicians, impose their system onto scripture.

---

*John Sanders is Associate Professor of Philosophy and Religion at Huntington College, Huntington, Indiana.

Several points need to be made regarding these general claims before surveying the chapters individually. First, by "the classical view" and "the doctrines of grace" the authors mean the Augustinain-Calvinist tradition. However, the claim that they represent "the" classical view cannot be supported for the simple reason that, as some of the authors in the book note, the early fathers along with the Eastern Orthodox, Anabaptist, Arminian, Wesleyan, and Pentecostal traditions along with many Roman Catholics have always affirmed "freewill theism" and rejected theological determinism. If any tradition has the right to the title "the classical view" it would seem the older and more widespread strand of the tradition, freewill theism, has the better claim. If the authors simply claimed they were defending the "classical Calvinist" view, I would have no qualms. Second, throughout the book the authors decry as "caricature" when Arminians claim that humans are puppets in the Calvinistic schema, yet they repeatedly claim that humans "save themselves" according to Arminian theology. Each side fails to see itself in the description of the other. Moreover, both camps believe the "plain teaching" of scripture supports their respective views. Both sides affirm the clear teaching of scripture to be exactly opposite positions. How shall we resolve these contestations? Will appeal to more scripture be of benefit? Should we conclude that the hermeneutical skills of one side are depraved while those of the other are elect? Apparently, on this issue, the Bible is capable of being read by very devout Christians in quite different ways. It would seem that some epistemic humility is in order. The doctrines of human finitude and the noetic effects of sin (sin distorts our reasoning) ought to chasten us from making extravagant claims about the correctness of our theologies. Moreover, if culture affects the thinking of all of us, then we should be cautious about claiming that our theological opponents are the only ones "pushed around" by cultural forces. None of our theologizing escapes being conditioned by cultural trends, and it is high time evangelicals not only admit this, but make it an active part of our hermeneutical processes. It simply will not do to have one side making the "culture" accusation of their opponents while claiming themselves to be cultural virgins.

Now let me turn to the individual chapters. The first three chapters of the book present a defense of specific sovereignty (everything that occurs is specifically ordained by God to happen) from the Old Testament, the gospel of John and the Pauline corpus. They cover many of the standard Calvinist texts used to support meticulous providence and so provide a beneficial survey. The opening chapter by Ortlund correctly argued that, according to meticulous providence, God cannot be said to "respond" to creatures since this would make God dependent upon creatures (p. 30). It makes no sense to say that everything that happens is precisely what God has ordained to happen and then claim that God is responding to something we do. I shall return to this point latter in the article. Ortlund's discussion of the Old Testament texts on divine repentance is very poor. He fails to interact with any of Terence Fretheim's detailed studies of these texts.[2] If someone is going to claim that the three dozen or so texts affirming that God changes his mind do not really inform us what God is like, then they need to take Fretheim's thorough discussions into account. Morover, in this chapter and throughout the book the well-know "pancausality" texts are cited and interpreted to teach that God specifically ordains each and every calamity that occurs (e. g. Amos 3:6; Isa. 45:7). It would be good to see these authors interact with the work of Fredrik Lindström who thought the Bible taught divine pancausality, but, after a thorough analysis, came to the conclusion that the biblical authors do not teach this.[3]

Thomas Schreiner presents a well-researched and irenic study of Romans 9 and individual election. The chapter seeks to counter two views. First, Schreiner argues that Craig Blomberg and others are wrong to see Romans 9 referring to "historical destiny" rather than salvation. Although the original references about Jacob and Esau in the Old Testament may well refer to peoples (nations) and not individuals, Schreiner believes that Paul applies these texts to the salvation of individuals. Though I think Schreiner is correct that Paul is applying these texts to the topic of divine election to salvation, I do not believe Paul is addressing the Calvinist-Arminian formulation of this debate. It is so difficult for us today not to read our debates into the text. Schreiner also rejects the notion that Romans 9 is about "corporate" rather than individual election. Here he discusses William Klein's book on the topic.[4] Schreiner uses the analogy of buying a professional baseball team to argue that election involves specific individuals, not merely an abtract entity. When you purchase the franchise (an abstract entity), he says, you also purchase all of the individual players and coaches that are included. Well, this is true if you buy an existing franchise, but if you purchase the right to a brand new franchise, say the Geneva Supralapsarians, there are no individual players or coaches at the time of purchase.

John Piper's chapter argues that though the Arminian "pillar texts" (e. g. Jn 3:16; 1 Tim 2:4) speak about God's love for all, they do not override unconditional election. He argues that there are "two wills" in God: one that all people enjoy salvation, and the other that only those specifically chosen by God will enjoy salvation. Piper, following Jonathon Edwards, correctly identifies a similarity here between the Calvinist and Arminian perspectives since Arminians claim that God wills that all people enjoy salvation and also that God wills that only those who exercise faith in Christ will enjoy salvation. Hence, there are two wills or, as I would prefer to say, two areas about which God makes decisions. The difference, he notes correctly, between Arminians and Calvinists lies in where each view locates God's higher commitment.

Whereas Arminians locate it in God's desire to grant us the freewill necessary for a relationship of love, Calvinists locate the higher will in God's desire to manifest "the full range of God's glory in wrath and mercy" (p. 124). For Piper and others in this book, God's glory would not be fully displayed unless God both saves some and damns others.[5] Calvinists are often asked why God does not redeem everyone when it seems it is within the divine power to do so. The typical Calvinist response is to say that God is not obligated to save anyone (p. 245). But, according to these authors, if God were to save everyone then the full force of God's wrath would not be displayed and if none were saved then the full force of God's love would not be displayed (e .g. p. 85; 124). That is, the divine glory needs some people to be redeemed and some to be damned. Though there is nothing in the creature that obligates God to save some of them, it is the case that the divine glory obligates (necessitates) God to save some people and to damn others in order for the divine nature to be fulfilled. Consequently, God needs human beings for redemption and damnation in order for God himself to be fulfilled.

By far the longest chapter in the book is Wayne Grudem's fine study of the warning passages in Hebrews. He argues that the specific terms used in 6:4-6 may legitimately be read as describing either genuine Christians who have fallen away or as referring to non-Christians who were attracted to the gospel but then lost interest. However, he argues that only one of the terms used in Hebrews to describe the truly regenerate is found in 6:4-6. From this and other arguments he concludes that the warning passages are directed against people who have experienced many of the blessings of the gospel but who were never actually saved in the first place. Without taking anything away from Grudem's solid work, I would like to suggest that John Wesley was correct that arguing about whether genuine Christians can become unsaved is a moot point until we first answer: How do we know whether one is actually saved now? After all, both those who say genuine believers can lose their salvation and those who argue that those who fall away were never genuine believers to begin with, are looking at precisely the same people.

D. A. Carson picks up this issue in his essay on assurance. He has a helpful study on what should and should not be the basis of our assurance. Though our works are some evidence that we are truly saved, Carson believes the Puritans went overboard with this. He suggests that our assurance of salvation is based primarily on the objective work of Christ and secondarily on our own works and the witness of the Holy Spirit. Moreover, he says that we will not attain any "absolute, epistemologically tight Christian assurance" (p. 276). Nonetheless, he does claim that Calvinism provides a psychological comfort that is impossible for Arminianism. This is because, for Calvinism, the believer's security is in God, not in any introspection of conscience or observation of works. However, Carson overreaches here because the doctrines of unconditional election and the perseverance of the saints provide assurance for the believer only if we can confidently identify ourselves as one of the elect.[6] Granted, our assurance is in Jesus. But how do we know that we actually are in Jesus? The Arminian will question whether she is deceiving herself that she is a genuine Christian while the Calvinist will wonder whether he is truly one of the elect. After all, perhaps God has simply ordained that I "look like" one of the elect when I am actually not. How can I know the difference? Evangelicals still have a ways to go in developing a theology of assurance.[7]

S. M. Bough's chapter on foreknowledge claims that it means "to choose," and so the Arminian view of election will not work. Although the chapter contains some helpful research, Bough repeatedly makes claims that go way beyond his evidence (an error not limited to his chapter alone, however). Even more distressing is the caustic tone and use of fallacious reasoning against his opponents. For instance, because the openness of God view agrees on one point with Socinianism, Bough calls it "Neo-Sociniansim." Since view A has one point in common with view B, views A and B must be identical. Given such reasoning, we could arrive at all sorts of interesting connections. For instance, Baptists agree with Roman Catholics that Jesus is the messiah so Baptists must be "Neo-Catholics." Since Calvinists agree with Stoicism on divine determinism, Calvinists are "Neo-Stoics." It is unfortunate that some evangelicals use such deceitful practices in order to disqualify their opponents a position at the dialogue table.

Bruce Ware's chapter seeks to demonstrate that the biblical teaching on divine election, calling and grace supports a Calvinistic soteriology. Ware begins by noting that "Calvinists and Arminians have more points of agreement than disagreement." Nonetheless, he believes that Calvinism provides a better cumulative case for explaining the data of scripture for these three doctrines. Ware surveys a number of favorite Calvinist texts and explains them clearly.

Schreiner's second chapter in the book seeks to refute the Wesleyan notion of prevenient grace. He briefly explains and then critiques four arguments used in favor of prevenient grace. Schreiner concludes that the idea of prevenient grace is not taught in scripture but is an imposition read into scripture in order to solve logical problems and justify God's love. Though I do not agree with all of Schreiner's exegesis, I do believe that he is correct that some of the biblical texts used to support the notion of prevenient grace do not do so. True, the texts may be read in a way compatible with the Wesleyan teaching, but they do not necessarily support the Wesleyan teaching. However, I see the same thing being done by many of the authors of this book—the texts used to support Calvinism may be read in ways compatible with Calvinist teaching, but they do not necessarily support Calvinist teaching. Doing theology is much more complex than most evangelicals allow. There is no easy way to "disprove" either Calvinism or Arminianism for they are complex theological formulations integrating scripture, logic, personal and social proclivities, and traditions. Evangelical theology needs to come of age, recognize these complexities and learn to live with epistemic humility.

J. I. Packer's chapter articulates the nature of God's love, both universal and particular. Packer says that "God loves all in some ways" and "he loves some in all ways" (p. 283). God grants blessings to all, but loves some in a way that regenerates them. He calls this teaching "strong meat, too strong for some stomachs" such as for the Arminians. Of course, Arminians do not find the meat too strong, but too rancid. Moreover, Packer claims that Arminians do not allow for the mystery of God's ways, but instead make God into the image of a giant man who is frustrated and disappointed. However, Arminians may counter that they are not anthropomorphizing God, but simply acknowledging God's theomorphizing humanity.

The three final chapters discuss sovereignty in daily life, prayer and preaching. Jerry Bridges claims that the type of sovereignty we affirm makes a big difference in the way we live our daily lives. He says that every detail of our lives, including every instance of blindness, cancer, and loss of job, is woven by divine sovereignty into the framework of God's eternal plan. Consequently, we can trust God that everything that happens to us is for the best: to "bring glory to himself and good to his aching child." Does Bridges mean that each and every instance of suffering is for the individual good of the sufferer? The rape and murder of a young girl is for her good? It would be more believable if Bridges said, following the Stoics, that such instances of evil were somehow for the overall good rather than each individual's good. Furthermore, he says that God ordains everything that happens to further the divine glory. But he also says, "that all our plans should aim for the glory of God" (p. 296). My question is: if everything, including my sin, does, in fact, further the divine glory, then what sense does it make to say we "should" aim for the divine glory? How can we fail to enhance the divine glory given meticulous providence? More on this below.

A typical criticism of Calvinism is that it reduces the motivation for evangelism and the urgency of prayer. This is incorrect, however, as C. Samuel Storms shows. For the Calvinist, prayer and evangelism are the divinely ordained instruments through which God has decided to work. God not only ordains the end that Gary will be saved on a particular day, he also ordains the means by which Gary will hear the gospel and be saved. Hence, Calvinists have certain motivations for prayer and evangelism even though they may not be all identical to those available to Arminians. Regarding our prayers for the unsaved, Storms says that our prayers do not render "God's choice contingent."

God's decisions, according to the authors of this book, are never dependent upon our prayers. Inconsistently however, Storms twice says that God is "pleased to ordain that he will save them in response to the prayers of others" (pp. 316, 320). Use of the word "response" by a proponent of meticulous providence is inappropriate because it implies that God is reacting to something we have done which God has not ordained. That Storms does not really mean that God "responds" to our prayers, however, is evident when he later says that "from the human perspective" it might be thought that "God's will for Gary is dependent upon me and my prayers" (p. 320). But God is not dependent upon my prayers since God also "by an infallible decree, has secured and guaranteed my prayers as an instrument." Hence, it "as though he were prevailed upon by prayer" but God is not actually prevailed upon. Earlier in the book, Ortlund correctly observed that, according to specific sovereignty, God does not respond to humans (p. 30). What Storms should have said is that God may be said to save Gary "after" my prayer but not in response to my prayer.[8] Why then do Storms and others continue to say God "responds" to our prayers? Could it be that the cultural forces of American evangelicalism are shaping their theology? Evangelicals will not buy into a theology in which God does not respond to our prayers so it is not surprising that many Calvinists would fudge at this point.

I will close the review of this book by quoting Carson: "we will always have some mystery. The important thing will be to locate the mystery in the right place" (p. 273). This is quite correct and brings out a fundamental difference in theologies. Whereas Arminians locate the mystery in heart of sinful humanity—why humans spurn the divine love is the mystery of iniquity—Calvinists locate the mystery in the heart of God—why God chooses some for salvation and not others.

God of the Possible

General providence, the view that God does not meticulously control everything, is the second "tale" of providence. Greg Boyd defends this view in his popular level introduction to the open view of God. He first wrote much of this material for pastors and laity in his denomination, the Baptist General Conference, who were receiving misinformation from Boyd's critics. The openness of God view affirms that God created *ex nihilo* and sovereignly chose to endow humans with the libertarian freedom necessary for a relationship of love to develop. Openness teaches that God enters into genuine give-and-take relations with us. God, of course, does the initiating, but unlike classical theism in which God cannot receive, proponents of openness believe that God does receive some things from us. God truly responds to our prayers and our actions. Open theism is, in large part, a derivation of Arminianism, which is why Bruce

Ware calls it "neo-Arminianism" in contrast to "classical Arminianism." There are two areas in which openness departs from classical Arminianism. First, whereas most Arminians have held that God is timeless (experiences an eternal now) open theists maintain that God, at least since creation, experiences before and after (temporal progression). Second, and clearly this is the lightning rod issue, classical Arminians have affirmed what is called **simple foreknowledge** whereby God simply "sees" all that we will do in the future but God does not determine or cause us to do what we will do. Thus, God has **exhaustive definite foreknowledge** (EDF hereafter) of all future contingent events. Proponents of openness, however, affirm a view called **presentism** wherein God knows all the past and present exhaustively and that part of the future that is determined to occur (e. g. earthquakes and God's decisions to act unilaterally). God does not have EDF of future human decisions. Rather, God has beliefs about what we will do based upon our habits, character, circumstances and the like. Hence, some of the future is definite or closed and some of the future is indefinite or open. Some of the future is open and does not become definite until God and humans make it definite by their actions.

The bulk of Boyd's book is given over to an explication and defense of presentism as a biblical and theologically sound understanding of divine omniscience. The debate is not whether God knows all that can be known (omniscience). Rather, it is about what can be known. The debate concerns "the nature of the future: Is it exhaustively settled from all eternity, or is it partly open? That is the question at hand, nothing else" (p. 17). For Boyd, God is omniscient. It is just that the future actions of beings with libertarian freedom do not yet exist so there is nothing there for God to know. Just as omnipotence is not denied by saying that God cannot do the logically impossible, so omniscience is not denied by saying that God cannot foreknow the logically unknowable. Half of the book is devoted to expounding biblical texts, both those that are used to support the open view and explaining how an open theist might interpret the texts typically used in support of EDF.

In chapter one Boyd explains the varieties of EDF and the reasons why thoughtful Christians arrived at this view. He then seeks to interpret texts such as the prediction of Peter's denial and Psalm 139:16 in ways compatible with presentism. Chapter two marshals a wide array of biblical texts used to support presentism. Some of these evidences are: (1) God expresses "regret" (Gen. 6:6; 1 Sam. 15:10); why would God do that if he always knew these things were going to happen? (2) God confronts the unexpected where God thought Israel would do one thing when she, in fact, did another (Isa. 5; Jer. 3:19-20, 19:5). (3) God gets frustrated with Moses' resistance (Ex. 4:10-15) which seems incongruous if God always knew Moses would go. (4) God tests people to discover what they will do (e. g. Deut. 8:2 and Gen. 22 where God tests Abraham and says "now I know that you fear me"). (5) God speaks in indefinite terms of what may or may not be (Exod. 4:1-9), and uses words such as "if" (Ex. 13:17), "perhaps" (Ezek. 12:3), and "might" (Jer. 26:19). (6) God strives with people trying to get them to believe and is grieved when they resist him (Isa. 63:10; Eph. 4:30; Acts 7:51)—why would God strive with people he always knew would not believe anyway? (7) People may be blotted out of the book of life (Rev. 22:19), and (8) God changes his mind in response to what people do (Exod. 32:14; Jer. 18; 2 Kings 20:1-6).

Chapter three explores the difference openness theology makes in everyday life. Boyd addresses the liberating nature of living with possibilities instead of prescribed pathways for divine guidance. He rejects the "myth of the blueprint," the notion that God has everything laid out for us to follow. Boyd claims that the urgency of prayer in the open view is the strongest of any theological position because God may or may not do something because we prayed or failed to pray. The problem of evil and suffering is discussed, wherein Boyd argues that we need not feel anger at God for "doing this to me" since these are not part of the divine plan. He tells a particularly poignant story of a young woman whose husband abused her and destroyed her life's dream of becoming a missionary. Though much of the practical applications of openness theology are in line with classical Arminianism, there are distinctives, particularly when it comes to divine guidance since, according to open theism, God does not know with absolute certainty what beings with freewill will do in the future. Some classical Arminians think this a terrible defect in openness thought since they suggest that if God possesses EDF, then if God foresees something is going to happen that God does not want to happen, God can prevent it from happening. However, Boyd is correct that the Arminian view of simple foreknowledge—where God simply sees the future—does not do God any good. The reason is simple: if God knows the actual future, then God cannot change the future since this would make his foreknowledge incorrect. For example, suppose that God has eternally foreseen my death in a car accident on a specific day. Your prayers that I arrive safely are useless since God has foreseen the actual, not the possible, future and cannot change it. The problem with the traditional Arminian view of foreknowledge is that God is "cursed with the ability to foresee disaster while being unable to do anything about it" (p. 101). Simple foreknowledge is useless for providence.

The final chapter of the book answers eighteen common questions and objections raised against the open view.[9] For instance, has anyone else ever held this view in the history of the church? How do you explain the anthropomorphic expressions in scripture about God's arms and eyes? Does not the open view "limit God?" What is the relationship between God and time?

Although his answers are brief and written for a popular audience, Boyd does a good job overall of providing possible answers to these questions. I say "possible answers" because not all proponents of openness agree with one another regarding all the details of the position. At times, Boyd uses biblical texts that do not support the open view. For instance, rhetorical questions in scripture (pp. 58-59), though compatible with openness, do not provide evidence that God does not know the future. Nonetheless, Boyd accomplishes his objective of giving a readable introduction to the open view.

God's Lesser Glory

Bruce Ware's book is an invective against open theism.[10] He rails against publishers, such as InterVarsity, Baker Books and Christianity Today, for even discussing this issue. He laments that the Baptist General Conference, after several years of debate, failed to rule openness theology out of bounds. Fortunately, says Ware, the national meeting of the Southern Baptist Convention passed several changes to their doctrinal statement, one of which affirms that God has EDF, thus ruling out presentism as a viable theory. However, Ware fails to mention that the state conventions have to ratify such changes and the largest groups of Southern Baptists, including the Texas Baptist Conference, have refused to endorse the changes. Ware and John Piper seem to believe that open theism is the most serious threat to the church today. It will "destroy churches" if left unchecked.

The book is divided into three parts: describing open theism, critiquing open theism biblically and theologically, and criticizing how openness theology applies to the Christian life. Chapter two correctly identifies open theism as a subset of classical Arminianism and clearly explains the arguments used by open theists to critique the views of omniscience known as simple foreknowledge and middle knowledge. As with *God of the Possible*, this book also deals primarily with whether or not divine omniscience includes EDF.

Chapter three gives some of the theological arguments for the open view. For the most part, Ware states these correctly, though with some exaggeration. Though Ware acknowledges that any view that affirms libertarian freedom for humans entails God taking risks, he believes that the open view implies a greater degree of risk taking on God's part than in classical Arminianism (pp. 48-9). However, this is wrong. For simple foreknowledge, it may be said that once God decided to create this world and then previsioned all that would happen in this world, God "learned" about all the things humans would do against his will—all of the risks God would take. When God begins to create he is aware of all the risks. However, this does not lessen, in the least, the actual risks God takes because what God previsions is not under his control. Hence, a God with simple foreknowledge takes precisely the same risks as does

50

a God with present knowledge.[11]

In the next chapter Ware attempts to rebut the biblical arguments (see the summary in Boyd above) used by open theists in support of their view. Ware opens the chapter by claiming that the denial of EDF is the watershed issue separating open theism from all forms of "classical theism" including Calvinism and traditional Arminianism (p. 66). Again, this is not the case. Though Ware correctly states the providential uselessness of simple foreknowledge (p. 37), he fails to understand the wide-ranging import of this. If the traditional Arminian view offers no providential advantage over presentism, then EDF simply cannot be the watershed issue. In the history of the church there have been two major understandings of God. The first, developed by the early fathers and held by the Eastern Orthodox and Arminians, is that God has chosen to be, for some things, affected (conditioned) by the creatures. God grants humans libertarian freedom such that God does not control our actions. God genuinely responds to our prayers and what we do. I call this major strand of theology "freewill theism." The other major understanding of God, developed by Augustine, Aquinas, Calvin and others, denies that God is in any respect affected by creatures—God is impassible. God grants humans compatibilistic freedom whereby we are free to act on our strongest desires, but our desires are determined by forces beyond our control. God never responds to what creatures do, rather creatures respond to what God has decreed they do. This view, known as classical theism, affirms that God is absolutely unconditioned by any being external to God, so God is strongly immutable and impassible.

The great divide separating the freewill and deterministic theistic traditions is actually (1) divine conditionality (including impassibility and immutability) and (2) the type of freedom God decided to grant humanity. Classical theism affirms God's absolute unconditionedness and compatibilistic freedom while freewill theism affirms that God is affected by us and that God grants humans libertarian freedom. At times, Ware admits that his real gripe is against all forms of freewill theism, including traditional Arminianism, and not merely against openness (pp. 42, 48, 143, 153, 208, 214, 223, and 226). Though Ware spends most of his time addressing the denial of EDF, he seems to understand that this is not the crucial issue (though highlighting it will certainly help sell books).

If one of the two watershed issues between classical and freewill theisms is divine unconditionality and its attending doctrines of impassibility and immutability, then what are we to make of Ware's claims that God is affected by us in that God has emotional responses to what we do? God does not, he says, change in his purposes, will or knowledge (p. 73), yet God can "literally change" (pp. 73, 92) in his emotional experiences to what we do as those situations arise in time. Ware calls this "relational mutability." Several comments are in order. To begin, if Ware is repudiating strong formulations of impassibility and immutability and saying that we can actually affect (condition) God, then he should beware of throwing around the charge of heresy since the Council of Chalcedon anathematized anyone who says God is passible or changeable.

Moreover, it is not clear to me what Ware believes about God's relationship to time. It seems that he affirms divine timelessness or sempiternity (all time at once), yet he says, "God literally sees and experiences in this moment what he has known from eternity" (p. 73). However, this seems to suggest that a timeless deity experiences time which, as Aquinas and Calvin clearly understood, is contradictory. Timelessness just means that God does not experience "moments." A number of evangelicals want a timeless being who nonetheless experiences events along with us in history. This is due, in part, to our desire for a "personal relationship with God." However, the great luminaries of the faith (as well as contemporary Christian philosophers) understood that a timeless being cannot experience any sort of change since change involves time.[12] A timeless being cannot be said to plan, deliberate, respond, regret, grieve, or get angry. That is why classical theists have maintained that these biblical expressions are anthropomorphisms that do not actually inform us about the way God is. If Ware wants to attribute responding and grieving (p. 92) to a timeless deity, then he will have to explain how it does not contradict the metaphysics of timelessness.

In a similar vein, it is incoherent to affirm both that God's will is never thwarted or frustrated in the least detail (p. 149) and also affirm that God has changing emotional responses to what we do. How can a deity who ensures that everything happens precisely as he wants it to happen, grieve over what happens? Is God unstable? Again, the great classical theists understood that these affirmations are contradictory. Clearly, Ware either has to revise more of the divine attributes of classical theism and move closer to freewill theism or he must return to standard classical theism.

Chapter five presents numerous biblical texts in support of God having EDF. The bulk of the chapter focuses on Isaiah 40-48. Ware interprets these chapters to mean that God puts his very claim to deity to the test: "If I can accurately predict what will happen then I am God, if I fail, then I am not God. "[H]is exclusive claim to deity, set in contrast to the false gods, demands that God *as God* get *everything* right" (p. 109). Ware does a good job of bringing out much of the meaning in these passages. It is disappointing, however, that he does not interact with Boyd's explanation of these same texts. According to Boyd, God does not put his deity on trial by claiming to accurately predict the future, but by claiming to be able to announce something and bring it about

(Isa. 46:10-11, 48:5; see Boyd, pp. 29-31). In other words, the test concerns divine omnipotence not foreknowledge. There are a number of biblical prophecies that are problematic for proponents of presentism to explain and Ware discusses them. More work needs to be done by proponents of presentism on various biblical texts.

Ware's remarks on "conditional predictions" are somewhat baffling. *"Conditional predictions*, by their nature, give to God a 'back door,' as it were. If things don't go as he hoped or thought, he can always change what he had said. In all such cases, we *cannot rightly expect exact fulfillments* of these predictions" (p. 137, emphasis his). After belaboring the point that God puts his very deity at stake by predicting the future with 100% accuracy, Ware now says that we cannot expect God to accurately predict the future all of the time. If that were not bad enough, what sense does it make to affirm that God's will is always accomplished (p. 149) and also to affirm that things may not "go as he hoped or thought?" How can they fail to go as God foreordained they should go?

In the next chapter, Ware raises three objections to open theism: it has an excessively immanent view of God, it believes that God takes risks, and it implies that God cannot achieve all of his purposes. Are these criticisms of openness only? "To a great degree, the openness proponents are saying only what their Arminian colleagues have long argued" (p. 143). Yet, Ware believes that the denial of EDF exacerbates these problems. As I explained above, however, simple foreknowledge functions for divine providence in precisely the same way presentism does.

Chapters seven through nine critique openness while explaining the Calvinistic view of prayer, guidance and suffering. Ware writes: "if divine guidance is an evolving reality, it would seem that one would need regularly to keep seeking God's leading on each specific question or burden, even if one had sensed strongly just what the Lord's leading was on that matter." If so, "How can you tell whether to persevere in difficulty?" (p. 181). This is an accurate description of the openness position, but if it is a "problem," it is a problem for Ware's theology as well. The Calvinist God may be guiding you into something for a time, all the while planning to lead you out of it after a time. Calvinists do not believe God guides you into one thing forever. True, whatever you are doing at the moment is precisely what God has ordained you to do, but God may have ordained you not to persevere in some endeavor and so stop what you were doing and switch to something else. Hence, the Calvinist, just as much as the open theist, has to regularly seek God's leading and question whether God wants him to persevere.

Regarding suffering, Ware accuses the Arminian God of being "foolish" to create a world of beings with libertarian freedom over which God cannot control. Using the Joseph story, Job, and Romans 8:28, he argues that the "Christian" God is in total control such that every "evil" that occurs is actually for the good. Ware does observe, correctly, that openness does not entirely solve the problem of evil since God could prevent each and every instance of moral evil, but chooses not to do so. Again, it is disappointing that Ware fails to even mention the responses open theists have given to this question.

In the final chapter Ware claims that, "In my view, every other understanding of divine providence to some extent diminishes the sovereignty and glory of God. It brings God's wisdom and power down to the level of finite human thinking" (p. 220). Moreover, "The conclusion that God's glory is diminished by libertarian human freedom is impossible to avoid" (p. 226). Here, Ware lays his cards on the table and indicts every form of freewill theism, including traditional Arminianism, for diminishing the divine glory. Again, this is why the watershed issues dividing this debate are divine conditionality and human freedom—not the denial of EDF! Moreover, there is a subtle problem in Ware's accusation: is it actually possible for freewill theism to rob God of glory if God exercises specific sovereignty? No, it is not, and the reason why is easy to see. According to Ware, God foreordains everything that happens and everything that happens is for his own glory. Nothing occurs that can detract from the divine glory. Well then, how can freewill theism (including openness) lessen God's glory if God ordained it for his own glory? Is God, for his own glory, foreordaining that his own glory be diminished? Hence, given Ware's own theology, it is impossible for open theism to lessen God's glory and so the thesis (and title) of Ware's book is shown to be incoherent on Ware's own terms.

Endnotes

[1] *The Grace of God, The Will of Man: A Case for Arminianism* (Grand Rapids, Mich: Zondervan, 1989) and *Grace Unlimited* (Minneapolis: Bethany Fellowship, 1975).

[2] Terence Fretheim, "Divine Foreknowledge, Divine Constancy, and the Rejection of Saul's Kingship," *Catholic Biblical Quarterly*, 47, no. 4 (Oct. 1985): 595-602; *Exodus*, Interpretation (Louisville: John Knox, 1991); "The Repentance of God: A Key to Evaluating Old Testament God-Talk," *Horizons in Biblical Theology* 10, no. 1 (June 1988): 47-70; "The Repentance of God: A Study of Jeremiah 18:7-10, *Hebrew Annual Review* 11 (1987): 81-92; *The Suffering of God: An Old Testament Perspective*, Overtures to Biblical Theology (Philadelphia: Fortress, 1984).

[3] See Lindström, *God and the Origin of Evil: A Contextual Analysis of Alleged Monistic Evidence in the Old Testament*, Frederick H. Cryer trans. (Sweden: CWK Gleerup, 1983).

[4] William Klein, *The New Chosen People: A Corporate View of Eleciton* (Grand Rapids: Zondervan, 1990).

[5] For criticisms of Piper's thesis see my *The God Who Risks: A Theology of Providence* (Downers Grove, Illinois: InterVarsity Press, 1998) pp. 217-219, 241-242.

[6] See the excellent essay by William Abraham, "Predestination and Assurance" in Pinnock, *Grace of God*, pp. 231-242.

[7] It is small wonder why evangelicalism has popularized an answer to this question by promoting a liturgical rite which, when performed, grants one assurance that one is a genuine believer. By reciting the "sinners prayer" parents and friends assure you that you are an actual Christian now.

[8] See my *God Who Risks*, pp. 269-271 for more discussion.

[9] For more questions and more answers from a number of proponents of openness visit the websites: www.opentheism.org and Christus Victor Ministries at www.gregboyd.org

[10] Not all classical theists are so caustic, however. For a more civil discussion that makes use of many of Ware's objections see Chris Hall and John Sanders, "Does God Know Your Next Move?" *Christianity Today* (May 21, 2001): 38-45 and (June11, 2001):50-56. Also see our forthcoming book with Baker, *Divine Debates*.

[11] I have explained this in some detail in my "Why Simple Foreknowledge Offers No More Providential Control than the Openness of God," *Faith and Philosophy* 14, no. 1 (1977): 26-40 and the abbreviated version of this in my *God Who Risks*, pp. 200=206.

[12] For a discussion of the literature on God and time see *The God Who Risks*, p. 319 n. 78.

Old Testament Prophecy
Recent Publications
by David W. Baker*

Over the last several years, numerous studies of various elements of
the Old Testament prophetic books have appeared. In this essay, a number of
these will be reviewed and evaluated. This article is not intended to be
comprehensive.[1]

Introduction

E.W. Heaton is a British Old Testament scholar whose 1977
introduction to the prophets has recently appeared in a new edition.[2] The author
self-consciously addresses the needs of the lay reader rather than the scholar,
so the footnotes rarely cite secondary sources, mainly indicating scriptural
passages supporting the claims made in the text. There is a useful bibliography
at the end of the book, so those who wish to pursue matters raised further may
do so. It has been updated with works as recent as 1993.

Heaton, in a very readable, and very English, style, divides his book
into ten chapters. 'Making Sense of the Old Testament' explores the history of
OT interpretation from the early period through the middle ages to today. He
sees it best understood as the records of a peoples encounter with their God,
and the reinterpretation of these stories as time went on. In chapter 2, the
writing prophets are briefly introduced in the context of their times, which for
Daniel is the second century BC, making him not properly one of the regular
prophetic books, and for Isaiah is three distinct periods, since it is seen as a
composite rather than a unity. 'The Vocation of the Prophets' explores their
societal roles as both individuals and institutional functionaries. Here he
overviews various topics such as ancient Near Eastern parallels and the
puzzling urim and thummim. 'The Preaching of the Prophets' looks at the
prophetic message forms and the righteousness of their person.

In an analysis of individual prophetic books, Heaton divides the
chapters into 'judgment without promise' (Amos., Isaiah, Micah). He sees these
as lacking hope, so needing to relegate passages of promise such as Amos 9:11-
15 to an addition by a later author. This is a more liberal approach to Scripture
where what should be found in it based on some interpretive preunderstanding
controls what is actually written in it. 'Salvation through judgment' (Hosea,

---

*David W. Baker (Ph.D., University of London) is Professor of Old Testament
and Semitic Languages at ATS.

Jeremiah), 'Salvation after Judgment' (2nd Isaiah, Ezekiel), and 'Salvation in the Restored Community' (Haggai and Zechariah, anonymous prophecy [mainly 3rd Isaiah, with excerpts from other prophets as well) round out the brief overview of the content of the books. The final two chapters explore the proposed movement from oral sermon to written text, as well as later editing and interpretation, and a look at Daniel against the background of apocalyptic, including that of the Qumran community and the early church. Heaton also touches on the topic of Jesus and prophecy.

The book will properly find a place in college and seminary libraries, where it provides a succinct, readable introduction to the more liberal view of the prophets. Teachers and preachers will be well served by reading it critically, especially noting what the prophets actually said as recorded in Scripture, carefully comparing that with the claims made here.

Another British author, John Eaton, almost simultaneously produced another elementary level introduction.[3] He has his eye toward the reader, who would probably be in college or a Bible study, in that he includes various and questions for personal research, discussion, consideration (looking for contemporary parallels) which are good stepping stones beyond the book and into the Book. All of the prophets receive at least some mention and discussion, and a 2 page bibliography supplies resources for further reading. His approach to such matters as dating is mainstream, assuming but not arguing for a late Daniel and tripartite Isaiah. For those looking for a readable text from this perspective, Eaton will serve you well.

In a much briefer and more popular format, John Sailhamer of Western Seminary has one of the books in his "Zondervan Quick Reference Library" on Biblical Prophecy.[4] It provides one page summaries on a number of aspects of prophecy which are designed to be readable in no more than a minute. There are seven sections in the book. "Introduction," "Hermeneutics," "Biblical Theological Foundations" discussing the kingdom of God and the various biblical covenants, "OT," "NT," "Central Themes" of restoration, redemption, messianism, Israel and the church, the tribulation, rapture, millennium, and heaven, and "Theological Systems," i.e. covenant theology and dispensationalism. There is also a concluding glossary defining fifteen terms.

The list of topics shows Sailhamer's dispensational interests, but he does do an admirable job in presenting various positions in such a brief space. The volume, as the entire series, would do well in a church library.

Studies

A.	Ronald E. Clements, an British Baptist and emeritus professor in London, has written on aspects of the prophets for a number of years. In a 1996 he collected fifteen of these studies and published them together with an introduction in which he provides an overview of 'The Interpretation of Old Testament Prophecy, 1965-1995.'[5] Clements' own work provides a useful entré into the field over this period, since he is one of the major contributors. His introduction focuses on four major issues of the period, form critical studies of the prophets (what kind of literature are their writings?), Isaiah (unity/diversity, historical background), formation of the literary form of the prophets' writings, and interpretation of the prophets.

The essays themselves are collected into six parts. The first concerns the historical and political background of some of the prophecies, as well as the messianic hope, the second explores aspects of the interpretation of Isaiah (7:10-17 and its messianic interpretation, Deutero-Isaiah's development of earlier themes, and the book's unity), the third, Jeremiah (1-25 and the Deuteronomistic History, and hope in the book), the fourth, Ezekiel (prophecy in crisis times, and redactional history of chapters 1-25). The last two parts look at apocalyptic (the reading of Scripture and the canonical process, and apocalyptic's origins) and the prophetic canon (structuring of the prophetic oracles as a literary device, prophecy as literature and theology, and prophetic editing) respectively.

The book is a fitting summary of the work of a leading scholar in this field. It contains useful material for the serious student of the prophets, and should find a place on all seminary and Bible college library shelves. There is material of interest to the pastor, but the more scholarly nature of the work would probably mean that her book funds could better be spent elsewhere. Also, since the articles are all reprints, they all are available from the original sources.

B.   The Israeli scholar Uriel Simon has also produced a volume of seven collected essays on the prophets, all but one published previously.[6] Simon teaches at Bar-Ilan University in Israel and directs the Institute of Jewish Bible Research there. His goal in this volume is to provide a literary reading of the text, paying special attention to what the narrator says and how he says it. This type of study is based on the objective text more than any putative sources, whether literary or historical. Factuality is secondary to literary craft in this type of study.

This series of studies goes beyond others reviewed here in that it involves the 'former prophets,' the historical books which provide the background for the 'latter' or writing prophets. The stories he studies are: Samuel's birth (1 Sam 1:1-28; 2:11a, 18-21) and call (1 Sam 3), Saul and the witch at Endor (1 Sam 28:3-25), David's confrontation by Nathan (2 Sam 10:1-

12:31), the episode of the young prophet and the old man of God (1 Kings 13:1-32a + 2 Kings 23:16-18), Elijah versus Baal (1 Kings 17-19), and Elisha and the Shunemite woman (2 Kings 4:1-8:6). All of these episodes show the importance of prophetic actions, providing a needed foil to the idea that they were just men of words.

This type of study is different from a commentary, in that it looks at a story as story, seeing it in its unity rather than as simply a collection of constituent parts. Plot and character play a larger role than do individual words and historical details, the grist of a commentary. This final form type of analysis is a welcome addition to, and even an advance over, studies which analyze and dissect a text to death. Here its life and vitality are explored. This is a technical study, however, and uses literary jargon and linguistic description which will need some work by the uninitiated in order to be able to understand. An interesting element for most readers of this review is the common reference to Jewish interpretations of the stories, and aspect which is too often neglected in Christian interpretation.

This volume should be in all libraries interested in biblical and literature studies.

C.   A 1997 collection "offers an entrée into the methodological pluralism of biblical studies" (back cover).[7] It contains 7 chapters by as many authors on topics such as: new looks at prophecy in the Mari archives (Herbert Huffmon of Drew University), the nature of prophetic literature (David Petersen of Iliff School of Theology), rhetoric in Jonah (by the editor from the University of Capetown), the prophet's religious and social role (David Noel Freedman of UC- San Diego), charisma and the prophets (Ronald Clement, emeritus from Kings College, London), the unity of Isaiah (Rolf Rendtorff of the University of Heidelberg), the conclusion of Joel (by James Crenshaw of the University of North Carolina), and prophecy in art (with illustrations; by Zefira Gitay, an art historian also from Capetown). The book shows that an approach to a text or a genre cannot be monolithic, and that insights can be gained from numerous different vantage points. This book will be for more specialist libraries.

D.   Three recent works study different aspects of the prophecy of Isaiah. They show the breadth and depth of topics and questions which can and must be addressed in biblical studies.

1. The broadest of these works is a collection of twenty-eight essays by as many scholars from around the world in honor of the sixty-fifth birthday and retirement in 1996 of the Dutch Catholic scholar W. A. M. Beuken.[8] This

is a useful and important volume in its own right, and well illustrates the various approaches which can helpfully illuminate a text. The essays are divided into four sections. The first, 'Isaiah and his Book,' looks at aspects of the biblical book as a whole. Of the four essays in this part, two (by Clements and Hermisson, the latter in German) explore the central, and literarily uniting, motif of Zion, one (by Sweeney) explores Isaiah's reworking of the Davidic covenant in Isaiah, and the fourth (by Gitay), explores the act of reading, building on the author's interest in rhetoric and textual function.

Section two, 'Proto-Isaiah,' consists of eight essays. They illustrate different approaches and breadths of study, ranging from a study of historical information in Isaiah 1-39 (by Schoors), through a suggestion regarding literary origins (of 36-39, by Vermeylen), to analyses of much shorter text sections (1:29-31 as an early example on 'inner-biblical interpretation' of 6:13, by Williamson; the literary unity of 8:19-23, in German by van der Woude; whether 11:1-10 is to be seen as universal or particular, in German by Zenger; the linguistic area of domain analysis applied to 12:1-6, assisting in an appreciation of the communicative function of the text, by van Wieringen; an analysis of metaphor in general, and then concentrating on 25:10a, by Doyle; and a close reading of 27:10-11, by van Grol).

Section three, 'Deutero- and Trito-Isaiah,' includes seven articles. Their interest spans the identity of Deutero-Isaiah (by McEvenue, suggesting a woman, the female identified as the herald in 40:9), history and eschatology in Deutero-Isaiah (where Leene suggests that the he 'borrowed the basic structure of his view of ...[these] from the Enthronement Psalms'); a form-critical analysis, using a discourse analysis of 40:12-42:13 to explore lawsuit, debate, and wisdom connections (by Dijkstra); a phrase in 40:20 (van Leeuwen); a close reading of 42:10-12 (by Prinsloo); the Cyrus oracle (44:24-45:7) illuminated by syntax, versification and structure (by Fokkelman); and the structure and redaction of 60:1-63:6 (by de Moor).

Section four, 'Intertextuality and Wirkungsgeschichte,' contains nine articles dealing with aspects of Isaiah being a user of texts produced by others (Gen 1-3 in 65:16b-25, by Steck, and a producer of texts and motifs used by, or at least found in, others (Ezekiel 20:32-44, by Lust; LXX 49:1-6 by van der Kooij; Habakkuk, by van Ruiten; Wisdom of Solomon 3:1-4:19, by Beentjes; Job 16-19, by Bastiaens; the rabbinic Pesiqta de Rav Kahana 16, by Teugels; Matthew's christology [Matt 1:23; 4:15-16], by Weren), and finally, the phrase 'knowing Yahweh' as it occurs throughout the Old Testament, by Vervenne).

While the articles are scholarly, and some quite technical, the breadth of topic should provide material of interest to all readers. Even those without technical or literary competence in some of the areas will find useful and stimulating information here. Though probably only appearing in academic libraries, the volume does deserve a look by all interested in this, one of the key Old Testament books.

2. A more narrowly defined work by Hugh Williamson of Oxford University investigates the composition and transmission of Deutero-Isaiah.[9] He opens with a chapter on recent Isaiah study, showing evidence suggesting multiple authorship of the book and categorizing scholarship during the last century into six approaches to the authorship question, in particular as regards First and Second Isaiah. His particular interest for the volume is the "the extent to which, if at all, chapters 40-55 of Isaiah were directly influenced at the point of composition by the form which chapters 1-39 had assumed by that time" (27). In other words, were they originally separate works, or was Deutero-Isaiah (D-I) aware of and influenced in any way by Isaiah of Jerusalem, who he assumes to be two different people. He concludes that not only did D-I know the earlier work which he saw as being prophecy anticipating his own time, so felt free to use and edit earlier material to show the close connection between the periods and the two parts of the literary work. This useful, technical work will need to be consulted by all who are working on Isaiah and the history and development of OT prophecy.

3. The third, and most technical and topically narrow volume explores the subject of word-order, and variations within it, in Deutero-Isaiah.[10] Setting himself within the field, Rosenbaum states that "this study will utilize a functional approach to language, in particular Functional Grammar, as well as insights and terminology from Russian Formalism, Prague School linguistics and Discourse Analysis" (1). The functional approach explores how language serves as a medium of communication, an inductive approach to language study, in contrast to a formal approach which is more deductive. The original language citations, of which there are many, are presented in transliterated Hebrew with accompanying abbreviations designating the syntax of the clause, literal interlinear translations into English, and a more flowing, idiomatic English translation. Linguists will find the work valuable, though the lay reader, and even most specialist biblical scholars will value the work, but probably only after it has been divested of technical jargon. This kind of primary research and analysis is vital, but so is its 'translation' into a form usable to others outside the field of technical linguistics. For technical libraries.

E.   While studies of the verbal rhetoric have been appearing for some time, analyses of non-verbal rhetoric, such as that undertaken by Kelvin G.

Friebel, are much rarer.[11] His is a revised 1989 PhD thesis completed under Michael Fox at the University of Wisconsin–Madison. The author's choice of Jeremiah and Ezekiel is good, since there are so many sign-acts used in the books. He asks whether the acts were actually performed, or whether they were just a symbolic literary construct, how they communicate, how they fit into rhetorical theory, and how they compared with other, extrabiblical examples of nonverbal communication. He looks at what he reckons is a unique such prophetic act at Mari, as well as numerous non-prophetic acts in the area of the Near East. A further area of exploration which would be fruitful is the iconographic evidence. Since there is much extant material from Mesopotamia during the time when the two prophets were active, a comparison of literary and representational instance of the sign-acts should be mutually illuminating.

F.   The minor prophets and their use in the pulpit is the subject of a study by Elizabeth Achtemeier.[12] She is a good choice for writing such a volume due to her academic and practical experience in classroom and pulpit. She recently retired form teaching Bible and homiletics at Union Theological Seminary in Virginia. For each prophet, Achtemeier lists 2-3 recommended commentaries, usually including her own, brief historical and theological overviews. She then has several selected passages for which she provides comment regarding their place in the lectionary reading cycle, features to note in the text, and possibilities for preaching. It is a well thought out volume, though each reader would probably think other texts should have been highlighted. Also, it will seem too sparse to most readers, which could also be a goal for the book, to drive the reader back to the text and to the study in order to delve even further into the major themes and truths held in these 'minor' prophets.

G.   A different kind of study was undertaken by Else Holt for her doctoral research at the University of Aarhus in Denmark.[13] Due to the tardiness of this review, and the short print runs of such works, it is unfortunately already out of print. The volume is a revision of a thesis finished in 1990 under Knud Jeppesen at the University of Aarhus in Denmark. Its purpose is 'to make a traditio-historical examination of the traditions about Israel's past as they appear in the book of Hosea: what is their background, and how does Hosea use them?" (14). She is thus asking a literary question rather than a historical one. Historical veracity is not a prerequisite of literary use- they are two different categories. She does make the refreshing observation, however, that the burden of proof does lie with those denying the authenticity of one passage or another, in contrast to a strictly minimalist approach which can deny anything not externally verifiable.

The two main historical elements Holt explores are Jacob (Hos 12) and Israel as God's covenant elect. Since she does not hold that the final form of the Pentateuch yet existed until later, she feels that Hosea worked with more fluid traditions in his reinterpretation of the character of Jacob. She determines the following scenario: Hosea uses and interprets traditions known to him; editors (his disciples?) gather these traditions; these editors place them in a framework of exhortation to Judah, showing the nations history in a positive light and urging the new hearers to learn from it. She also shows that Hosea's discussion of the elect people of the covenant is also based on historical traditions. As part of this study she includes a comparison of the cult of Yahweh with that of Ball, and a study of the word *sidq*.

Holt's work is an important reminder of the separation between historical veracity of statements made in a work and a study of the composition of a work. From a more 'maximalist' position, I would like the affirmation of the former along with a study of the latter, but they are separate issues. The book is suitable for academic collections.

H.   The changing person and role of the prophets is the subject of the revised doctoral research which William Schniedewind undertook at Brandeis University.[14] The author traces the shift between the prophet who received and delivered the living 'word of God' during the pre-exilic period to the post-exilic prophet who was charged with receiving and interpreting the word. They moved from oracle to hermeneut. While Schniedewind does not note them, there seem to be parallels to the same shift with the scribes, who also were originally channels of divine revelation but took upon themselves the interpretative role. It is the latter which is condemned in the NT, since they seemed to have held their interpretations to be on a similar level of authority as that of the original divine revelation. His approach is to start with the portrait of prophecy reflected by the Chronicle, whose post-exilic viewpoint upon pre-exilic prophecy proves enlightening.

Schniedewind opens with a detailed analysis of titles used of the prophets, and the inspiration formulae (e.g. 'Thus said the Lord") which they used. Based on these elements, he groups prophetic speeches in order to determine the roles of the prophets and their words. It is here he sees the movement toward inspired interpreter of traditional texts, a role similar to that suggested above by Williamson for the author of Deutero-Isaiah. There are chapters looking at the levitical singers (1 Chron 25:1-6) and their role as 'teaching priests' as relates to the concept of inspiration (concluding that their music was inspired, according to the Chronicler, but that they were not prophets), the relationship between the king, especially David, and prophecy, and the prophets as historians in their acknowledged use of sources.

The volume is well-written and accessible. It uses unvocalized and untransliterated Hebrew, but translations allow the non-Hebraist access to the discussion. The work will need to be consulted for all those interested in prophecy and the history of the religion of Israel.

I. Larry McQueen published a Pentecostal interpretation of Joel in 1995.[15] He seeks to set the classical Pentecostal text of Joel 3:1-5 (English, 2:28-32) into its OT context before taking the usual hermeneutical step of looking at it through Acts 2. The author first introduces Pentecostal hermeneutics, with emphases on an experiential pre-understanding, Scripture as living, and the place of the community in interpretation. He then sets out his understanding of Joel as a literary unity composed in the early fifth century BC.

One chapter looks to Joel's literary structure and the place in it of the promise of the Spirit's outpouring. It then notes the varied genres of lament, salvation, and judgment, and themes of the day of the Lord and Zion. It then looks at the Spirit promise in light and context of these elements. A second chapter looks at the themes of Joel, particularly that of the Spirit, in the NT (Luke-Acts, Paul, John, Hebrews and Peter). McQueen then traces the use of these themes through the history of Pentecostalism up to the mid-1990's. The book is a useful exercise in textual analysis from one denominational perspective, a task which has many applications for different texts as well as different traditions. The volume will be of interest to Pentecostals, those interested in hermeneutics, and students of both Joel and the Holy Spirit.

J.　　　Richard Schultz explored to important topic of the use of verbal parallels (or quotations) in the prophets in a revision of his 1989 Yale thesis.[16] There are so many apparent quotes in the corpus, and there has never been an adequate method developed to study them, so this is an important endeavor. Following good thesis form, Schultz starts by looking at the history of research. He points out various issues which make the problem especially difficult: dating, textual transmission, prophetic 'schools,' the growth of exegesis, the text and its 'authority,' and canon. In order to develop his own methodology, Schultz looks at 4 non-prophetic literatures: ancient Near Eastern early Jewish, proverbial sayings and others quotations in the OT, and western literature.

Schultz sets out his own method as having three elements: the use of both verbal and syntactic correspondence in order to first identify a quotation, a combination of synchronic and diachronic analysis looking to both historical and literary contexts, and an awareness that a quotation can have varied functions. As a test of his method, Schultz analyses 5 passages from Isaiah which are either quoted in Isaiah or in other prophetic books. The book is foundational for future study of the OT prophets, and even beyond, since parallels exist beyond their boundaries. The volume needs to be in all theological libraries.

Commentaries

The Twelve

A.   A recently inaugurated series, "Berit Olam: Studies in Hebrew Narrative & Poetry" recently released a two volume work on the Minor Prophets.[17] Sweeney opens with a currently 'hot' topic, the formation of the 12, ably surveying suggestions that it came into being diachronically, over a lengthy time period, or synchronically, all in one period. He admits the importance of the question, but his commentary format proscribes detailed and definitive analysis. Each book is given a lengthy treatment in the commentary proper. This consists of: an   overview discussing canonical location, historical background, themes, critical and theological issues; the commentary proper, and a section of further readings, both other commentaries and more detailed studies.

Accessability to a wide range of readers is kept in mind through transliteration of Hebrew, Greek and Aramaic. All should benefit from the careful, readable presentation of suggested interpretations. Sweeney keeps his eye firmly on the OT, not showing interest in latter development of interpretation or use in the NT or the contemporary church. An element of this serviceable set which will distinguish it from many such is its discussion of the interpretational ramifications of the canonical setting of the various books.

B.   While not technically a commentary series, an addition to the "Westminster Bible Companion" should be made here.[18] Brown very briefly seeks "to explain the biblical book in its original historical context and explore its significance for faithful living today" (back cover). Aimed at lay readers, it very briefly introduces each book, provides each section of the text in the NRSV, and comments on each section, looking at motifs and themes within the section and their development elsewhere. This is a useful starting point for those wishing to encounter the prophets for the first time, but most will soon want to delve deeper into some of the riches which are available. This volume, and the series, could find a place in church and academic libraries

C.   The series "The Forms of the Old Testament Literature" is also not technically a commentary, but rather an introduction to the form critical study of each biblical book. The first on the minor prophets appeared in 2000.[19] While not a complete commentary, students of the text will find useful information on Nahum through Malachi. Each prophetic book starts with a bibliography covering the entire book, a structural outline and discussion of the content of entire book, as well as discussions of genre, historical and literary setting, and intention, with another briefer bibliography concerning these latter matters. Smaller sections are also analyzed from each of these perspectives, as well as a look at text criticism. The book concludes with a well-annotated glossary of genres and formulas.

There is no actual exegesis or application. The series should be in all academic theological libraries, but most preachers and church teachers would find other resources much more productive for their needs.

Hosea

Two commentaries have recently appeared from T&T Clark in Edinburgh, and show well the British excellence in exegetical work.[20] One, an addition to the International Critical Commentary series, explores Hosea.[21] In it A.A. Macintosh of St John's College, University of Cambridge, provides a careful and extremely detailed analysis of this important prophecy, concentrating especially upon text critical issues, which is one of the strengths of the series. The introduction, covering almost one hundred pages, spends thirteen of these on text critical sources. Comment on these is also included in the discussion of every passage in the commentary itself.

The series itself started almost a hundred years ago, but only produced volumes on some the biblical books. The last few years have seen its rebirth, with some of the gaps being filled, and replacements written for previous volumes. In the Old Testament series, Jeremiah has been covered in two volumes by William McKane.[22]

The volume starts with a brief overview of the book's contents, and an extensive bibliography of twenty-seven pages. An introduction covers canonical location, language (reflecting the northern prophet's ow idiolect), form and style, composition (a literary work, transmitted and effected by Judean redactors), historical background (reflecting the period 750-720 BC), Hosea's thought/theology, and has a time-table of the period.

The commentary proper consists of the author's own translation of a verse at a time. Notes on the translation, generally Hebrew usage and grammar, uses untransliterated and untranslated Hebrew. The following comment section is more accessible, however, using transliteration and translation. The comment is sensible and thorough in matters linguistic and historical, though those seeking theological application will need to look elsewhere. Each section concludes with the evidence from other texts and versions.

This is an excellent and useful representative of this kind of technical commentary. While mainly directed toward the scholarly community, interested students and pastors will also find material of use, even though this would not be the first commentary on the book to which they would most naturally refer. The price will most probably limit its use in other than libraries, but all serious seminaries and Bible colleges should have it, and the entire series.

Joel

A.   A resuscitation of the venerable "New Century Commentary" is being undertaken by Sheffield Academic Press. A new volume on the series is on Joel and Amos by Richard Coggins, formerly of King's College, London.[23] Coggins begins by discussing the concept of 'the twelve,' and then briefly explores issues of dating. He proposes that both the prophecies were only brought together in the second century BC, though some of their elements may have circulated earlier, even, for Amos 'possibly from a time when Israel had its own king' (7). For each prophet there is a specific introduction concerning issues of date, authorship, unity, genre, etc., followed by the commentary proper. It proceeds verse by verse expounding on matters historical, textual, lexical, and literary. Any Hebrew used is in transliteration so all should find it usable. For those seeking a competent, mainline approach to these two books in a manageable size, Coggins will serve well.

B.   A more theological and applicational approach from an evangelical perspective is provided by David Prior in "The Bible Speaks Today" series.[24] The series sets itself the task of falling between the sermon (contemporary and accessible but light on exegesis) and the commentary (exegetical but without an eye to practicality and readability). It well fills a needed niche, while not denying the critical importance of both of the other genres. While not a traditional commentary, Prior does keep one eye firmly on the 'first horizon' of the biblical text, seeking to determine, as far as possible, date, author and setting. He also keeps his other eye on the 'second horizon' of contemporary application. He is quite comfortable looking to the NT in a much fuller way than most OT commentators, and also few there are who refer to *Schindler's List* and UNICEF figures on atrocities to children in Rwanda. Preacher and teacher will greatly appreciate Prior's efforts, and it should serve as a reminder to even the most serious scholar that there should be at least some practical relevance to even the most esoteric of study. These prophets do indeed have much to say to us in our own lives of uncertainty and atrocity.

Amos

A new edition of a commentary by Gary Smith, professor of OT at Midwestern Baptist Seminary in Kansas City.[25] This edition brings the bibliography up to date, and incorporates it more fully into the discussion by greatly expanding the number of footnotes, especially in the introduction. Smith does an excellent job in interpreting this very important book against its historical, geographical and religious background. Pastors and students would be well served in having this as a primary resource for studying the book, and it would find a useful place in seminary, college, and even some church libraries. The new publishers are to be commended, as are the original publishers, for establishing such an occasional series for commentaries of excellence which have not been commissioned for some established, ongoing series.

Jonah

The Anchor Bible series provides biblical commentary from across the theological spectrum, from conservative to liberal, Protestant, Jew and Catholic. Jonah, belatedly noted here, appeared in 1990 from the pen of the department chair in religion at the University of North Carolina at Chapel Hill.[26] He, as one with interest in the language and history of Mesopotamia, is a good choice for this prophet. He views the book as a composite with unifying features. As regards dating, he surveys 4 different kinds of evidence which have been brought to bear, coming tentatively down to a post-exilic date. He also has brief sections on the use of Jonah in Jewish and Christian liturgy. Sasson sprinkles the commentary with special discussions of such matters as ancient storms, animals in narratives, and Hebrew poetry. He then concludes the body of the book with a discussions of genre or literary classification, and also of Hebrew narrative art, very useful questions to ask of all writing, but particularly of Jonah.

The book contains much transliterated Hebrew, not all with proximate translation, some will find it heavy going. There is much here to justify the care and diligence needed in reading, so this book should not be ignored by any interested in Jonah. It, and the its series, needs to be in every serious theological library.

Micah

Also from Britain is the commentary on Micah by William McKane, Scottish emeritus professor at St Andrew's University.[27] The volume seems to be self-standing, not part of a series, even though the publisher is home for the esteemed "International Critical Commentary" series. It is an odd book, starting in without preamble on suggested textual additions. The author states his compositional thesis to be "that only Micah 1-3... is to be assigned to the eighth century prophet Micah, that the book of Micah bridges the centuries and that its history spans the pre-exilic, the exilic and the post-exilic periods" (7). He suggests a redaction history for the collection, and gives it several different *Sitze-im-Leben*, from the original 8th century prophecies to their use by exilic and post-exilic writers as a source for liturgical laments at the fall of the nation.

The commentary proper is accessible mainly to scholars, since Hebrew and Greek scripts are used, as are untranslated foreign quotes. The work is especially strong on text criticism, one of the special interests of the author, as well as the history of interpretation. Specialist libraries will find a place for this volume.

An established team of commentators, Francis I. Andersen and David Noel Freedman, have co-authored the Anchor Bible Commentary on Micah.[28] Like their other joint works (commentaries on Hosea and Amos in the same series) it is thorough and exhaustive in its coverage. This is illustrated by its 12 page index of authors cited, and its 67 page bibliography which, while claiming not to be exhaustive, is a goldmine of resources for those studying the book.

The frontal material includes a time line of kings and events from the period reflected in Micah (mid-eighth to late sixth centuries BC), a synoptic date chart of five kings (Uzziah/Azariah, Jeroboam, Jotham, Ahaz, and Hezekiah) mentioned by 4 prophets (Amos, Hosea, Isaiah, Micah) as determined by 7 contemporary experts on the time period, and two maps. The introduction proper looks at text, canonical placement, contents of the constituent parts of the book, the traditional divisions of the book as found in early manuscripts in Greek and Hebrew, the book's organization, previous studies and research methodologies, the relationship between Micah and Jeremiah (which share numerous items of vocabulary and theme), the book's literary integrity ("the book as a whole shows some signs of overall integration," 27), and scribal transmission.

The commentary itself is exhaustive in matters linguistic, historical, sociological, and philological. Poetics is also an interest of both authors, so it receives attention as well. Hebrew is almost always transliterated, as is Greek, usually with a translation close enough to allow even non-linguists to follow the argument, though some of the linguistic points themselves are esoteric enough to be beyond most lay readers. One of the strengths of the authors is placing the interpretation of the text within the context of the history of scholarship, so their references to others are numerous. This volume, and the series to which it belongs, needs to be in every serious biblical studies library.

Nahum

The *Historical Commentary on the Old Testament* is a good series, judging by the previous volume reviewed in this journal,[29] and the volume on Nahum does honor to the series.[30] The author teaches at the Theological University in Kampen and at the Free University in Amsterdam, continuing the Dutch tradition of the preceding volume and of the series editors. The series projections show wider scope than this, with a wide range of recognized scholars taking part. The author takes Nahum to be a pseudonym of a writer in Jerusalem about 660 BC, using earlier writings of Isaiah and the Psalms as well as Mesopotamian literature. Based on strophic analysis, he sees the entire book as 'a well-structured unity' (5). Spronk looks briefly at the book's theological context and the history of its interpretation before moving to the commentary proper.

The latter contains the author's translation, a section entitled 'essentials and perspectives' which discusses genre, historical setting, and theology. The 'scholarly exposition' which follows includes a bibliography with a history of exegesis and the author's own exegesis proceeding from canto (e.g. 1:1-11) through canticle (e.g. 1:1-3a) through strophe (e.g. 1:1) to word. Individual Hebrew words and phrases are given in Hebrew script which is usually unvocalized and untransliterated, so some of the argument will be beyond those without some linguistic fluency. The volume is especially strong in literary and philological material, though all with a serious interest in Nahum will need to consult it.

Habakkuk

Francis I. Andersen also recently published an Anchor Bible commentary on Habakkuk (see Micah above).[31] It follows the form of the series, and exhibits the same strengths as have already been mentioned. He does provide useful excurses on aspects of Hebrew poetry, including its language, use of verbs, chiasmus, scansion, and items which occur once in a passage but have double-duty grammatical functions, as well as a useful look at the categories of grammatical gender, specifically as it relates to *ruahi*, 'wind, spirit.' This volume is necessary for all serious students of Habakkuk.

Zephaniah

Another Anchor Bible volume has recently been published by Adele Berlin, who teaches Hebrew Bible and ancient Near Eastern literature at the University of Maryland, College Park.[32] Her contribution is much more modest in scope than other of this series mentioned here. In addition to the usual format of the series, she is cognizant of, and cites from, Jewish commentary on the book. She also has useful sections on intertextuality, author and date (an implied or fictive author to whom the book was ascribed in the post-monarchy period) and historical setting (the 7th century reign of Josiah). She does helpfully point out that those who date the author and events as portrayed in the text itself do not have to ask the same questions as those who put post-exilic words into a pre-exilic setting. The comments are useful, though their relative brevity (covering less than 90 pages) might lead some to other commentators for a fuller treatment, or they might be seen as a refreshing breeze after going through all of the detail of some of the previously mentioned works.

Zechariah and Malachi

The well-established, mainline commentary series 'The Old Testament Library,' is represented by a volume covering Zechariah 9-14 and Malachi written by David Petersen, professor at Iliff School of Theology in Denver.[33] It concludes a work published in its first part over a decade ago, and represents the more liberal end of the theological spectrum.[34] The latter does not come through too strongly here, since on any reckoning, the prophecies are relatively late. Petersen dates them to the Persian period (late sixth-early fifth centuries BC). He does a very good job in providing a historical, religious and social picture of that period, drawing on recent scholarship based on textual and artifactual resources. He brings out such points as the multiple Yahweh temples of the period, indicating that God was worshiped in places other than the Jerusalem Temple. There also seems to be evidence of religious syncretism at these shrines as well.

Petersen also analyzes the literary structure and form of the prophecies. He sees Zechariah 9-14 as a separate work than 1-8, consisting of a collection of 'originally diverse material.' Malachi he sees as an example of the diatribe genre, similar to a dialogue, using only the words of one party, with quotes from the other party. The analysis helps in understanding the book.

Following his own translation with notes on textual and grammatical matters, Petersen presents an interpretation of the text itself. Hebrew is transliterated and usually also translated. The commentary is a good look at the book as it fits into the Old Testament, with generous citations of illustrative OT passages. Those who look for comment on later, New Testament referents will be disappointed, however. All academic biblical studies libraries should have this book, and it will repay consultation by those interested in these two passages.

From a completely different theological tradition comes the Malachi volume in the Anchor Bible by Andrew E. Hill, who teaches at Wheaton College.[35] It is good to see increasing evangelical involvement in such high-profile commentary series. His preliminary material is much lengthier than is regular, with a useful glossary and extended discussions of literary (authorship, unity, genre, structure, form, literary features [with 25 different ones identified], message, and theology) and historical aspects relevant to the book, dating the prophetic oracles (near 500 BC; the discussion is supplemented by an appendix indicating the range of 7 different dating positions held by some 75 scholars), Malachi in the NT and in subsequent liturgy. Hill also includes very useful appendixes on: an analysis of the postexilic prophets based on a typological linguistic model initially developed by Robert Polzin and refined by Hill, a discussion of intertextuality or textual interrelationships between Malachi and other books, and the vocabulary of Malachi. This especially rich literary analysis, accompanied by good historical and linguistics analysis, makes it a worthy addition to this series, and a necessity in all theological libraries.

Endnotes

1. For a more detailed overview of the state of play of prophetic studies over the last quarter century, see David W. Baker, "Pondering the Prophets," in *The Face of Old Testament Studies*, ed. David W. Baker and Bill T. Arnold. Grand Rapids: Baker Book House/Leicester: Apollos, 1999, 266-294.

2. E. W. Heaton, *A Short Introduction to the Old Testament*. Oxford/Rockport, MA, 1977, 1996. xi + 202 pp., paper, $13.99.

3. *Mysterious Messengers: A Course on Hebrew Prophecy from Amos Onwards*. London: SPCK, 1997/ Grand Rapids and Cambridge: Eerdmans, 1998. 214 pp., paper, $18.00.

4. John H. Sailhamer, *Biblical Prophecy*. Grand Rapids: Zondervan, 1998. 93 pp., paper, $6.99.

5. Ronald E. Clements, *Old Testament Prophecy: From Oracle to Canon*. Louisville: Westminster John Knox, 1996. x + 278 pp. hardcover, $29.00. The introduction is found on pp. 1-19.

6. Uriel Simon, *Reading Prophetic Narratives*, trans. Lenn J. Schramm. Indiana Studies in Biblical Literature; Bloomington: Indiana University Press, 1997. xx + 363 pp, hardcover, $49.95.

7. Yehoshua Gitay, ed., *Prohecy and Prophets: The Diversity of Contemporary Issues in Scolarship.* Semeia Studies. Atlanta: Scholars Press, 1997. viii + 174 pp., paper, $24.95.

8. J. van Ruiten and M. Vervenne, ed., *Studies in the Book of Isaiah: Festschrift Willem A.M. Beuken.* Bibliotheca Ephemeridum Theologicarum Lovaniensum CXXXII; Leuven: University Press/Peeters, 1997. xx + 540 + 7 pp., paper, np.

9. H.G.M. Williamson, *The Book Called Isaiah: Deutero-Isaiah's Role in Composition and Redaction* (Oxford: Clarendon, 1994), xviii + 306 pp., cloth, $65.00.

10. Michael Rosenbaum, *Word-Order Variation in Isaiah 40-55: A Functional Perspective.* Studia Semitica Neerlandica; Assen: Van Gorcum, 1997. xii + 259 pp., paper, $63.00.

11. Kelvin G. Friebel, *Jeremiah's and Ezekiel's Sign Acts: Rhetorical Nonverbal Communication.* JSOTSup 283. Sheffield: Sheffield Academic Press, 1999. 535 pp., cloth, $95.00.

12. Elizabeth Achtemeier, *Preaching from the Minor Prophets.* Grand Rapids: Eerdmans, 1998. xii + 143 pp., paper, $14.00.

13. Else Kragelund Holt, *Prophesying the Past: The Use of Israel's History in the Book of Hosea.* JSOTS 194; Sheffield: Sheffield Academic Press, 1995. 160 pp., cloth, $41.00.

14. William M. Schniedewind, *The Word of the Lord in Transition: From Prophet to Exegete in the Second Temple Period.* JSOTS 197; Sheffield Academic Press, 1995. 275 pp., cloth, $41.00.

15. Larry R. McQueen, *Joel and The Spirit: The Cry of a Prophetic Hermeneut.* Journal of Pentecostal Theology Supplement Series 8. Sheffield: Sheffield Academic Press, 1995. 125 pp., paper, $14.95.

16. Richard L. Schultz, *The Search for Quotations: Verbal Parallels in the Prophets.* JSOTSup 180. Sheffield: Sheffield Academic Press, 1999. 395 pp., cloth, $88.00.

17. Marvin A. Sweeney, *The Twelve Prophets*. Collegeville, MN: Liturgical Press, 2000. xlii + 802 pp., cloth, $89.90.

18. William P. Brown, *Obadiah through Malachi*. WBC. Louisville: Westminster John Knox Press, 1996. xii + 209 pp, paper, $17.00.

19. Michael H. Floyd, *The Minor Prophets*, Part 2. FOTL XXII. Grand Rapids: Eerdmans, 2000. xviii + 651 pp., paper, $49.00.

20. The second is McKane's work on Micah discussed below.

21. A.A. Macintosh, *A Critical and Exegetical Commentary of Hosea*. Edinburgh: T&T Clark, 1997. xcix + 600 pp., cloth, $69.95.

22. W. McKane, *Jeremiah*, 2 vol. Edinburgh: T&T Clark, 1986, 1996.

23. Richard James Coggins, *Joel and Amos*. Sheffield: Sheffield Academic Press, 2000. xii + 170 pp., paper, $14.95.

24. David Prior, *The Message of Joel, Micah & Habakkuk: Listening to the Voice of God*. Leicester/Downers Grove: InterVarsity, 1998. 279 pp., paper, $14.99.

25. Gary V. Smith, *Amos*, A Mentor Commentary. Gaenies House, Fearn, Ross-shire IV20 1TW, Great Britain: Christian Focus Publications, 1998; originally Grand Rapids: Zondervan, 1989. 398 pp., hardcover, $29.99.

26. Jack M. Sasson, *Jonah: A New Translation with Introduction, Commentary, and Interpretation*. AB 24B; New York: Doubleday, 1990. xvi +368 pp, cloth, $32.50.

27. William McKane, *The Book of Micah: Introduction and Commentary*. Edinburgh: T&T Clark, 1998. xiv + 242 pp., cloth, $49.95.

28. Francis I. Andersen and David Noel Freedman, *Micah: A New Translation with Introduction and Commentary*. The Anchor Bible 24E. New York: Doubleday, 2000. xxv + 637 pp., cloth, $42.50.

29. Cornelis Houtman, *Exodus* I. HCOT; Kampen: Kok Pharos, 1993, reviewed in *ATJ* XXVIII (1996) 100 .

30. Klaas Spronk, *Nahum*. HCOT; Kampen: Kok Pharos, 1997. xxii + 153 pp., paper, np .

31. Francis I. Andersen, *Habakkuk: A New Translation with Introduction and Commentary*. The Anchor Bible 25. New York: Doubleday, 2001. xxii + 387 pp., cloth, $45.00.

32. Adele Berlin, *Zephaniah: A New Translation with Introduction and Commentary*. AB 25A; New York: Doubleday, 1994. xxii + 165 pp., cloth, $29.00.

33. David L. Petersen, *Zechariah 9-14 and Malachi*. OTL; Louisville: Westminster John Knox, 1995. xxii + 233 pp., cloth, $29.00.

34. David L. Petersen, *Haggai and Zechariah 1-8: A Commentary*. OTL; Philadelphia: Westminster, 1984.

35. Andrew E. Hill, *Malachi: A New Translation with Introduction and Commentary*. AB 25D; New York: Doubleday, 1998. xliv + 436 pp., cloth, $37.95.

The Best of the Best on Spiritual Formation: A Review Article
by Jerry R. Flora*

Aiden Wilson (A.W.) Tozer captured the minds and hearts of many Christians in the last generation. As pastor, editor, and author he produced substance and style that sounded prophetic. His pen seemed to be dipped first in fire, then in ice, as he both scalded the North American church and plumbed the depths of God's reality. His books *The Pursuit of God* (1949) and *The Knowledge of the Holy* (1961) quickly gained attention as near-classic in their dimensions.

Although Tozer had little formal education, wide reading and prayerful living prepared him for his task. At one point he drew up a list of books for those who want to explore "the deep things of God" (Snyder 1991, 231). But the list contains a shock. Among the 35 titles only seven come from Protestant writers. Apparently this leader who described himself alternately as an evangelical and a fundamentalist found 80% of his spiritual nurture in books written by Catholics.

As the twentieth century dashed to its finish-line, matters began to change. An explosion of publishing occurred in the area of spirituality and spiritual formation. The playing field broadened to include spiritualities of various religions, revival of old paganisms, and the so-called New Age spirituality. Along with this came a renewal of interest in the best of Christian literature, the goal of A. W. Tozer's quest.

New anthologies of devotional literature arrived on the scene in the 1990s, each of them trying to convey something of the richness of Christian spiritual writing. In this article I want to review several of these collections and offer a few recommendations among them. The bibliography at the close will give complete publication data for your further exploration.

1

Richard Foster has been a leader in Christian spiritual formation ever since his first book, *Celebration of Discipline*, appeared in 1978. Other distinguished publications have followed, climaxed by *Prayer: Finding the Heart's True Home* (1992) and *Streams of Living Water: Celebrating the Great Traditions of Christian Faith* (1998). Foster's writings always show

---

* Jerry Flora (Th.D., Southern Baptist Theological Seminary) is Professor ot Theology and Spiritual Formation at ATS.

depth of commitment, breadth of awareness, gentleness of spirit, and a striving for balance. Working alongside through much of the writing has been his friend and associate, James Bryan Smith.

Early in the 'nineties the two men collaborated to produce *Devotional Classics: Selected Readings for Individuals and Groups* (1993). This anthology introduces 52 great writers of the Christian church from its beginnings to the present. The selections were originally 4-page study and discussion tools for use in small-group settings. Each contains an introduction to the author, excerpts from his or her writings (printed in two-column format), a Bible selection relevant to the theme of the excerpt, reflection questions, suggested exercises, and concluding personal thoughts by Dr. Foster. The material has found ready acceptance in many quarters, thanks to the respect in which Foster is held and its flexible, user-friendly approach.

The book is a chunky paperback (approximately 7.5 x 9.25 inches) of 353 pages (including three indexes), organized topically. After a section on "Preparing for the Spiritual Life" (eight writers) it introduces five "great streams" of Christian tradition: the prayer-filled life (contemplative), the virtuous life (holiness), the Spirit-empowered life (charismatic), the compassionate life (social justice), and the Word-centered life (evangelical spirituality). Since its publication, Foster has concluded that there is a sixth "stream" of Christian tradition, the sacramental life (incarnational).

The book's greatest strength is this topical arrangement, along with the clear language used throughout and the inclusion of selections from Scripture. The format allows readers to explore up to a dozen writers in one stream of tradition. Of the 52 authors, all but four come from the western church, both Catholic and Protestant (rather evenly divided). The exceptions are Gregory of Nyssa and John Chrysostom from the ancient East and, more recently, Sundar Singh of India and China's Watchman Nee, both of whom were heavily influenced by English writers. Given the history of Christianity, women will always be under-represented in such collections, but thankfully there is a good handful here.

The book's greatest weakness is the obverse of its strength. How does one pigeon-hole a writer? John Wesley, for example, could fit in all the five categories proposed above. Foster admits this but feels the value to be gained is worth the risk. A few dates might be questioned, especially the birthdate of the book's first writer. C. S. Lewis was born in 1898, not 1900. The date of Sundar Singh's mysterious death is given as possibly 1933, but he disappeared in 1929, never to be seen again (Foster and Smith, 1993, 313). Apart from such quibbles, this is an excellent, clear, balanced introduction to great (mostly western) devotional writers topically presented. It was produced as a resource for both individual and group use, and it meets that goal. (A similar volume,

Spiritual Classics (2000), is now available as a complement to *Celebration of Discipline*.)

2

Robert Llewelyn is an Anglican priest noted as warden of The Julian Shrine at All Hallows Church, Norwich, England. This small chapel is built on the site of the cell where, in the 14th-15th centuries, Julian of Norwich lived and prayed. An anchoress (a solitary intercessor and spiritual director), Julian is the first known woman to write a book in English. *Revelations of Divine Love* is its traditional title, but Julian called her visions merely *Showings*. She has gained a large following in the past generation for reasons which we cannot explore here. In 1980 Llewelyn edited a much-abridged version of her book under the title *Enfolded in Love* (England) or *Daily Readings with Julian of Norwich* (USA). This began a whole series of small devotional anthologies introducing classic writers to the reading public. He then collected many of those into *The Joy of the Saints: Spiritual Readings throughout the Year* (1988).

This paperback of 374 pages offers meaty introductory material by Llewelyn, one-page readings for every day of the year, brief biographical notes on the writers, and an author index. Like the pocket-size books of which it is composed, *The Joy of the Saints* is visually inviting, with ample margins and occasional small drawings. The readings follow no discernible pattern nor are all those by any author grouped together. Rather, the reader experiences through the year a significant one-page selection for each day prepared by some great Christian writer of the past. The 4th-century desert fathers are the earliest, and the latest is Therese of Lisieux (d. 1897).

One might expect that Llewelyn's connection with Julian and the Julian Shrine would dispose him to prefer her writing above all others, and that is indeed the case. Following at some distance are Francis de Sales, Augustine, William Law, Martin Luther, John of the Cross, and John Wesley in that order, plus seven others. Aside from the desert fathers and Isaac of Syria, all represent the western church. Males predominate, but Julian of Norwich, Margery Kempe, Teresa of Avila, and Therese of Lisieux offer feminine voices. Since no writers are later than the 19th century, it is important that they be presented in clear, contemporary English, and that is happily so. The book's strength is its invitation to encounter a smaller number of authors in greater depth than Foster and Smith can offer, together with its arrangement in daily readings (as brief as four lines but never longer than one page).

3

Day by Day with the Early Church Fathers (1999) is both like and unlike Llewelyn's anthology: Alike in that this too is a book of one-page daily readings in no discernible sequence, followed by biographical notes. Unlike in that the 39 authors here all come from the early church, with no writer later than John of Damascus (d. A.D. 749). The division is about even between East and West, but no women are among them. Augustine appears most often, followed in order by John Chrysostom, Cyprian, and Origen. The compiler-editors are J. Alan Sharrer, Christopher D. Hudson, and Lindsay Vanker, but there is no hint of who they are, what they do, or their qualification for this task.

Two items from the introductory pages help to identify how the book was produced. (1) "The devotional readings in this book have been carefully selected from the 38-volume series *The Early Church Fathers*, first published in 1885. Each ... devotion was edited in a procedure that updated the language yet preserved the original meaning the church father intended" (Sharrer, Hudson, and Vanker 1999, iii). (2) "All Scripture references in this book are taken from the *Holy Bible: King James Version*" (copyright page).

The volume is somewhat narrow in format (approximately 5.5 x 9.25 inches), a hardback of 389 pages. The introduction is a single page, followed by daily readings of one page each. Small medieval woodcuts appear at the top of every page (a different one for each month), then a scripture passage and the text from the early writer, often accompanied by a sidebar highlighting one sentence from that text. The book concludes with biographical notes on the ancient authors (more full than in Llewelyn) and a detailed index of the source for each day's reading. January 1 ("Tears and Joy"), for example, is identified as coming from John Chrysostom's *Homily 6 on Matthew*, paragraph 8.

The strength of this anthology is its focus on writers of the early centuries with an even distribution between West and East. By limiting itself to the King James version of the Bible and the 1885 translation of the church fathers, the book needs no acknowledgment of authors or publishers, nor copyright permission for anything it includes. All is in the public domain, and all is available without permission and without cost, making the publisher's task easier (and cheaper). But readers deserve at least some identification of the editors and more helpful introduction than a mere page.

4

Another volume of readings from the early church is *Drinking from the Hidden Fountain: A Patristic Breviary. Ancient Wisdom for Today's World* (1993). I find this book to be a visual and tactile pleasure. It is a sewn

paperback with a plasticized cover, good quality paper, and a very handy size
(5 x 7 inches). Here are daily readings from about 45 writers grouped so that
each month's material follows one theme. May's excerpts, for example, are
titled "Come to me, O God, that I may come to you." A meaty prologue
precedes the readings, and they are followed by biographical notes, a general
index month by month, and an index of sources.

Most of the writers come from the eastern church with John
Chrysostom predominating, followed in order by Basil (the Great) of Caesarea
and a close race between Maximus the Confessor, Augustine of Hippo,
Clement of Alexandria, Defensor Grammaticus, and Cyril of Jerusalem. In
addition to Augustine, the West also offers Tertullian, Ambrose, and Boethius.
Three authors break out of the early church period: Simeon the New
Theologian and Niceta Stethatus from the East and the great western monk,
Bernard of Clairvaux (d. 1153), the latest author to be quoted. The collection
includes no female writers.

The editor, Jesuit scholar Thomas Spidlik, first published this
anthology in Italian in 1971, then went on to produce *The Spirituality of the
Christian East: A Systematic Handbook* (1986). The latter volume displays
massive scholarship and must be described as magisterial. Its chapters are
stunning in their compression and documentation. The bibliography runs to
more than 50 pages, citing works in a half-dozen languages. Thus when Spidlik
edits *Drinking from the Hidden Fountain* and identifies the ancient source for
each of its readings, one can infer that he himself translated everything in the
book before Paul Drake rendered it into English.

This is indeed "a patristic breviary," a prayerbook mostly from writers
of the ancient church. The selections invite the reader to linger, pray, and
incorporate their wisdom into daily living. Its handy size and meticulous
scholarship make it doubly attractive to anyone serious about encountering the
best from the eastern church's first millennium.

5

Near to the Heart of God: Daily Readings from the Spiritual Classics
(1998) is the most extensive of the anthologies considered thus far, if that
means the number of writers who are included. Foster and Smith have 52, but
this book has 60 (not counting "anonymous"). Here are readings for every day
of the year, each of them titled and preceded by a short biblical passage, then
followed by a suggested personal response. The book concludes with 18 pages

of biographical notes and index, recommended additional reading, and indexes of scriptures and topics.

The editor, Bernard Bangley, is a Presbyterian pastor and author of several books centered on outstanding devotional writers. In a warm, personal introduction he describes his procedure: "What I have done is to paraphrase their writings into clear, simple, modern English.... I have not put any words into their mouths.... The metaphors, examples, and illustrative comments in this book are in the original material.... I have resisted every temptation to introduce new elements. They aren't needed. These pages were lively when they were first written and remain lively today" (Bangley 1998, vii-viii).

The book achieves this goal. It is a pleasure to read, often surprisingly contemporary. Bangley's favorite among the five dozen writers is Francis de Sales followed in order by Thomas a Kempis, Guigo I, and Teresa of Avila. Although these are all Roman Catholic, about half the writers are Protestants, while four come from the Orthodox church (John Cassian, Evagrius Ponticus, Pseudo-Macarius, and the author of the 19th-century *Pilgrim's Tale or The Way of a Pilgrim)*. Their dates stretch from the late first century (Hermas) to the 19th ("the pilgrim"), and eight of the 60 are women. The selection shows some special interest in the British Reformation of the 16th-17th centuries.

If one wants to begin reading in the greatest Christian devotional writers, this book might be a place to start. Its simple, modern English makes it easy to focus on the substance without getting stuck in outdated style. In fact, Bangley and Harold Shaw Publishers have gone one step further. They have produced a sampler, *Morning and Evening with the Spiritual Classics: 40 Days of Meditations* (1999). Here are 80 selections from the larger volume offered in a slim pocket or purse size (3.5 by 6.25 inches), costing only $2.99. This is an ideal place to start. From it one can graduate to the larger volume and on to the others reviewed here.

6

Finally, we may consider a different kind of collection, one arranged in chronological sequence. *Invitation to Christian Spirituality: An Ecumenical Anthology* (1999) is the work of John R. Tyson of Houghton College. An acknowledged expert on the life and thought of Charles Wesley, Tyson here collects material from 76 writers in a paperback of 474 pages. The book opens with a 50-page "invitation" in which the editor discusses the nature and themes of Christian devotion. Then begins the march through church history in five periods: the ancient church (21 writers), the medieval era (11 writers), the Reformation era (10 authors), modern spirituality [roughly 1600-1900] (17 authors), and contemporary spirituality [the 20th century] (17 writers).

Tyson offers "an ecumenical anthology," but inclusivity remains elusive. The East, for example, disappears after the early church. Even then, the absence of John Chrysostom--possibly the greatest of all eastern fathers--seems egregious. Other notable omissions include John Bunyan (*The Pilgrim's Progress*), George Fox (founder of the Quakers and author of a famous journal), William Law (whose writings influenced the Wesleys and many after them), John Woolman (whose *Journal* details a one-man civil rights movement prior to the American Revolution), and one of the 20th century's most widely noted authors, Henri Nouwen. On the other hand, we can thank Dr. Tyson for including more women (18) than any other anthology reviewed here. He also offers selections from contemporary writers who need to be noticed; for example, the African American Howard Thurman, Mother Teresa of India, Peru's Gustavo Gutierrez, and Archbishop Desmond Tutu of South Africa.

Tyson writes a brief introduction to each period of church history and several paragraphs for each person included, then come one or more excerpts from the writings of each author. The book concludes with a detailed general index and a scripture index. It is the most complete of all the collections reviewed here and the only one to move in historical sequence. Those are its strengths. Among weaknesses are the omissions detailed above and the use of older translations for some of the works that are excerpted. If you are looking for a church-historical survey of great devotional writers which is fairly complete, this is the book.

7

In closing, let me briefly mention several works related to those reviewed here. (1) A fine complement to Tyson's anthology is Bradley Holt's *Thirsty for God: A Brief History of Christian Spirituality* (1993). A college professor and former missionary in Africa, Holt offers in 150 pages all a short text should be. He begins by discussing four biblical relationships: with God, ourselves, others, and the earth. Then he traces the history of Christian devotion through the same five periods as Tyson, but using other titles. (He calls the medieval period "the European era," arguing that Christianity, after an explosive missionary start, shrank back into a European enclave within the larger world.) The book includes discussion questions, spiritual formation exercises for each chapter, a timeline, glossary, bibliography, and indexes. This is an ideal short survey, the best of its kind in print.

(2) Another brief guide is *The Inward Pilgrimage: An Introduction to Christian Spiritual Classics* (1996) by Bernhard Christensen. This simply written "introduction," first published in 1976, is again available, this time with a new foreword and questions for reflection/discussion by Bradley Holt. What

Dr. Christensen does is to introduce, describe, and offer short quotations from sixteen devotional classics taken in chronological order. Beginning with Augustine and the desert fathers, they conclude with Evelyn Underhill and Dietrich Bonhoeffer. The surprise in the collection may be Brigid Emily Herman's *Creative Prayer*, happily available once more in a new, fresh editing (1998). If you want to put just your toe into the water of devotional classics, then Christensen's book is one to consider. Its only drawback is the appearance in the new edition of some distressing typographical errors.

(3) A good follow-up might be the series called Upper Room Spiritual Classics. These are pocket or purse-size paperbacks of 72 pages, each introducing the work of one devotional master. Beginning in 1998, the Upper Room has released five of these each year. They are available in 5-volume annual sets or in individual volumes ($4.95 each). These are one of the best buys on the market: a fine introduction, carefully chosen excerpts from each writer's work (in gracefully contemporary inclusive language), and suggestions on how to read for personal and group formation. Hearty thanks to the publishers and the editor, Keith Beasley-Topliffe, for work well done!

(4) *A Practical Guide to Spiritual Reading* (1994) goes beyond excerpts to complete works worth exploring. The author, Susan Annette Muto, possesses encyclopedic knowledge of the church's devotional literature, and her "guide" is a comprehensive handbook. Part I is 50 pages of help for this kind of reading. Part II (150 pages) details three reading programs involving scripture and the literature of spirituality. Part III offers an annotated bibliography that is 75 pages long. In an appendix Dr. Muto sets out "a three-part, twelve-month cycle of readings ... for classroom or home study purposes" (Muto 1994, 303). I know of nothing quite like this compendious volume.

(5) Another unique collection is *Amazing Grace: Hymn Texts for Devotional Use* (1994). Here are the words of more than 200 of our best hymns printed without musical notation as the poems they really are. The editors, Bert Polman, Marilyn Kay Stulken, and James R. Sydnor represent the Christian Reformed, Lutheran, and Presbyterian churches respectively. "This volume is really a home hymnal instead of being a part of the church pew furnishings.... The Hymn Society in the United States and Canada endorsed and recommended the publication of this hymnal" (Polman, Stulken, and Sydnor 1994, viii-ix). Its compact size (4.5 by 6.5 inches), clear layout, and ample indexes make this a valuable companion for devotional use.

(6) Many collections of prayers are on the market, but few can rival *The Oxford Book of Prayer* (1985), edited by Bishop George Appleton of the Church of England. This anthology contains more than a thousand prayers, the great majority from within the Christian faith. In addition to prayers from scripture, there seem to be prayers from all periods and places the church has

existed. The three longest sections organize their material around the Lord's Prayer, the Apostles' Creed, and prayers from other religious traditions. Ample indexes of authors, sources, and subjects round out this excellent volume of 399 pages, available in both cloth and paper bindings. It is a treasure of material for pondering and praying.

Treasures to be admired, wealth to be gained, breadth to be explored, depths to be plumbed—our faith abounds in possibilities of discovery. We owe it to ourselves and our Lord, the church and the world, to discover and utilize the best of the best. As A. W. Tozer is reported to have said, "Life is too short to waste time reading books. You must read only the best." If I were beginning, I would choose Christensen's *The Inward Pilgrimage* together with Bangley's sampler, *Morning and Evening with the Spiritual Classics*. After that, perhaps the Upper Room Spiritual Classics, and the banquet is served. Enjoy the best of the best!

Works Cited

Appleton, George, ed. 1985. *The Oxford Book of Prayer*. New York: Oxford University Press.

Bangley, Bernard, ed. 1998. *Near to the Heart of God: Daily Readings from the Spiritual Classics*. Wheaton, IL: Harold Shaw Publishers.

_____. 1999. *Morning and Evening with the Spiritual Classics: 40 Days of Meditations*. Wheaton, IL: Harold Shaw Publishers.

Christensen, Bernhard. 1996. *The Inward Pilgrimage: An Introduction to Christian Spiritual Classics*. Minneapolis, MN: Augsburg Fortress.

Foster, Richard J. 1978. *Celebration of Discipline: The Path to Spiritual Growth*. New York: Harper & Row, Publishers.

_____. 1992. *Prayer: Finding the Heart's True Home*. Harper San Francisco.

_____. 1998. *Streams of Living Water: Celebrating the Great Traditions of Christian Faith*. Harper San Francisco.

Foster, Richard J., and Emilie Griffin, eds. 2000. *Spiritual Classics: Selected Readings Individuals and Groups on the Twelve Spiritual Disciplines*. A Renovare Resource for Spiritual Renewal. Harper San Francisco.

Foster, Richard J., and James Bryan Smith, eds. 1993. *Devotional Classics: Selected Readings for Individuals and Groups*. A Renovare Resource for Spiritual Renewal. Harper San Francisco.

Herman, Brigid E. 1998. *Creative Prayer*. Ed. Hal M. Helms. Brewster, MA: Paraclete Press.

Holt, Bradley P. 1993. *Thirsty for God: A Brief History of Christian Spirituality*. Minneapolis, MN: Augsburg Fortress.

Llewelyn, Robert. 1980. *Daily Readings with Julian of Norwich*. Vol. 1. Springfield, IL: Templegate Publishers.

_____. 1988. *The Joy of the Saints: Spiritual Readings throughout the Year*. Springfield, IL: Templegate Publishers.

Muto, Susan Annette. 1994. *A Practical Guide to Spiritual Reading*. Rev. ed. Petersham, MA: St. Bede's Publications.

Polman, Bert, Marilyn Kay Stulken, and James R. Sydnor, eds. 1994. *Amazing Grace: Hymn Texts for Devotional Use*. Louisville, KY: Westminster John Knox Press.

Sharrer, J. Alan, Christopher D. Hudson, and Lindsay Vanker, eds. 1999. *Day by Day with the Early Church Fathers*. Peabody, MA: Hendrickson Publishers.

Snyder, James L. 1991. *In Pursuit of God: The Life of A. W. Tozer*. Camp Hill, PA: Christian Publications.

Spidlik, Thomas. 1986 [Italian 1978]. *The Spirituality of the Christian East: A Systematic Handbook*. Trans. Anthony P. Gythiel. Cistercian Studies Series 79. Kalamazoo, MI: Cistercian Publications.

_____. 1993 [Italian 1971]. *Drinking from the Hidden Fountain: A Patristic Breviary. Ancient Wisdom for Today's World*. Trans. Paul Drake. Cistercian Studies Series 148. Kalamazoo, MI: Cistercian Publications.

Tozer, A. W. 1949. *The Pursuit of God*. Camp Hill, PA: Christian Publications.

_____. 1961. *The Knowledge of the Holy: The Attributes of God and Their Meaning in Christian Life*. New York: Harper & Row, Publishers.

Tyson, John R., ed. 1999. *Invitation to Christian Spirituality: An Ecumenical Anthology*. New York: Oxford University Press.

Upper Room Spiritual Classics. 1998- . 15 vols. to date. Nashville, TN: Upper Room Books.

BOOK REVIEWS

David Noel Freedman, Allen C. Myers, and Astrid Beck (editors), *Eerdmans Dictionary of the Bible*. Grand Rapids, MI: Eerdmans, 2000. 1459 pages. Cloth. $45.00.

Eerdmans has produced a fine-quality, truly comprehensive one-volume Bible Dictionary. As the editor-in-chief points out in his preface, the genre of "Bible Dictionary" is actually two-fold. The multi-volume "dictionaries" are intended to be encyclopaedic in their coverage of each topic, being at once comprehensive (insofar as they treat most every topic imaginable) and exhaustive (insofar as they go into respectable depth on each topic). This volume should not be seen as competing with such resources (e.g., *The Anchor Bible Dictionary* or the *IVP Dictionary of the New Testament*), but rather with similar one-volume resources that are much more restricted in the depth of treatment possible.

Within its class, however, this resource distinguishes itself on a number of fronts. First, it is truly comprehensive. The sheer number of entries (over 5000) alone gives strong evidence of this. One will find entries not only on the canonical books, the apocrypha, major pseudepigrapha, and texts from the Dead Sea Scrolls, but also articles on a broad array of archaeological, historical, theological, and even cultural topics related to the Scriptures and the world in which they took shape. Second, its selection of contributors has, in general, been judicious. Major articles tend to be allocated to world-class scholars who have distinguished themselves in the relevant areas (e.g., James Crenshaw on Psalms, Paul Redditt on Zechariah, Joel Marcus on Mark, Craig Koester on John, Victor Matthews on Kinship, and Sara Mandell on the Hasmoneans). Moreover, the range of contributors reflects in a fair and balanced way the range of scholarship and confession. That is to say, while an individual article will betray an author's bias, the range of biases represented is exceedingly fair. Some of the assignments may not be as optimal as was the case in Freedman's larger dictionary, the *Anchor Bible Dictionary* (i.e., fewer of the articles are actually assigned to scholars who have produced significant monographs or articles on the subjects), but, remembering the different goals of the two kinds of dictionary, this does not in the end detract from the value of the present work.

Each article provides an overview of the subject and concludes with several resources for further study. In every case, the user should bear in mind that the multi-volume dictionaries (such as the two mentioned above) will provide fuller treatment and fuller bibliographic suggestions, and so should be consulted next for further study. The more-than-5000 articles written by over 600 contributors are attractively complemented by over a hundred maps and photographs scattered throughout and by sixteen pages of color maps at the back of the volume. For ready-reference (and for value), the *EDB* is a choice resource that I would highly recommend for pastors, students, and lay persons.

David deSilva

Ferdinand E. Deist, *The Material Culture of the Bible: An Introduction*, edited by Robert P. Carroll and Philip R. Davies. Biblical Seminar 70. Sheffield: Sheffield Academic Press, 2000. 348 pp., paperback, $29.95.

This important book has an unfortunate history. The author, Ferdinand Deist, a leading South African Old Testament scholar, died of a heart attack in 1997, before the completion of the volume. The editorial mantle was taken up by the British OT scholar Robert Carroll, who himself died in 2000. The final editorial work was completed by Davies. The material was deemed of sufficient import to bring to a conclusion, even though the concluding syntheses were not complete upon Deist's death.

As the title indicates, the volume sets out to explore Israel's culture, though the title is ironically inappropriate. Deist looks to exegetical and social-scientific approaches to OT study, most particularly anthropology, to help in interpreting the biblical text What is ignored, however, is the material evidence itself, that is what has been unearthed by archaeologists. For example, in a brief section on the technology of war, he looks to the Bible for categories and terminology of implements and calamities of war, but makes no reference to artifacts or even contemporary illustrations which would add visual impact to his theme, e.g. the scenes of the siege of Lachish from reliefs from Sennacherib's palace. This is an unfortunate lacuna which, while making the book shorter, also makes it less useful.

In the first chapter Deist looks at definitions of 'culture,' and he asks the question whether the biblical text reflects the culture it portrays or a later, post-exilic culture. He argues that, while it might have reached its final form after the exile, it does contain genuine reflections of an earlier period. In the second, technical chapter, Deist explores theories of culture, and in the third he looks at language and meaning. He then moves to less theoretical areas when he explores in turn the environment, the economy, technology, social organization, political organization, and very briefly, the topic of social control, including honor and shame. This is currently a very hot topic, and would undoubtedly have been greatly expanded in the finished work. The volume concludes with a 22 page bibliography and indexes of references, subjects, Hebrew terms, and authors.

In spite of its tragic incompleteness, the volume is a mine of wealth for the biblical exegete, even though the technical nature of the introductory can be heavy reading. For example, the chapter on the economy shows the value of the great linguistic detail into terms for and the societal import of, property, labor, distribution, and consumption. Among other things it shows the great importance played by the cult and its maintenance in the Israelite economy. While the volume will usefully be supplemented by other works by such authors as John Walton and Victor Matthews, and we look forward with anticipation to the soon to be released *Life in Ancient Israel* by Philip King and Lawrence Stager which we hope to review next year. This volume should be in all seminary and specialist libraries. David W. Baker

F. Brown, S. R. Driver, C. A. Briggs, ed. *The Enhanced Brown-Driver-Briggs Hebrew and English Lexicon.* CR-ROM version. Oak Harbor, WA: Logos Research Systems, 2000. $49.95.

Logos is again to be thanked for making important research material available in its Logos Library System format. In this format, searches can be made through all elements of the library, so making it a powerful tool.

The *Lexicon* has a long history in English since its publication by Clarendon Press in Oxford in 1906. This is apart from its earlier incarnations in Latin and German starting in 1833. This form is 'enhanced' in that it has added several referential numbering systems to the 1906 version, including the numbers for *Strong's Exhaustive Concordance, The Theological Wordbook of the Old Testament* (ed. G. A. Archer *et al.* [Chicago: Moody, 1980]), and those developed by E. W. Goodrick and J. R. Kohlenberger III for *The NIV Exhaustive Concordance* (Grand Rapids: Zondervan, 1990). These numbers have been added at the beginning of each word entry. It is unfortunate that the latter number follows the abbreviation "GK," which is a common abbreviation for the venerable Hebrew reference grammar of Gesenius-Kautsch. Another enhancement is the inclusion at the appropriate place in the text of the "Addenda et Corrigenda" taken from the 1951 English corrected edition. The Strong's numbers and corrections had previously been incorporated by Jay Green in his edition of BDB published by Hendrickson in 1979. He also added an index of Strong's numbers, Hebrew forms, and BDB page numbers which students found very useful. For some reason, Hendrickson opted to delete the Hebrew words from this index in their 1996 edition, making the result much less user friendly. This new electronic edition concludes with alphabetized indexes of Hebrew and Aramaic derivative forms, allowing students to be able to smile yet again.

This lexicon is the current tool of choice for most introductory Hebrew courses. While this format is more expensive than either the Hendrickson or Clarendon editions, its ease of use and portability should make it attractive to those who do not have a hard copy. For those who do, suggesting it as an appropriate Christmas or birthday gift would give you something much more useful than another tie. The CD versions should be in every academic biblical studies library which has electronic holdings.

David W. Baker

Ludwig Koehler, Walter Baumgartner, and J.J. Stamm, ed. *The Hebrew and Aramaic Lexion of the Old Testament CD-ROM Edition.* Leiden: Brill, 2000. $399 (individual) – $999 (institutional site license for up to 25 users).

Brill (www.brill.nl) and Logos Research Systems (www.logos.com) are to be commended for their continued vision of making major academic works available in electronic format. This important work, part of the printed version of which was reviewed in an earlier volume of this *Journal* (28 [1996] 150-151), is part of the increasing number of resources accessible using the Logos Library System, which is included on the disk. Minimum system requirements include: a Pentium 60 computer using at least Windows 95 with an SVGA monitor, 25 MB free disk drive space and a 4x CD-ROM. If more space is available, the product can also been downloaded to run off the computer hard drive rather than the CD. The CD is accompanied by a 26 page 'User's manual.'

This version of *HALOT* is able to function as a stand-alone module, as part of an existing Logos Library, or on a network, and installation instructions are given for each of these options. When used with the Logos Library, it is seamlessly integrated so that searches and other functions can easily include *HALOT* along with the other books. The ease of its use in electronic form makes this a much more usable tool than the 4 volume printed set. The CD also has the distinct advantage of being considerably less expensive than the printed version, which runs approximately $551. While it is still very expensive for individuals to purchase, serious students of Hebrew and the Bible will need access to *HALOT*. If they don't already have it in printed form, this would be a wise choice. This form should be available in serious academic, seminary, and specialist libraries which have electronic holdings.   David W. Baker

"Hebrew Speaktionary" CDROM by Living Israeli Hebrew (ph. 800-98-5698), $19.95.

If you have been looking for a simple way to learn everyday Modern Hebrew vocabulary, you should consider this electronic tool. It is simple to use. A plethora of words have been arranged under 29 categories, from animals to directions, time, clothing, food, electronics, Jewish festivals, and more.

To strengthen your fluency in office hardware, for example, click on "Business & Office." A further click on "stapler" within the English wordlist will bring a color photo of a stapler to your monitor. Click on the picture, and a native speaker will say "*shadchan*" in crisp tones. The picture is triple-captioned: English, transliterated Hebrew, and Hebrew script (consonants only, as is typical for Modern Hebrew).

Learners young and old alike will find this tool appealing. It would be useful for classroom use as well as part of a self-study program.

To summarize, Hebrew Speaktionary's strengths are that it is highly visual, it offers wide variety, and it presents authentic pronunciation. Drawbacks? If your goal is to converse in Modern Hebrew, you will need a different tool to learn how to string words together. If your interest is Biblical Hebrew you may be intrigued to discover how many ancient words have been retained in Modern Hebrew (house is still *bayit* today). At the same time you will be hard-pressed to fasten much ancient value to the remaining words in this program (including *shadchan*).   Paul Overland

Sandra Landis Gogel, *A Grammar of Epigraphic Hebrew*. SBL Resources for Biblical Study 23. Atlanta: Scholars Press, 1998. xx + 522 pages, hardback, $44.95.

Hebrew is rare among written languages in that the majority of its early written remains are included in only one book, the Old Testament. By word count, there is far more Hebrew material from the period up to the return from the Babylonian exile found inside the Old Testament than there has been found outside it. This is not to say that there is no useful extra-biblical material, which is definitely not the case. The relatively small corpus, the often broken nature of the texts, and the diversity of genre, find spots, and publication have resulted in only little synthetic study of this material. It is to address this lack that Sandra Gogel wrote this volume.

Gogel states that: "This book provides a grammar of the extra-biblical Hebrew inscriptions of Palestine which have been attributed by various archaeological, historical, and paleographic analyses to the period between the tenth and sixth century B.C. These pre-Persian inscriptions comprise a corpus of epigraphic Hebrew inscriptions (including ostraca, graffiti, and seals) which previously has never been studied comprehensively."

The book begins with a description of the texts mined for grammatical information, starting with the 10th century Gezer Calendar through the 6th century inscription from Khirbet Beit Lei, a total of 348 inscriptions. There follow chapters on phonology (including a useful, lengthy discussion of *matres lectionis*), morphology, and syntax, as well as a lexicon of almost a hundred pages. A very useful feature for a volume of this type is the inclusion in an appendix of transliterations and English translations of all the relevant texts. This is valuable in that it makes the text self-standing, not necessitating constant searching for the actual texts under discussion. The book concludes with a 28 page bibliography covering material up to 1998.

The volume is very well conceived and executed. It will be used by Semiticists, and should be in seminary, academic and specialist libraries, where it will be a standard for years to come.   David W. Baker

Botterweck, G. J., Helmer Ringgren, and Heinz-Josef Fabry, eds. *Theological Dictionary of the Old Testament*, Vol. 9, mārad-nāqâ. Trans. by David E. Green. Grand Rapids, Mi.: Wm. B. Eerdmans, 1998, xxvi + 563 pp.

This volume in the O.T. counterpart to the successful *Theological Dictionary of the New Testament* contains a high number of articles on theologically significant terms. The articles on *mishpāṭ* (justice, judgment), *nhm* (regret, repent, comfort) and *nephesh* (throat, desire, life, self, person), among others, offer especially full treatments of terms that do not always translate easily from Hebrew to English.   Following the series format, entries discuss the etymology, semantic field, and particular uses, and where possible, semantic parallels in other ancient Near Eastern languages.   The entry on *nābî'* (prophet, prophesy) is an example of how wide the exploration of a term may range.   It begins with the assertion that the root is derived from West Semitic (as opposed to a proposed Egyptian etymology) and then proceeds to discuss the origin, use, and derivation of the term in Eblaite, Akkadian, and Ugaritic.   (In these and other languages the root seems to denote one who has been called or named.)   This is followed by a survey of the phenomenon of prophecy in Mari, Canaan, and Assyria.   The wider linguistic and religious context of the root thus established, the discussion then moves, respectively, from the use of the root in Amos, in prophetic narratives before Amos, in prophetic literature from Hosea to the Exile, in exilic prophecy, and in the postexilic period.   Reading the article from beginning to end thus not only gives the reader a sense of the term and its usage but also a capsule survey of the development of prophecy in Israel.

Students using this work will want to be aware that most of the entries are grounded in German scholarship and generally assume the models of composition and development that are common in that context. Many of the articles are also somewhat dated. (A survey of footnotes and bibliographies yields a preponderance of citations from the 1950's through the 1970's, with infrequent references to literature since then.) However, this is problematic in only a few cases, such as the article on *mishpāhâ* (clan), which should be consulted along with more recent work on the kinship system of ancient Israel. The student, therefore, will want to resist the impulse to consider any of the articles as the "last word" and will use this resource along with others for lexical study. As a tool for acquiring a fuller understanding of the semantic world of biblical Hebrew, *TDOT* still has few equals.   L. Daniel Hawk

G. Johannes Botterweck, Helmer Ringgren, Heinz-Josef Fabry, ed. *Theological Dictionary of the Old Testament*, vol. X. Grand Rapids: Eerdmans, 2000. Xxiv + 592 pp, $48.00. Vol. XI, 2001. Xxiv + 615 pp, $50.00.

These volumes complement the earlier well-known series on the New Testament (G. Kittel's *TDNT*; English translations, 1964-) in a series which itself started in English translation in 1974. The first volume under review contains 80 articles by 53 contributors, and the second, 83 articles by 53 contributors. They were originally published in German in 1986 and 1987–1988, respectively, so the translation and English publication process has been very slow.

There are numerous articles in both volumes of major theological (e.g., X-'avenge, revenge,' 'forgive,' 'serve, worship,' 'long time, forever,' 'transgression'; XI-'help,' 'Most High,' 'hold back,' 'make, do, act,' 'time,' 'redeem,' 'pray, prayer'), ethical (e.g., X- 'loan; practice usury,' 'charge interest,' 'seduce,' 'pledge, loan'; XI-'poor,' 'stand surety,' 'rich, wealth'), historical (e.g., X- 'Sodom,' 'Sea of Reeds,' 'Sinai,' 'Eden'), and socio-religious (e.g., X- 'Succoth,' 'scribe,' 'ruler, prince,' 'Hebrews'; XI- 'city,' 'burnt offering, sacrifice,' 'young woman [virgin],' 'people,' 'circumcise,' 'Astarte') importance. These volumes, and the series as a whole, deserve a place in any serious theological library. Most pastors and teachers, however, would probably find themselves better served by making the *New International Dictionary of Old Testament Theology and Exegesis*, ed. W. van Gemeren (Grand Rapids: Zondervan) their first choice for such a reference work.   David W. Baker

Jerome T. Walsh. *Style & Structure in Biblical Hebrew Narrative*. Collegeville, Min.: The Liturgical Press, 2001

Although there have been many fine studies on the stylistic features of biblical Hebrew narrative, it has remained for the present work to give a comprehensive treatment of the various devices utilized in its structuring operations. Walsh addresses the topic by examining structures of organization, disjunction, and conjunction. Following a brief introduction, he catalogues and describes a range of devices by which

Hebrew narrative organizes units and subunits, sets boundaries that demarcate them, and links them together to achieve continuity.

Symmetry and repetition, the distinctive attributes of classical Hebrew literature, receive the fullest treatment. The author first orients the reader through a description of such operations as symmetry and asymmetry, repeated elements, repetition as an organizing principle, balance between associated subunits, and the interpretative access provided by symmetries. Various types of symmetrical structures are then discussed: reverse symmetries (such as concentric and chiastic structures, wherein latter elements oppose former ones), forward symmetries (where symmetry is created through simple parallelism), alternating repetition (e.g. an A B A B A structure), partial symmetries (inclusion and epitome), types of symmetries with multiple structures, and instances of asymmetry (wherein a symmetrical pattern is established but disrupted by a significant deviation). Walsh illustrates each of the structures here, as throughout the book, with analyses of multiple textual examples. Part II continues the investigation by identifying structures that mark the boundaries of narrative units. Here Walsh explains how changes in characters, locale, time and narrative voice can signal a new direction in the story, and how repetition of information already known, unnecessary repetition of subject nouns, and unnecessary interruptions of direct speech with "and X said" accomplish the same objective. The section concludes with a discussion of the ways that units can be marked by disruptions of narrative sequence. Part III, the shortest section, moves in a different direction and explores devices that render a continuity between narrative units and subunits. These include various forms of "threads" (significant unifying elements or patterns in one unit that are repeated in a following unit), "links" (non-significant repetitions such as catchwords), and "hinges" (a combination of threaded and linked elements).

One of the first tasks in the exegesis of narrative is the identification of narrative units and the description of the way the units are connected to each other. Students sometimes find this task difficult and often undertake it apart from a sense of Hebrew narrative's distinctive features. This accessible book therefore provides a welcome and important resource and will benefit both students and seasoned interpreters alike.

L. Daniel Hawk

Wilfried Warning, *Literary Artistry in Leviticus.* Biblical Interpretation Series 35. Leiden: Brill, 1999. xv + 256 pp., cloth, EUR 70/ $82.00.

When one thinks of the book of Leviticus, literary artistry is not usually the first thing that comes to mind. How can a book detailing sacrifices and clean and unclean things be artistic? This slightly revised 1997 thesis from the SDA Theological Seminary seeks to address that issue. In his own words, Warning aims at "ascertaining the structuring significance of terminological patterns and their respective contribution to the overall artistic outline of the extant text" (2).

In his review of previous discussions of levitical structure, Warning makes the pointed observation that the widely varied approaches to biblical studies, and even more, one might add, the diverse outcomes from these approaches, "are most likely indicative of the ineluctable subjectivity inherent in each approach including the present one" (7).

In order to somewhat alleviate the subjectivity, the author's interest is in the present Masoretic Text, not in any putative pre-text. He seeks to see how it, rather than some hypothetical, reconstructed text is structured by its author/editor.

In his overview of present understanding of the priestly writings, Warning classifies approaches into 4 groups, those saying that P is: 1) a multilayered work from the preexilic period; 2) a multilayered work from the exilic/postexilic period; 3) an editorial reworking of previous material and not an independent source at all; 4) originally from the pen of Moses, along with the rest of the Pentateuch. He mentions names of several scholars working within each of these camps. He then looks at some who have specifically worked on aspects of structure, namely Y. Radday, W. H. Shea, M. Douglas, and C. R. Smith. Warning himself takes a rhetorical critical approach to the book, seeing the 37 divine speeches as the elemental building block of the book. He analyzes the speeches' microstructure ('the interrelation of distinct and different parts') and the macrostructure of the text of Leviticus as a whole.

Warning spends one chapter looking at the divine speeches, marked by 'and Yahweh spoke/said to Moses/Aaron.' He points out that the theologically central chapter 17, which details the Day of Atonement, is also central to the structure of the book as he determines it. What he does not do is justify including both the Hebrew verbs 'say' (2 times) and 'speak' (35 times) on the same level as speech indicators, when they numerically seem to not be equal, though he does note ties between the two passages introduced by the first verb.

Through verbal repetition of numerous words, the sevenfold repetition of words and forms, chiastic structures, and positioning in the seventh or twelfth and second and second-to-last positions, the author seeks to show the purposeful, and thus unifying, structure of the book of Leviticus. Readers will find some examples convincing and some problematic, but the study does indicate that one must take structuring seriously. As Warning notes, the study has implications for an atomistic approach to the composition of the book. Such structuring, if objectively verifiable, leaves problematic any suggestion that the work might be a simple collocation of numerous sources and not a deliberate structure drafted by a skillful author or editor.

While the book is helpful, it is not for the lay reader, since much unvocalized, untransliterated, and usually untranslated Hebrew is used, as would be expected in a scholarly work of this nature. What is not expected is the lack of careful editing, which is unfortunate and troubling, especially for such an expensive book and from a generally careful publisher. The book is published with an added page of 31 errata items. I also note in checking to see if I might be mentioned in the bibliography (a human trait we all engage in!), that there is a typo in that entry, so one wonders how many others there might be in the bibliography and elsewhere which were not caught. While the book should be in serious theological libraries, it should be used with care so that any misprints might not cause undue consternation.   David W. Baker

V. Philips Long, ed. *Israel's Past in Present Research: Essays on Ancient Israelite Historiography.* Sources for Biblical and Theological Study, Volume 7. Winona Lake: Eisenbrauns, 1999, xx + 612 pp.

The question of history, as it relates to the testimony of the Old Testament, has rarely been as difficult to address as it is presently. The paucity of external data for key periods of Israel's history, continuing debates over the composition of the texts, and profound disagreements over assumptions and methods have prevented scholars from approaching a consensus on tasks as basic as describing the historiographical impulse in ancient Israel, defining the relationship between the biblical text and archaeological models, or writing a history of Israel. As a result, the scholarly literature is massive both in volume and perplexity. Long, however, has succeeded in editing a superlative anthology that (despite the disclaimers in his preface) gives the reader a comprehensive grasp of the scope of the current discourse as well as the various approaches that configure it.

Long's decision to focus primarily on methodological discussions rather than specific historical studies or issues (e.g. the appearance of Israel in Canaan, the Israelite monarchy) makes this volume particularly useful to those interested in the historical witness of the Old Testament. Long divides the collection into six parts. Each begins with an introduction that orients the reader to the topic addressed within it. Parts 1 and 2 put the discussion of history in context. Part 1 consists of three essays. The first (by John H. Hayes) surveys the study of Israelite and Judean history from the Renaissance to the present, while the latter two (by Mark Brettler and Rolf Rendtorff) address the present lack of consensus amongst biblical historians. The three essays in Part 2 (by William W. Hallo, H. Cazelles, and A. R. Millard) explore biblical historiography within the context of the intellectual climate of ancient Near East.

Parts 3 and 4 are concerned with the multiplex character of history writing in Israel and the methodological challenges it raises. Long groups the essays in Part 3 into three categories. Essays by John J. Collins, John Van Seters, R. N. Whybray, Philip R. Davies, and Gerhard Maier discuss the Old Testament's antiquarian character (i.e. its interest in representing the past). Two more essays, by J. Alberto Soggin and Claus Westermann, explore its aspectual character (i.e. its theological perspective and didactic intent). The section concludes with two essays by Long and L. Alonso Schökel that address the artistic character of biblical historiography. The essays in Part 4 then take up the task of how a history of Israel should be written. Contributions by Diana Edelman, K. Lawson Younger, Jr., Siegfried Hermann, J. Maxwell Miller, and Ferdinand Deist discuss, respectively, how the Bible and material remains may be assessed and utilized as sources, how we should understood the notion of history and ideology, the importance of exegetical study, the role of the historian's own biases and perspectives, and what models are appropriate to describe the process of historical change. Two additional essays (by Niels Peter Lemche and Baruch Halpern) take widely divergent positions on the role biblical materials ought to play in writing history. The section concludes with essays by John Barton and Herbert H. Klement that examine the impact of literary critical approaches.

Part 5 comprises representative treatments of historical issues. Essays by Roland de Vaux, Thomas L. Thompson, and John Goldingay discuss the thorny issue of evaluating the historicity of the patriarchal narratives. Richard Hess assesses archaeology's contribution the early history of Israel in Canaan, while J. G. McConville argues, through a study of major themes, that the Deuteronomistic History preserves authentic historical remembrance. Hans Walter Wolff and Hans-Dieter Neef examine the appropriation of historical traditions in the prophets, and Gary N. Knoppers asserts that, despite their bias, the books of Chronicles are reliable and useful sources for reconstructing Israelite history.

The volume concludes with an essay by the editor that looks forward to future developments and offers proposals for continuing dialogue and refining methods. The essay is necessarily brief but nevertheless provides an informative perspective on where the discipline is headed. In the same spirit I would add a couple of observations. First, we might expect an increasing dialogue between history and sociology, not so much in the application of Marxist social models (although this will no doubt continue), but rather in what sociology can contribute to our understanding of such things as everyday life, social structure, social movements, and the shaping of identity. (On this topic, see *Community, Identity, and Ideology : Social Science Approaches to the Hebrew Bible*, Charles E. Carter and Carol L. Meyers, eds., SBTS 6, Winona Lake, Ind.: Eisenbrauns, 1996). Second, I look for an increasing engagement with the challenges posed by the New Historicism and particularly with its insistence on the role ideology plays in the production and interpretation of historiographical literature. Although currently a small minority, scholars working along these lines have already raised important questions about the ways the exertion of political power may have shaped the composition of biblical texts and, more directly, how political ideologies have profoundly influenced the way Israel history has and is being written. (Here I am thinking, for example, of Keith Whitelam's *The Invention of Ancient Israel: The Silencing of Palestinian History* [London/New York: Routledge, 1996] as well as recent assessments of W. F. Albright.)

The essays in this volume represent an impressive cross-section of the wide-ranging discussions associated with the history of Israel and the historical witness of its texts. For those wanting to explore the fascinating questions of history, this is the place to begin.   L. Daniel Hawk

Antony F. Campbell and Mark A. O'Brien. *Unfolding the Deuteronomistic History: Origins, Upgrades, Present Text.* Minneapolis: Augsburg Fortress, 2000. vi+505 pages, paper, $37.00.

This book annotates the text of Deuteronomy-Kings according to the Deuteronomistic History theory. The 'unfolding' of the title, therefore, is meant in rigorously critical terms. Campbell and O'Brien are well known for their previous work on the subject, and the volume shows the marks of their study. The form of the Deuteronomistic theory is their own modification of the principal current theories. A Josianic 'DH' is preceded by older forms of the material, and followed by exilic revisions. The principal older material is found in a 'Conquest Narrative' (Joshua), a 'Deliverance Collection' (Judges), and a 'Prophetic Record', already identified by Campbell in 1 Samuel 1-2 Kings 10 (*Of Prophets and Kings*; CBQMS 17; Washington, 1986). The exilic revisions come in more than one form ('royal focus' and 'national focus'). The form of the theory is thus indebted in part to Noth, but also to Cross's double redaction and indeed Smend's concept of multiple exilic revisions (as is O'Brien's *The Deuteronomistic History Hypothesis: a Reassessment* (OBO 92; Freiburg, Switzerland, 1989), but is distinct from both.

The book is best described in terms of its layout. It consists of the biblical text in double columns, marked in various ways to represent the literary provenance of individual sections (sidelining, double-sidelining, italics etc.). The coding is set out in footers, which vary somewhat according to the part of DH under consideration. The biblical text is annotated with comments, keyed to the text by a kind of footnoting system, and falling into three parts (corresponding to the three terms in the book's subtitle): 'Text signals' (a basic commentary designed to highlight literary-critical issues); 'text-history approach' (commenting on the composite nature of the text, where this is perceived), and 'Present-text potential'. The last of these is intended to provide reflections on how this potential 'may be exploited in all fidelity to the text in order to fuel imagination in its use' (p. 1). The three divisions of comment are not all pursued regularly to the same degree, since that is not always thought to be necessary, as when large tracts of text are from the same level of tradition. Then the 'Present-text potential' predominates, and the comment becomes rather expository.

The concept of the book is a serious attempt to deal with both diachronic and synchronic aspects of reading the Old Testament, in recognition that an older form of biblical criticism, concentrating on textual origins, had not proved widely acceptable, yet insisting that honest reading may not dispense with diachronic study. The result is sometimes a little uneasy. The 'present text potential' can still be rather source-oriented, e.g. 'The text of chaps. 16-18 [of 1 Samuel] cannot be read as a unity. Attempts to do so invariably deal only with part of the text, not its total horizon' (p. 260). The 'diachronic' mode is thus kept firmly in the foreground. Even so, the expressed interest in theological interpretation does come through.

An Introduction explains the nature of the book, offers an overview of scholarship on DH, and gives an outline of the theory that will be followed. There is an index of biblical references, and two sets of tables bearing on the composition of DH: the first, 'Patterns and Judges', tabulates motifs and expressions in Judges in relation to each judge; the second displays four patterns of judgment-formula in Kings.

The book is a useful text for the critical aspects of courses on the Historical Books.   Gordon McConville, University of Gloucestershire.

Richard D. Nelson. *The Historical Books*. Nashville: Abingdon., 1998.

Having read, and been much impressed by, Nelson's *Raising up a Faithful Priest* several years ago, my appetite was whetted for a further volume from this interesting and insightful scholar. His examination of the Ancient Israelites' sacrificial system through the lens of anthropology, cultural studies and social psychology provided a stimulating perspective of Leviticus which offered a possible and intriguing rationale behind the priestly/sacrificial order. Nelson's insights emphasized the theology of shalom and the way shalom may have been achieved through sacrifice.

Imagine, then, my personal excitement when *The Historical Books* was published and available, for I am a devotee of these narratives. To my disappointment, Nelson has written a survey of the historical books of the Hebrew Bible, and a shallow one at that, for an audience which is perhaps studying these texts for the first time in either a Seminary or a church setting. It is a beginners primer if you like, to the historical narratives. As he surveys the various books Nelson presents themes and ideas which occur, such as land, leadership, prophecy, kingship, exile. Each book is presented as a separate unit within the whole of the historical material but Nelson doesn't explore the interrelationships between these units.

Recent scholarship has been debating the historicity of the so-called historical books and since the discussion has turned into a maximalist - minimalist debate in which one camp argues that the historical books are faithful accounts of historical events whilst the other argues that extra-biblical evidence suggests that the historical books do not present a faithful account of historical events, there has developed an interest in the nature of historical writing as a form. What is historical writing and what is its purpose? Nelson hints at this philosophical argument in part 1 and for me that is the most interesting section. To his credit, Nelson's notes and bibliography point the reader in the direction of further reading which could elucidate and inform in this debate, but ultimately it is a safe and uncritical survey.

Sadly, Nelson perpetuates the historical-critical approach to textual analysis when he discusses patterns of reading and his look at the historical events which undergird the historical books is cursory to say the least. For a scholar who explored the sacrificial system in such an intriguing way this book is by no means as thoughtful, careful or provocative. Dorothy Penny-Larter

Jonathan E. Dyck, *The Theocratic Ideology of the Chronicler*, Biblical Interpretation Series, 33 (Leiden: Brill, 1998), 256 pp., $86.00.

In this revision of his Ph.D. thesis, Dyck explores the relationship between the Chronicler's expression of his theocratic ideas (the combined spheres of religion and politics) and their consequences within his socio-historical context, the Jewish community living around Jerusalem during the late Persian period. The first two chapters are devoted to explaining Dyck's particular approach of ideological criticism, which is derived from the social sciences. He does not have an interest in the interpretation of the text as such, but rather in the contextual functions and social force of the text. He also surveys the research on the Chronicler's purpose, while making a major distinction between the author's conscious communicative intentions and motives, and a work's sometimes not so conscious contextual functions. Dyck adopts Ricoeur's three-stage analysis of ideology: distortion, legitimation, and integration/identity: "At the level of integration, ideology functions to preserve the [social] order.... At the level of legitimation, ideology serves to maintain systems of domination.... And at the level of distortion, ideology reifies and alienates..." (74). Dyck applies this three-stage analysis in reverse order to three readings of Chronicles.

In Chapter Three, Dyck compares and contrasts the identity of "Israel" in Chronicles and in Ezra-Nehemiah, discussing how that identity is defined by the exile.

For Ezra-Nehemiah, the exile was a watershed event that established the means for recognizing the true "Israel" as the returnees from exile. For the Chronicler, the exile created a chronological break that needed to be overcome by reestablishing Israel's identity. The Chronicler articulated a more encompassing concept of an "all Israel" theocracy, but one in which Judah and Jerusalem had a distinct place. His ideology of identity provided continuity between past traditions and the current community in such a way as to establish the "identity" of the power structures of the post-exilic community as well as the "identity" of the rest of the people of Israel, who were expected to believe in this social system.

In Chapter Four Dyck, argues from the point of view of legitimation that the Chronicler's ideology of identity of Israel sought to legitimate the role of Jerusalem as the focal point for those belonging to "all Israel." The Chronicler did not abandon the distinction the exile created between true Israelite, the returnees to Jerusalem, and non-Israelites (Ezra-Nehemiah), but transformed that perspective to give hegemony to the returnees over all of the land of Israel. Dyck claims that the Chronicler was a member of the ruling and priestly classes in Jerusalem, and represented their self-understanding. The Chronicler's work not only encouraged his community to claim its rightful place and to restore the theocratic kingdom, but also sought to exercise power by shaping the beliefs of the inhabitants of "all Israel," of whom some might not have welcomed such claims of hegemony.

In Chapter Five, Dyck turns to a reconstruction of the internal social context that the Chronicler was addressing. Although the details are based on inference, Dyck concludes that there was a system of hierarchies extending from the basic unit of Israelite social structure, the "houses of the fathers," up to the Second Temple, an institution fulfilling conflicting roles for the community, the local elite, and the Persian Empire.

Chapter Six examines the Chroniclers' work from Ricoeur's perspective of "distortion." Dyck argues that one should read Chronicles with suspicion. To the degree that the Second Temple was an oppressive force to some segments of the social structure, the Chronicler's legitimation of the identity of the Second Temple, Jerusalem, and "all Israel," functioned ideologically, and is distorted. There was a gap between the conscious claims of the Second Temple hierarchy and the beliefs of those dominated by it, a gap that the Chronicler's ideology bridged. Therefore, the Chronicler's rewriting of history with its theocratic ideology was a necessity (of which he was not necessarily conscious) driven by internal social forces in the interest of establishing the power of the dominant party, the Second Temple hierarchy.

Dyck's program is admirable: to identify the Chronicler's ideology and correlate his motives and intentions with contextual functions. He faces the problem, however, of being limited to the primary resource of Chronicles and Ezra-Nehemiah, with limited other evidence about the period in question, a problem that he does recognize (p. 51). Partly as a result, he both makes methodological claims and draws conclusions that are difficult to support. For instance, Dyck claims to able to separate the Chronicler's individual ideology from the Chronicler's expression of the ruling community's ideology, in order to focus on the latter; however, he does not clarify how the two can be distinguished within Chronicles. He sees Chronicles as an expression of the ideology of the dominant position, and yet states that the Chronicler "played no small part" in creating that position (p. 4). One wonders if Chronicles is an expression of an individual's ideology, or a window into the ideology of a community, or a work that established an ideology. He also states that the ideological consequences are not necessarily related to the Chronicler's intention, and that he will focus on the unintended consequences (p. 213), but one wonders how he will determine what the Chronicler did not intend? Moreover, one finds out in the last chapter that the ideological consequences, which are based on the hypothesis that the Chronicler was part of the ruling elite and upon the reconstructed social setting, are not necessarily actual consequences but potential ones (my wording), which exist within the given social relationships (see, pp. 165, 213-14).

The primary strength of Dyck's work is that he brings a different perspective through which to view the issues involving Chronicles and the Second Temple community. When Dyck says, "The trick is to generate belief. It is one thing to intend to urge one's audience..., quite another to successfully persuade one's readers.... It is the task of ideology to ensure the success of the perlocutionary act and to secure the belief... (p. 216)," he is describing the focus of classical rhetorical criticism. However, his ideological approach sets the rhetorical act in a specific context and focuses on the power roles at work among the different strata of the social setting. As a result, Dyck's reconstruction of the social structures and forces of the Second Temple community and their dynamic interplay with the work of the Chronicler will be of service to students of the Book of Chronicles and this era of Judaism.

Rodney K. Duke, Appalachian State University

Richard J. Clifford, *The Wisdom Literature*. Interpreting Biblical Texts Series. Nashville: Abingdon, 1998. 181pp.

Six compositions associated with Hebrew Wisdom are introduced in The Wisdom Literature: Proverbs, Job, Ecclesiastes, Wisdom of Ben Sira, Wisdom of Solomon, and Song of Songs. Clifford aims to give "just enough information to make you a good reader," focusing on "the world of the text." I believe he has succeeded ably.

Designed for the student with little background in biblical wisdom writings, this paperback alludes to the maze of scholarly theories without becoming needlessly entangled. Attention focuses instead on the larger issues of literary / historical context. Parallels stemming from ancient near eastern sapiential writings surface often in this volume. Each book is introduced by either a summary (Job) or sampling (Proverbs, Wisdom of Ben Sira).

Two chapters deserve particular note. In Ecclesiastes Clifford's approach shifts. There he summarizes five scholar's interpretations (from Zimmerli to Seow). The reader is left to select one of the views, or to develop one of his / her own. In Wisdom of Solomon a summary of Jewish activity in Egypt, combined with an overview of Hellenistic religion and philosophy provide insights vital to the understanding of this work from the first century B.C.

If one is looking for a verse-by-verse commentary or an in-depth discussion of critical issues, The Wisdom Literature will not satisfy. If, however, one is looking for a primer which will open the door both to the world of the text and to the text itself, this volume is a very strong candidate.   Paul Overland

E. John Hamlin, *Surely There is a Future: A Commentary on the Book of Ruth.* International Theological Commentary, Frederick Carlson Holmgren and George A. F. Knight, edd. (Grand Rapids, MI:Wm. B. Eerdmanns Publishing Co.) 1996. 82pp. + xi pp.

John Hamlin's brief treatment of the book of Ruth is a good, introductory-level commentary for someone unable to deal directly with the Hebrew text. It is not overly technical in its approach, but more than adequate for someone preparing a Sunday school lesson, a small group Bible study or a personal Bible study. A three-page bibliography leads the interested reader to books and articles that are also not overly technical in presentation.

Ruth is a highly-structured book, using chiasm, repetition and contrast, among other literary devices. The author shows awareness of these features and shows the implications of this structuring for readers in a straight-forward manner, without being tedious.

Certain cultural information is necessary for an understanding of the story and Hamlin gives background cultural data in brief form as well -- just what the reader needs to know to understand, for instance, the gleaning laws, Levarite marriage laws, land sale and transfer laws and customs that are basic to an appreciation of the story and of the motivations of its characters.

The commentary presents semantic data for relatively few words, just those that need clarifying for the sake of following the story-line or for illuminating an essential point. This is a strength of the work; consistent with the non-technical approach. However, in general Hamlin's explanations of word meanings are a weak point - the explanations are often strained. Perhaps this owes to an intent to bring out the "theological" sense of a term; a sense which at times just isn't part of the makeup of the word. For example, on p. 13 he writes, "The basic meaning of the Hebrew verb translated 'started' (*qum*) is to rise up out of a condition of lethargy, sorrow and discouragement." However, in fact, the basic meaning of the verb is much more simple, "to rise up, to begin, to confront (e.g. an enemy)." Any additional qualification of the meaning would only be a result of factors conditioned by the context. Nothing about "lethargy, sorrow and discouragement" is implied by the use of this particular verb in the context of chapter 1, verse 7 as cited by the author. The text of the narrative does at length show Naomi in this condition, but it is in no way implied by the use of this high-frequency Hebrew verb. Another example of misleading semantic data is found on p. 27. While the verb *gur* is often explained as meaning "to live as temporary residents," in fact it does not imply anything as to the intended time of the stay. Rather, it refers principally to the status of the residents, i.e., resident aliens who do not enjoy the full status and rights of natural residents. Elsewhere in the commentary definitions are accurate and helpful (e.g., hayil and go'el on p. 25). The reader will do well to use a lexicon or Bible dictionary to check the data presented.

Book Reviews

The application to the life of the church is helpful at points, but Hamlin uses the commentary to argue for the acceptance of women pastors -- a point irrelevant to the exposition of Ruth. This is a simple story of a woman who ministers to another in need, acting in a non-official , "Good Samaritan" capacity. It is also about a man who takes initiative to minister to someone in need of help and protection -- and in doing so serves as the protecting "wings" [Heb. *knaphim*] of the Lord. These two characters are contrasted with two others, a male and a female, who do not minister when presented with opportunity. Whether an argument for women pastors is to be made from other parts of scripture or not, the book of Ruth does not speak to the issue.

Theron Young, Portugese Bible Institute, Infantado, Portugal

Tod Linafelt and Timothy Beale. *Ruth and Esther*. Berit Olam: Studies in Hebrew Narrative and Poetry. Collegeville, Minn: The Liturgical Press. 1999.

In the introduction to his commentary on Esther Tim Beale writes, "On first reading it appears so simple, so whole, and its meaning so completely self-evident. Yet the closer one gets to this text, the more perplexing it becomes. Questions lead not to answers but to more profound questions" (ix). Both of these commentators delight in exploring texts and both explore with a delicious fascination these "simple" stories. We are in for a treat!

Tod Linafelt begins his commentary by dismissing the assertion that Ruth is a story of "utter simplicity and naivete", proposing that this an ambiguous text where meaning is uncertain and often unsettling, whose writer was a person of immense skill. It is these ambiguities which are to be negotiated by the reader and not necessarily solved. Immediately the reader of this commentary knows that Linafelt's careful and meticulous exegesis will offer possibilities for the reader to consider and not a definitive meaning. Already the traditional historical-critical approach to textual analysis has been compromised and Linafelt is entering into the scholarly discourse that surrounds the book of Ruth. There is an assumption here that the reader of this commentary will have already familiarized her/himself with Ruth criticism.

Linafelt's is the third new commentary on Ruth to have been produced in the last five years. During the last decade monographs and essays have accompanied the publication of scholarly material generated by and focused on the women in the Old Testament. Feminist scholars, structuralists, formalists and intertextual critics have found nuances and colors of meaning in a book which has lain hidden in the interstices of the Deuteronomistic History. Linafelt's commentary synthesizes much of this work, interacts with it, and claims for the book of Ruth a place in the canon as a critique of the Davidic monarchy and patriarchal historiography, an elevation of Ruth as a paradigm for womanhood, and, as an exploration of kinship relationships, recognizes the important thread of the feminine voice with its inherently alternative values which counterpoints and often undermines the powerful voice of the masculine in the biblical text.

The commentary is a conventional one offering expert linguistic and structural analysis and it is certainly a very scholarly document. Linafelt's reading is methodically careful and attentive; his deconstruction meticulous and thoughtful. Although only 80 pages in length this commentary is very "meaty". I am concerned that Linafelt has declined to explore the community and ethnic relationships evident in the text as part of his study of kinship relationships and that he has ignored the Covenant/legal issues impinging on those kinship relationships. Perhaps a cultural-historical, ideological perspective would prove illuminating. But within the confines of his objectives this is a flawless study and one very worthy of attention.

Esther on the other hand, remains one of my least favorite books of the Old Testament and Timothy Beale's commentary does not convince me otherwise. Beauty contests, drinking parties, public humiliation of persons claiming recognition of their human dignity, and violent brutality dominate the text. The ethnic barbarity perpetrated by both Persians and Jews leaves me with a bad taste in my mouth and convinces me that the current interracial and interreligious problems in Israel emanate from, and are exacerbated by, such biblical texts as Esther. Beale ignores the moral dimension of Esther and that is problematic in itself. Haman's anti-semitism is discussed, but negative Jewish attitudes to Persians are dismissed as later additions to the original text. Regardless of what was added later, this is the text we have and it reveals a ghetto mentality, a people that will seek revenge. No wonder God is hidden from view! Like Luther I really can't understand why Esther is part of the canon.

Dorothy Penny-Larter

A. Boyd Luter and Barry C. Davis *God Behind the Seen: Expositions of the Books of Ruth & Esther Expositor's Guide to the Historical Books* (Grand Rapids, MI: Baker Books) 1995. 377pp.

The treatments of Luter and Davis are, by design, popular and non-technical. They are more homiletic in style than strictly expositional. Both authors give reliable comments on the literary structure of the books, helpful for readers unaccustomed to picking up on
structural clues.

A. Boyd Luter's treatment of Ruth gets off to a rough start. Inaccurate historical, geographical and literary data detract from the quality of the work. For instance, the fields of Moab would not be visible at some 50 miles from Bethlehem (p. 25) even on the clearest of days. There is no evidence to suggest that Jews considered gentiles (anachronism?) as dogs in this period (p. 27). The "personal guidance of the Lord" is scarcely visible in the book (note, p. 35). In fact, the indirect nature of the Lord's guidance in the book is at the heart of the message. The term "Moabitess" is used in 2:2 and 2:21, contrary to the note on p. 74. Other inaccuracies could be listed. However, in later chapters the comments are more precise and helpful. The book is to be recommended for its treatment of Ruth's chastity in regard to her threshing-floor encounter with Boaz (pp. 56-57, 60). Equally well presented are the motivations for the kinsman-redeemer's declination to marry Ruth (pp. 70-73).

Barry C. Davis' work on Esther frequently introduces anecdotes and trivia which may be entertaining, but are irrelevant for the elucidation of the meaning of the text (e.g., Hawaiian "kapakahi", pp. 261-62). Alliterated outlines are a plus for some, but generally a minus to good exposition (e.g., p. 283).

Book Reviews

Important questions about Esther, Mordecai and Haman are left unanswered by the book of Esther. Perhaps the best indicators are to be found in the culture and historical context of the period of the book. For instance, is Esther the grand prize winner in the "Miss Persia" beauty contest, of which she was a voluntary participant? A series of Niphal verbs in 2:8, clearly passive in meaning, seem to point away from this conclusion of Davis. The decree of the king "was heard," the virgins "were gathered" and Esther "was taken" to the king's palace. Given the culture of the participants, it is more likely that Esther had no choice in the matter.

Is Mordecai a stubbornly proud Jew who refuses to bow to Haman because of a racial prejudice against Agagites (a.k.a., Amalekites)? Nowhere are we informed of a tension between Jews and Amalekites in this late period. An oblique reference to Haman as an Agagite would not point us in that direction. Mordecai's refusal to bow has an analogy in a source not too distant historically and geographically from Esther. Daniel's three friends also refused to bow (Dan. 3:8-18), to the praise of their character. It is at least as likely that Mordecai's refusal was based on religious zeal.

Based on these and other shaky conclusions, Davis concludes at the beginning of the commentary that Mordecai and Esther are carnal Jews who have forsaken the worship of the Lord. This colors his commentary throughout the rest of the book. The conclusion is at best based on an argument from silence. It is more likely that they are struggling to survive as exiled "hostages" in a hostile world, where choices are few and Jews are lowly esteemed. Reserve may be considered prudent in the face of mortal threat. Mordecai's refusal to bow to a pagan ruler and Esther's request for Jews to fast on her behalf (4:16) reflect the tension in which they lived. The "down-playing" of Esther and Mordecai's spiritual side is perfectly consistent with the message of the book. In a world where God is unseen and His name not mentioned, He still works to orchestrate events according to His will and protect His people.   Theron Young

Gordon F. Davies. *Ezra and Nehemiah*. Berit Olam: Studies in Hebrew Narrative and Poetry. Collegeville, Minn: The Liturgical Press. 1999.

Sometimes the application of an alternative and different interpretative methodology reveals a great deal of the text. Tricky passages are often illuminated and the reader finds a new level of understanding. Familiar passages not considered problematic can receive a different twist in the hands of a commentator. Often the reader is challenged to return to the text for another look, a further exploration in order to make sense of the material being examined. If nothing else then, the role of a commentary is to engage the reader in the hermeneutical process.

In this highly pedestrian, dismal commentary the offerings of rhetorical criticism in the discussion of Ezra-Nehemiah seem small indeed. Davies makes no attempt to explain the impact of his translation on the overall reading/rhetorical value of the text. He does not explore the way in which the text is constructed rhetorically, but takes a piecemeal approach to each translated section making little or no connection to the previously discussed material. Interesting features and issues emerging from his reading lie unexplored, this largely because the commentary is a servant of rhetorical criticism rather than rhetorical criticism being in service of textual examination and interpretation. What a disappointment.   Dorothy Penny-Larter

James A. Wharton, *Job* (Westminster Bible Companion Series). Louisville, KY: Westminster, 1999. ISBN0-664-25267-2.

The importance of Job's questions will grow only greater as Western culture ages. Despite medical advances, health is not indomitable. Despite sophisticated national defense systems, a democratic metropolis holds no guarantee against devoted terrorism. Indeed, "No faith question is more central than the agonized 'Why?' addressed to God," (p. 1).

In *style*, Wharton's volume is less of a commentary, more of a reading guide. The layout is not verse-by-verse, but section-by-section. In fact, some sections are rearranged (all Eliphaz's speeches are grouped together) to help the reader grasp the flow of his arguments. Footnotes are nonexistent, resulting in a more relaxed "read". Text-critical and word studies notes are few. But where included, they are quite significant. E.g., in 13.11a should we read, "Though he slay me, yet will I trust in him" [KJV] or "See, he will kill me; I have no hope" [NRSV]? Did God simply "answer" Job from a whirlwind, or did he by his answer verge on "rescuing" him? This latter example becomes pivotal as Wharton explains his all-important interpretation of God's reply.

Careful not to claim the "last word" in *interpretation*, an important piece of his scheme surfaces in Wharton's view that *by the very act of answering Job*, God was offering his validation of Job's integrity. And this, despite the confrontational tone found in God's answer. As a result, Job's compliant response expresses more an acceptance of the conflict (since God has affirmed his servant's integrity) rather than a resolution of it. This seems to explain Wharton's conclusion expressed much earlier, that "the function of Job, from time of its inclusion among the Holy Scripture...has *never* been to provide answers to the questions it raises. Rather it has functioned...as a means of keeping the questions urgent and contemporary" (p. 2, ital. original).

One of the important gauges of a resource's value stems from the author's *grasp of the subject*. In this regard Wharton demonstrates a wonderful breadth. A casual reader easily becomes lost in the lengthy cycles of dialogue with Job's friends. Wharton crystallizes the message, waking up the reader so he/she does not miss an important piece of the logical puzzle.

To summarize, if you are looking for a technical resource with significant linguistic and bibliographic information you will need to look elsewhere. But if you desire a guide pointing the way through the maze of Joban dialogues, a seasoned professor offering a fresh perspective on the "upside-down trust" expressed by Job in God (and by God in Job?—see p. 159), Wharton's work will prove refreshing and useful.   Paul Overland

Book Reviews

Konrad Schaeffer, *Psalms* (Berit Olam: Studies in Hebrew Narrative and Poetry. Collegeville: Liturgical Press, 2001) pp.xlv + 399. $ 49.95.

Readers of the psalms have been greatly blessed in the last few years by a series of studies which have refocused attention on the primary purpose of the Psalms, to teach us to pray. J. C. McCann's *A Theological Introduction to the Book of the Psalms* (1993), E. Zenger's *A God of Vengeance?* (1996) and R. E. Murphy's *The Gift of the Psalms*(2000) are all fairly popular works of this genre. But with Schaefer's commentary we have something really substantial, yet at the same time quite accessible. It is based on the Hebrew text, always transliterated and translated, and the latest developments in Psalm studies.

His lengthy introduction discusses the nature of Hebrew poetry, its use of repetition and parallelism. Here he draws heavily on the work of Kugel and Alter, who have taken us well beyond the insights of Robert Lowth. Then he discusses the way the psalter is organized as a book, not as a random anthology, developing the ideas of Wilson and others.

The most valuable and longest section of his introduction is entitled 'A School of Prayer'. 'In the Psalter a believing poet speaks to God about God. Across the centuries worshiping communities and individuals have adopted this book to express their own faith and devotion.'(p. xxv) For Schaefer, though, the words of the psalmist are not just human words, but God's word and they show us how and what we ought to pray for. The symbolic language used in the Psalms enables the modern reader to identify with the sentiments of the original poet. The pain and joy of the psalmist become ours as we pray the psalms.

Sometimes of course the psalms express feelings that the modern Christian is uncomfortable with, for they seem incompatible with the view that we should forgive our enemies. But Schaefer argues that they give expression to central human emotions that we should express to God. We should be angry with oppressive institutions and wicked perpetrators. He asks rhetorically 'Does one pray to a God who tolerates persons or systems which treat people unjustly?'(p.xliii) The difficulties we face using these psalms serve 'as an invitation to enter more deeply into the mystery of God's word. The vexing problems and fearful insecurities of life, the travails that afflict every human being are all reflected in the Psalter.'(p. xlv)

The commentary itself is full and thorough, explaining the structure of each psalm, its relationship to adjacent psalms, and its place in the psalter as a whole. Careful attention is given to the exegesis of each line of the psalm, and their reuse in New Testament contexts is often noted. But the form-critical analysis that has so dominated psalm scholarship is rarely mentioned in the commentary and only briefly discussed in an appendix. This seems a healthy development, as much of such discussion is not very fruitful. However I do think the interpretation could have been given a sharper focus if Schaefer had reflected more on the fact that the psalms had been collected and arranged in their present order sometime in the post-exilic era. Their cries for help and affirmations of faith in those difficult days for the people of God become the more pointed and poignant when read against the exilic situation. The titles of the psalms, whether authentic or not, give an insight into the editors' understanding of these texts.

But these are minor grouses about a great commentary. From now on it will be one of the first I consult when I work on the psalms, and every theological student should be encouraged to read at least the introduction. If the church could take on board the insights of this commentary and the works mentioned above, its worship could be transformed and made more fit to be offered to Almighty God.

Gordon Wenham, University of Gloucester

Michael V. Fox, *Proverbs 1-9* (Anchor Bible Series). New York: Doubleday, 2000. ISBN 0-385-26437-2.

At an SBL panel of authors in Nashville last fall Professor Fox was asked, "What is distinctive about your commentary on Proverbs?" He replied that the Anchor Bible publishers gave him free rein to organize his work as he wished. The result was a combination of verse-exposition together with excursive sections that illuminate larger issues of wisdom literature. This aspect of book design will present itself as one of the first features striking any who peruse his volume.

Is such freestyle an asset in commentary writing? If you are looking for an in-depth treatment of Proverbs, Fox's format offers a clear advantage. Reading his work is like sitting in a captivating Bible lecture presented by someone so steeped in the text that a single biblical phrase evokes a string of insights and associations ranging far beyond the immediate text, while nonetheless very illuminating for the present passage.

For example, after treating the introduction of 1.8-9, we meet segments entitled "Fathers as Teachers", "Mothers as Teachers", and "Ornament Imagery in Proverbs". Again, following detailed examination of 1.10-19 we read of "The 'Deed-Consequence Nexus'" argued 45 years ago by K. Koch—a concept serious students of wisdom literature need to be aware of. In another segment we are invited to probe more carefully the identity of "The Gang" which tempts youth in ch. 1. Exactly what sort of persons may this group have represented in the world of the young, impressionable audience?

If one lacks the patience to "stay tuned" through these excurses which break through the fabric of the commentary, it is possible to fast-forward from one verse-exposition to the next. But that would result in missing some of the best that Fox has to offer.

In addition to excurses scattered through the exposition, more substantial essays gather toward the end of the volume. One appropriately gives Fox's view concerning Lady Wisdom: exactly who should we understand her to be? After reviewing several scholarly options he concludes, "Lady Wisdom is indeed godlike, but that is a literary guise, and we should grant the author and readers the literary competency needed to use and read tropes in an appropriate manner" (354). He offers a presentation that in my opinion is as convincing as it is refreshing. Minute issues are treated as well, such as one and one-half pages of shrunken print explaining perplexing problem of rendering *'amon* (artisan, constantly, or ward/nursling?) in 8.30.

Further assets in this work should be noted. International wisdom of the ancient world is very well represented, both in introduction and throughout the commentary. Special attention is given to *peshat* (literalist)-oriented Jewish commentators of the medieval era. Fifteen pages unfold careful word studies of Hebrew synonyms for "wisdom" and "folly". Textual traditions are conveniently summarized, followed by extensive text-critical notes at the back.

Is there room for differing with this impressive work? Certainly. Some will question, for example, whether he has convincingly argued that "it is improbable that many—if any—of the proverbs were written by Solomon" (p. 56). Others will wonder whether he is correct to infer that "[t]here is little logical progression from lecture to lecture [of Prov. 1-9], nor is there any evident organizational principle in their disposition" (p. 324). Do points of discussion such as these detract from the overall value of the volume? Clearly they do not; they only incite reexamination and invite scholarly debate. This work will be a regularly-referenced volume in my future study of Proverbs.   Paul Overland

Walter Brueggemann, *Isaiah*, Westminster Bible Companion Commentary Series, Louisville, KY: Westminster John Knox Press, 1998. 2 vols. ISBN 0-664-25524-8 (vol. 1) and 0-664-25791-7 (vol. 2).

Three questions are useful when deciding whether to purchase a commentary. First, does the author bring qualifications meriting publication of a volume such as this? Second, do the author's conclusions concerning specific critical questions lead to teaching that will be most useful to me? Third, do insights in typical passages significantly deepen my grasp of the message found there?

As far as Dr. Brueggemann's qualifications are concerned, he is highly respected in the field of Old Testament. Among the scores of seminar presentations available at Society for Biblical Literature meetings, his sessions are routinely "standing room only." One has only to read his *Theology of the Old Testament* to appreciate the breadth of grasp he has attained in the field of Hebrew Bible.

Concerning specific questions, two may be worth mentioning. First, Brueggemann follows the current consensus that detects three time periods within Isaiah: 8th century BC for chs. 1-39, 6th century exilic for chs. 40-55, and 6th century post-exilic for chs. 56-66. This conclusion seems rather assumed than explained. Perhaps in another of his works Dr. Brueggemann has accounted for this conclusion. I would have appreciated more information at this point. But that omission is likely due in part to the intended audience of the Westminster Bible Companion series. The expressed objective is to serve dedicated laity, whose patience for and interest in scholarly detail may quickly wear thin.

The dating/authorship question has a bearing on a second critical question, how one views the announcement that Cyrus, a Persian emperor, would rescue exiled Israel (44.28, 45.1). Some view this as having been recorded after-the-fact, which, though easier to believe, is problematic for the reasoning of Isaiah. In this section God is arguing that his credentials exceed those of false gods precisely because he can foretell the future. Brueggemann views the announcement as genuinely predictive, preserving the force of logic in this section (p. 75). Admittedly, the predictive impact would be greater were this section (with chs. 1-39) attributed to Isaiah of the 8th century.

Finally, do insights in typical passages significantly deepen one's grasp of the message found there? Often the answer is a resounding "yes." Without burdening the lay reader with Hebrew, Brueggemann skillfully draws on his rich knowledge of history and language to unfold texture and tenor within the text. At times I differ with interpretive conclusions (such as his assessment of Isa. 53 as better describing a suffering nation than a solitary redeemer), yet after the reading of other passages I emerge indebted for insights gained. Paul Overland

John N. Oswalt. *The Book of Isaiah: Chapters 40-66.* New International Commentary on the Old Testament. Grand Rapids, Mi.: Wm. B. Eerdmans, 1998.

Among the many commentaries on Isaiah published in recent years, Oswalt's is the most comprehensive. While recent commentaries have concentrated on such aspects of the book as composition, rhetorical forms, historical context, or theology, this commentary addresses all these elements – and more. The volume begins with an introduction that discusses the issues of composition, content, and structure as these relate to Isaiah 40-66, followed by an outline of the contents and an extensive bibliography. (A thorough introduction precedes the first volume of the commentary, published previously.) Each passage typically begins with the author's translation, an overview of the passage with attention to structure and scholarly discussion and then proceeds to verse-by-verse commentary. Copious footnotes appear throughout, and occasional excurses and "special notes" are inserted at relevant points. The volume concludes with indexes of subjects, authors, scriptures, and Hebrew words.

Oswalt makes a strong case that these chapters, as well as those that precede them, are the work of the 8th Century prophet Isaiah. Supplementing arguments made in the introduction of the first volume, he links the mainstream critical hypothesis of a 2nd and 3rd Isaiah (or an extended compositional history) with a deficient view of biblical prophecy (one that makes no place for supernatural prediction). He then develops this argument throughout the body of the commentary. A particularly forceful point in the argument is made in the discussion of those prophecies that predict the rise of Cyrus. The prophecies present Cyrus as an instrument of Israel's deliverance from captivity and point to his victory over Babylon as a demonstration of YHWH's will and power. None of the gods of Babylon, argues the prophet, could ever have conceived such a thing. It is entirely unforeseen, an authentically new historical circumstance that points to YHWH's uniqueness and sovereignty as Creator. (See, for example, the comments on pp. 103-04 199-207, 270-72.) Oswalt argues that if these texts were composed, as is commonly supposed, shortly before 540 B.C.E. (when Babylon fell), the central point they make is undercut. Why would an anonymous prophet argue that the triumphs of Cyrus represent YHWH's unimagined new work when this could easily be surmised from contemporary events? Even pagan prophets could do the same. To carry the intended impact the prophecies would have had to be revealed supernaturally, well before events pointed to Cyrus' ultimate triumph.

Oswalt's arguments for the compositional unity of Isaiah 40-66 are well-developed and well-informed. However, one wonders whether he has created an unnecessary dichotomy. (See especially the Special Note on p. 192.) It does not necessarily follow that positing a "Second Isaiah" involves a rejection of supernatural prediction and a denial of the testimony of the book about itself, especially given our

Book Reviews

(highly individualistic) notions of authorship and how little we really know about the composition and transmission of traditional materials in the ancient world. ("Accepting the evidence as given" versus holding that "evidence has been tampered with" seems a distinctively modern way of framing the issue.) Could there not be a mediating position, one that is open both to the possibility of a complex compositional history and to supernatural prediction? To be sure, the element of prediction seems moot if the materials in chapters 40-55 were composed in the mid to late 540's. But what if, for the sake of argument, they were composed before or around 550 B.C.E., when Cyrus overthrew the Median king Astyages? If this were the case, the prophet would be commenting on contemporary events and predicting their eventual outcome, something Isaiah of Jerusalem (and his prophetic colleagues) did as a matter of course. Explaining the meaning of YHWH's work among the nations and predicting its outcome in this context would have been no less remarkable than, for example, Jeremiah's or Habakkuk's predictions of Babylon's rise to prominence.

Apart from the debate on composition, Oswalt's view of Isaianic authorship affords keen insight into the unity of the entire book. He perceives the theme of servanthood as its unifying theme. Isa. 1-5 introduces the book by presenting the present and future of God's people. Isaiah's vision (Isa. 6) then represents a call to servanthood. The rest of the book then flows out of this vision. Correctly determining whom to trust (Isa. 7-39) forms the basis for servanthood. The vocation of a servant is laid out in Isa. 40-55, while the marks of servanthood, i.e. the divine character replicated in God's servants, unites the material in Isa. 56-66. The reader will note a theological sensitivity in the identification and description of this theme. Indeed, a depth of theological insight is perhaps the best feature of the commentary, outweighing even the author's lucid interaction with scholarly literature and rich linguistic analysis. Oswalt writes in an accessible narrative style that lapses easily into theological reflection. Breaking the mold of the "scholarly" commentary, he consistently explores the spiritual dimension of Isaiah's message, with an eye toward its relevance for Christian thought and life. In so doing Oswalt has given us a commentary that illumines both the intellectual power and the spiritual majesty of this "prince of the prophets."

L. Daniel Hawk

Johan Renkema, *Lamentations* (Historical Commentary on the Old Testament Series). Leuven, Belgium: Peeters, 1998. ISBN 90-429-0677-4. Paperback, 641 pages.

First impressions generated by Dr. Renkema's volume on Lamentations proved unfounded. When only five chapters of scripture result in more than six hundred pages of commentary one tends to expect tedious scholarly detail. Further examination revealed a volume that is indeed scholarly. But it is not tedious.

The solid, scholarly dimension appears in the author's level of ease when handling the original language and insights concerning literary structure. Quickly one observes that each segment of the commentary begins by reproducing the respective biblical phrase in pointed Hebrew (also translated). Careful attention is given to word meanings as the text is reviewed.

Insights on poetic structure form a hallmark of Renkema's work. Following careful surface-structural analysis, he has become persuaded that "we are dealing with a unified, 'one-piece' composition" (p. 72). He proceeds to provide structural summaries for each poem, discovering in them varying degrees of concentricity or external parallelism. Literary devices (inclusios, responses, external parallelism, and the like) are further summarized in a convenient format at the head of each subunit of poetry.

But lexical and poetic insights function for the author only as tools to achieve a greater project—the discovery of theological significance in the text. And here the richness of inspired scripture gleams most brightly under the scholar's lens. Consider an extract elucidating *chesed* (steadfast love) in 3.22. Declining the connotation of covenant-obligated love (since the covenant now lies shattered due to Israel's persistent rejection of God), Renkema proposes a different connotation: congeniality without binding obligation, a durable affection which is wholly voluntary. God no longer is bound to respond with compassion to his wayward bride. Yet he does so, all the same! From an example such as this, one can detect that the author employs the pick-axes of scholarship to mine rich gems from the text.

Whom will this work benefit? Certainly those will find value in Renkema's work who have an interest in discovering the high level of sophistication of which biblical poets were capable. In addition, any who value a slow-read of this pathos-filled portion of the Bible will discover rich insights surrounding the grief and resurging hope experienced by this poet-pilgrim of the 6th century BC. If possible, bring with you a bit of Hebrew (and German) ability to your reading of the commentary. Though not requisite, it will help.   Paul Overland

---

Daniel I. Block, *The Book of Ezekiel, Chapters 1-24* (The New International Commentary on the Old Testament). Grand Rapids, MI: Wm. B. Eerdmans, 1997.

Daniel Block's massive commentary will become a standard for Ezekiel studies for years to come. The commentary draws together the best insights of the two great Ezekiel commentators, Moshe Greenberg and Walther Zimmerli, and then moves beyond them. In the tradition of Greenberg, Block emphasizes the literary unity and artistry of Ezekiel. In the tradition of Zimmerli, Block leaves no linguistic or theological stone unturned.

Block's approach is guided by four simple questions, behind which lies a maze of potential complexity: "(1) Ezekiel, what are you saying? (the text-critical issue); (2) Ezekiel, why do you say it like that? (the cultural and literary issue); (3) Ezekiel, what do you mean? (the hermeneutical and theological issue); (4) Ezekiel, what is the significance of this message for me? (the application issue)" (p. xi).

The commentary on each textual unit begins with Block's translation, along with footnotes on text-critical matters. A second section, "Nature and Design," includes discussion of style, structure and literary context, followed by verse by verse exposition. A third section, "Theological Implications," summarizes "the permanent theological lessons of the unit" (p. xii).

The commentary's chief strength is its attention to detail. One finds, e.g., two pages on the Tammuz cult (8:14-15); identification of the divination techniques "belomancy or rhabdomancy" (21:26 [ET 21:21]); and citation of extrabiblical texts that describe the departure of the god from its temple as a prelude to foreign invasion (275-76).

Having said that, readers should not be deterred by the many details. One can easily dip into the commentary at any point and discover a nugget. The commentary both presents a thorough exposition of the text, and offers a clear restatement of Ezekiel's theological vision. Block does not hesitate to allow Ezekiel's challenges of Jerusalem's theological certainties also to address, and destabilize, some of our own theological and ideological "certainties."

Criticism of this commentary will seem like grasping at straws. Rather, two observations will suffice. The first pertains to how Block integrates the literary structure of composite texts with theological reflections on entire units. Consider the treatment of chapters 8-11. Although Block concedes that these chapters are composite, including, e.g., two unrelated oracles that are clearly editorial insertions (11:1-13; 11:14-21), he argues for the "literary cohesion" of chapters 8-11. Accordingly, the "Theological Implications" of the temple vision of chapters 8-11 occurs at the end of the entire unit, after the editorial framing of the entire unit in 11:22-25. The two "relatively independent" literary units (11:1-13; 11:14-21) lead Block to include two sections of "Theological Implications" prior to the "Theological Implications" section for chapters 8-11. Thus, although the entire unit has a logical coherence, as argued well on pp. 342-45, the theological implications of chapters 8-11 must be sought in three different places (pp. 340, 355, 359). The impact of Ezekiel's editorial art would have been enhanced had the "Theological Implications" of chapters 8-11 also presented an integrated theological reading of the entire unit. The only significant theological reflection on the editorial insertion of 11:14-21 occurs in an earlier section, which indicates that these verses represent "a promissory note of restoration" even before the judgment has come to completion, a kind of "light at the end of the tunnel" (p. 356).

The second observation concerns how the commentary allows the shocking dimensions of Ezekiel's words and actions to impinge on the "Theological Implications" of the text. The strength of the commentary is its consistent laying bare "The Enduring Theology of Ezekiel" (47). Because of this commitment to a "permanent theological message" (355), Block seems, at times, reluctant to engage in dispute or even in conversation with Ezekiel. When Ezekiel seems too strange or offers excessively violent imagery, Block seeks, rather than to offer resistance, to explain why we ought not consider the language offensive. Although it is clear that "No one presses the margins of literary propriety as severely as Ezekiel" (466), there seems often to be an explanation that softens the severity. Three examples follow that illustrate the complexity and the ambiguity inherent in wrestling with Ezekiel's troubling texts.

First, the commentary on 4:1-5:17 notes that we may be "offended by the sheer terror of Yahweh's pronouncements," and then suggests that we not allow our reactions to "detract from the profoundly theological nature of the message" (216). The value of shocking the audience has been blunted.

Second, in the Excursus on "The Offense of Ezekiel's Gospel" (467) Block examines and explains the objectionable images of sexual violence in chapter 16.

Defending Ezekiel against all charges of inappropriate language and violent imagery, Block suggests we not impose "anachronistic agendas arising out of alien cultural contexts" (469). Rather, it is "The intensity of the divine passion [that] determined the unique and often shocking style of the prophet" (470). In the "Theological Implications" that follow (520-22), Block allows for no arrogance or smugness in those who claim to be people of God today. The equivalent "shock value" today is not, however, suggested. Could we not imagine the story in reverse? God's people are the abusive or unreliable and absent father.

Third, the "Theological Implications" of chapter 23 helpfully notes that the people of God are "vulnerable to the seductive appeal of other allegiances" (764). But these implications do not at the same time address the problem of *militarism* as Israel's root problem. The text becomes an occasion, instead, for noting the destructiveness of marital infidelity.

A commentary as massive as this one that advocates profoundly at every turn *for* Ezekiel and his God, and *against* our own biases, complicity with evil, and idolatries, deserves our deepest respect. Although the commentary will be most useful for those who know Hebrew, its riches are not at all inaccessible to the reader who is looking for consistent theological reflection on one of the most difficult of Biblical books.

Gordon H. Matties, Concord College, Winnipeg

Ehud Ben Zvi. *Micah.* The Forms of the Old Testament Literature. Volume XXIB. Grand Rapids, Cambridge: Eerdmans.

Ehud Ben Zvi's commentary is not for wimps! It forms part of a 24 volume commentary series which aims to present form-critical analyses of every book of the Hebrew Bible "according to a standard outline and methodology". Primarily exegetical in nature these commentaries are seeking to bring consistency to the form-critical terminology and present an exegetical procedure that will enable both students and pastors to participate in analysis and interpretation themselves. The intended audience is a broad one, namely anyone engaged in biblical interpretation.

Each phase of the commentary begins with a structural analysis followed by an exceedingly close inspection/examination of the textual material. Minuscule attention is paid to formulaic literary structures, the grist to Ben Zvi's mill, and in conversation with a massive array of biblical critics, Ben Zvi includes references to reader-response criticism and intertextual criticism in order to broaden the cultural perspective of the texts. His analysis of the superscription is a case in point. Ben Zvi suggests that prophecy was intended for a reading audience and furthermore it was to be reread, studied and meditated upon. Inherent within this concept is the idea that the text was a product of a number of activities - writing, composition, editing, copying, distribution and archiving - all of which required particular economic resources. At this point Ben Zvi considers the ideological and theological purposes of these writings, the exclusivity of literacy, the role of power relations within the reading communities and the appropriation of texts by particular communities within society. He also suggests that "rereaders, and particularly those who meditate on the text, are aware of the entire text even as they reread its first line. They may make connections between different units not only according to their sequence in the book but in multidirectional and cross-linked paths".

The analysis of each section ends with a staggering bibliography and for these alone the commentary is well worth some attention. Ben Zvi is obviously a prodigious reader! But the commentary costs $35, so it can safely be asserted that students will find this tome a luxury outside the scope of their meager pocketbooks. Indeed, I suspect that this commentary will grace libraries and be purchased by an interested/participating clientele, but Ben Zvi's royalties may be limited! Thus, I am led to conclude that even though this is a worthy commentary the product is appealing to an exclusive minority despite the intentions of the contributors. Interesting, eh?   Dorothy Penny-Larter

John J. Collins, *Jewish Wisdom in the Hellenistic Age* (The Old Testament Library; Louisville, KY: Westminster John Knox, 1997. xii + 275 pp. Cloth.

John Collins, perhaps best known for his scholarly works on apocalypticism in general and Daniel in particular, here offers a rich and first-rate introduction to Jewish Wisdom texts from the intertestamental period and their historical, social, and cultural settings. The book begins with a discussion of the canonical wisdom literature as the traditional groundwork upon which the featured texts will build and to which they respond. The remainder of the book is divided into two parts: "Hebrew Wisdom" and "Wisdom in the Hellenistic Diaspora." The fullest treatment is accorded the Wisdom of Ben Sira, which is appropriate given its length and its importance for later generations of synagogue and church. Chapter Two introduces the reader to the historical setting of Ben Sira, exploring the cultural and political tensions in Judea a generation before the radical Hellenization Crisis and the Maccabean Revolt. A third chapter details the ways in which Ben Sira links Wisdom and its attainment with the doing of God's Law, the Torah, and keeping reverence for the God of Israel at the center of one's life. Chapter Four surveys the plethora of ethical topics and social situations treated in Ben Sira's curriculum. Chapter Five details Ben Sira's engagement of questions of theodicy. Finally, Chapter Seven examines Ben Sira's treatment of the history of Israel in the "Hymn to the Ancestors" (chapters 44-50) and his eschatological expectations. The final chapter in Part One examines the contributions of several of the Dead Sea Scrolls to our appreciation of Wisdom in Israel during the intertestamental period.

The second part opens with a fine treatment of the circumstances of, and the challenges facing, Diaspora Jews. Chapter Nine surveys the ethical teachings of the "Sentences of Pseudo-Phocylides," a text appropriately called "Jewish Ethics in Hellenistic Dress," since the form and, for the most part, the content of this text is not exclusively Jewish. Chapters Ten and Eleven focus on the Wisdom of Solomon, another of the Old Testament Apocrypha. After setting the text in its historical context, Collins first examines the importance of the belief in immortality for the author in his program of encouraging his hearers to pursue virtue and remain loyal to God's ways. Chapter Eleven explores the points of connection between Wisdom of Solomon and Greco-Roman philosophical teachings about God, the universe, and their interconnections, and then explores the author's critique of idolatrous religion, his treatment of Wisdom's actions in the history of Israel, and the vexing issue of universalism and particularism in this text. A final chapter synthesizes the findings of the whole book, showing the development of the Jewish Wisdom tradition from Ben Sira through Wisdom of Solomon under the growing influence of apocalypticism and Hellenistic philosophy.

Since the genre of review invites critique, I would take issue with Dr. Collins's labeling of the Golden Rule as the "centerpiece of New Testament ethics" (p. 76). Although perhaps the best known piece of ethical teaching in the New Testament, the ethics of the New Testament seems rather to be built around the imitation of Jesus: "do unto others as Christ did for you." I offer this criticism as a tribute to Collins's volume, for I cannot otherwise take issue with, nor point out deficiencies elsewhere in, his masterful treatment of the subject. I highly recommend it for students of Old Testament and early Jewish Wisdom, and for students of New Testament Background.

David A. deSilva

Peter Enns, *Exodus Retold: Ancient Exegesis of the Departure from Egypt in Wis 10:15-21 and 19:1-9.* Harvard Semitic Museum Monographs 57; Atlanta, GA: Scholars Press, 1997. ix. + 204 pp. $29.95.

The study of how early Jews and Christian read and interpreted their Scriptures is of perennial interest and importance. This revision of a doctoral dissertation, conducted under James Kugel (himself well known for his work on early exegesis of Scripture, as in his recent book *The Bible as It Was*), provides a thorough and careful analysis of the ways in which the Exodus story is developed in two specific passages in Wisdom of Solomon, itself largely a midrash on Exodus and other episodes from the wilderness wandering (at least in chapters 11-19). Enns shows how the details introduced by pseudo-Solomon are often the result of a close reading of other passages of Scripture that touch on the Exodus event, and that they have parallels throughout intertestamental and early rabbinic literature, showing them to be part of the Jewish cultural store of knowledge about the Exodus event. At certain points, however, Enns is able to discern and highlight pseudo-Solomon's own exegetical tendencies. As a study of intertexture and tradition analysis, this monograph stands as an exemplary model.

David A. deSilva

Jan Willem van Henten, *The Maccabean Martyrs as Saviours of the Jewish People: A Study of 2 & 4 Maccabees* (Leiden: Brill, 1997). xi + 346 pp. $144 (cloth).

This is a mature work by a scholar who has distinguished himself in the study of early Jewish and Christian martyrology, and most specifically in the study of 4 Maccabees. In this volume, van Henten explores the contributions of those who are remembered as martyrs and heroes of the Jewish people during the repression instigated under Antiochus IV, who chose death with honor rather than life with disobedience.

Van Henten first provides an introduction to each of the major sources for the Maccabean era martyrs, namely 2 and 4 Maccabees, in which the foundational work of his earlier articles is plain to see in full fruition. After a chapter in which he examines the historical setting of the martyrdoms, he explores the meaningfulness and motivations of the martyrdoms as expressions of complete faithfulness to God expressed through the strict observance of God's commandments. He then examines the political and patriotic dimensions of the martyrdoms, by which a few individuals become shining models of resistance, calling their nation to rally around the values that are worth dying for. A final chapter exploring the martyrologies as expressions of Jewish philosophy is followed by a summary.

This is an important work in the field of the study of 2 and 4 Maccabees, bringing together much of the scholarly conversation already extant and advancing that conversation in useful ways (for example, van Henten's conclusions about the provenance of 4 Maccabees, which are indeed strong, and his emphasis on the political aspects and results of the martyrdoms). David A. deSilva

Timothy Friberg, Barbara Friberg, and Neva Miller, *Analytical Lexicon of the Greek New Testament* (Grand Rapids: Baker, 2000). 439 pp. $40.00 hardcover.

An analytical lexicon provides two valuable kinds of help for the beginning reader of the Greek New Testament. First, it is a lexicon, a dictionary of Greek words with their range of English meanings. In this regard, the present volume serves about as well as any basic lexicon, although it should not replace one's reliance on the more in-depth and standard lexica such as the *Greek-English Lexicon of the New Testament and other Early Christian Literature* by Bauer, Arndt, Gingrich, and Danker, now in its third, revised edition. Second, it is a complete parsing guide to every form of every word that appears in the Greek New Testament. In this regard, the present volume does an exceptional job in terms of including not only the critical text of both the UBS and Nestle-Aland Greek New Testaments (taking into account multiple editions of each, no less), but also the standard editions of the Majority Text as well as the host of variants to be found in the critical apparatus of these various editions of the Greek New Testament.

The one potential drawback of the volume is that the grammatical tags are based on an abbreviation scheme that, while it has the benefit of being concise, is not always obvious. The compilers allowed only single-letter abbreviations, with the result that "R" is the abbreviation for the PeRfect tense (since "P" was already claimed for the Present tense), and "O" the abbreviation for a Passive DepOnent verb.

Since the grammatical tags are the main feature of, and reason for consulting, an analytical lexicon, and example of the system is in order here. The full grammatical tag of *egenometha* would be VIAD--1P. The user will then look to the guide of abbreviations. The first letter indicates part of speech (V=Verb; there are seven different parts of speech in the key). The user will then move to the specific block of symbols for Verbs and proceed: I=Indicative; A=Active; D=Middle Deponent; the two dashes indicate two columns of abbreviations skipped (those reserved for participles, showing case and gender); 1P= 1st person plural. It will take some time, therefore, for the user of this volume to become familiar with the grammatical tagging system, keeping the abbreviation and symbol key close at hand for a good many hours of use, but once the system is memorized through use it would serve as well as any other system. One benefit of the grammatical tags to be found in this volume is that they provide more grammatical information for adjectives, the definite article, conjunctions, and particles than would be found in other analytical lexica. The analysis also lists all the possible parsings of a particular form (since it will often happen that a particular string of Greek letters could be construed as two, three, or even four different forms).

This reference tool concludes with an interesting essay on deponency written by Neva Miller. She suggests that the verbs that grammarians tend to classify as "deponent" (middle form with active meaning) all fall within categories that would be well suited to the Greek middle in and of itself — verbs involving reciprocal interaction between subject and object, reflexive action, self-involvement, self-interest, and the like. This provides at least one plausible way of making sense of a concept with which beginning Greek students tend to struggle. David A. deSilva

Daniel B. Wallace, *The Basics of New Testament Syntax* (Grand Rapids: Zondervan, 2000). 334 pp. $29.99 hardcover.

This volume is a welcome abridgement of Dr Wallace's massive *Greek Grammar Beyond the Basics: An Exegetical Syntax of the New Testament* (Grand Rapids: Zondervan, 1996). The earlier volume has received deserved accolades as an up-to-date reference grammar, and included hundreds of discussions of specific New Testament texts introduced under the appropriate grammatical or syntactical headings. Those discussions are largely absent from the abridged volume, as are the sectional bibliographies. The *Basics of New Testament Syntax* volume, however, is keyed to the larger reference work. If one acquires both, therefore, one can use the shorter volume as a handy reference and consult the longer work for specific discussions of passages where one wishes even more detailed information or examples of how the grammatical or syntactic category might affect one's understanding of the text.

The *Basics* will serve the pastor or other student of the Bible who wishes to continue to grow in his or her mastery of Greek, providing a well-organized and fairly comprehensive guide to all the nuances of, say, the Aorist tense or the Subjunctive mood or the dative case that were not included in the first-year introductory language course. Indeed, a book such as Wallace's *Basics* provides an essential second tier in one's grasp of the highly nuanced language of the New Testament, without which one's exegetical abilities would be measurably diminished. For example, the beginning Greek student leaves Greek II with a basic awareness that the genitive case indicates description, one important kind of description being possession. Wallace offers, however, a twenty-page discussion of the twenty-four identifiable nuances that a noun in the genitive case could convey. As the student of the Word encounters, therefore, a noun in the genitive case that does not immediately appear to provide description or denote possession, he or she can turn to Wallace's work for a guide to all the possibilities, so that he or she might discern the precise nuance a New Testament author might be seeking to convey.

I would therefore highly recommend this text as a necessary resource for all who wish to continue to grow in their study of the New Testament in its original language. David A. deSilva

Book Reviews

Paul Barnett, *Jesus & the Rise of Early Christianity: A History of New Testament Times.* Downers Grove, IL: InterVarsity Press, 1999. Pp. 448, $29.99.

In a self consciously evangelical approach to New Testament background, Barnett describes his goal as "to show that Jesus himself is the 'engine' that drives the story of the New Testament. In other words, this book arose from the long-held conviction that the 'Christ of faith' was one and the same as the 'Jesus of history'" (p. 10). Barnett assumes the essential historicity of the gospels, and that the traditions they contain, were transmitted not orally but in written form through earlier documents or reminiscences. The historicity of Acts is assumed (see pp. 231-326), as is the so-called "South Galatian" hypothesis for Paul's letter to the Galatians (pp. 292-296). Pseudonymity in the New Testament is rejected.

Barnett's strongest contributions are in the discussion of the background of the gospels. He is reluctant, however, to observe the importance of the role of oral tradition in framing the forms of gospel narrative. His discussion of the gospels as "bioi" or, Hellenistic "lives," however, is in keeping with some of the recent research, which recognizes that the gospels would fit into a coherent genre of ancient literature. His discussion of the background of 1st Century Palestine is most helpful, demonstrating thorough familiarity with both primary sources and secondary literature.

Barnett's understanding of Acts and the epistolary literature, however, is not as strong or helpful. Little appeal is made to archaeological findings. Also, he tends to rely upon rather questionable hypotheses, such as those found in John A.T. Robinson's *Redating the New Testament,* which present unconvincing arguments for accepting either Peterine authorship of 1 or 2 Peter (see p. 325, n. 9) or an early date of Hebrews (see p. 374, n. 22).

Barnett accepts the so-called "South Galatian" hypothesis for dating Galatians as Paul's earliest letter, written before the Apostolic Council of Acts 15, continuing the tradition of British evangelical New Testament scholarship since Ramsey. The reader should be warned, however, that considerable evidence exists against the hypothesis (see the introduction of H. D. Betz, *Galatians* [Hermeneia; Philadelphia: Fortress, 1979]). Barnett draws this conclusion because he presupposes the basic reliability of Acts, as well as its traditional authorship by Luke, the physician and companion of Paul While this may be acceptable in many circles, readers need to be aware that this position is by no means the universal consensus.

Perhaps Barnett is most helpful when he demonstrates that the most likely explanation for early Christianity's ascription of messianic status to the person of Jesus of Nazareth is that such messianic consciousness derives from Jesus himself, and was confirmed by his resurrection from the dead. The use of Johannine chronology to inform and supplement the portrayal of Jesus' ministry in the Synoptics has found support in J.P. Meier's *A Marginal Jew,* although, surprisingly, that book is seldom cited.

Despite some of the shortcomings, the book is well documented, with good bibliographies at the end of each chapter as well as extended notes and helpful maps. While discussion of critical theories is sometimes neglected in the text, such issues are acknowledged in the notes. There are also numerous excurses, one of the most helpful being "Excursus 20a" (pp. 420-421), which describes some of the inadequacies of Crossan's work on Christianity in the 40's and 50's (*Birth of Christianity: What*

Happened in the Years After the Execution of Jesus. San Francisco: HarperCollins, 1998).

In short, Barnett's work can be used with profit in an evangelical setting among undergraduates or in lay Bible studies. While it should not be taken as the only, or indeed last word. it does provide balance to some of the more extreme claims of groups, such as The Jesus Seminar, that are propagated in the popular media. It does demonstrate that one can have both a historical consciousness as well as a vital evangelical faith.

Russell Morton

Craig L. Blomberg, *Neither Poverty nor Riches: A Biblical Theology of Material Possessions*, Grand Rapids: William B. Eerdmans Publishing Company, 1999, pp. 253, $20.00.

"It is easier for a camel to go through the eye of a needle than for a rich person to enter the of kingdom of God" (Mark 10:25). Anyone in the Church of North America who takes Jesus at his word and, at the same time, takes an honest look at the economic conditions of the rest of the world, should be disturbed by what troubled the disciples that day: If this is true, which of *us* can hope to be saved? Can we count ourselves as blessed of God, a land flowing with milk and honey because we have found favor in the eyes of the Lord? Or are we a country full of rich fools, living in luxury every day while a billion beggars lie at our gates?

In *Neither Poverty nor Riches: A Biblical Theology of Material Possessions*, Craig L. Blomberg navigates skillfully through difficult passages of Scripture, avoids the dangerous obstructions of social convention and unquestioned politico-economic loyalty, and anchors his work safely in the harbor of sound biblical exegesis. The current debate over the biblical perspective of material possessions rages from the impractical position of extreme asceticism to the ludicrous and self-serving tenets of the "health and welfare gospel." Blomberg proceeds inductively, not dismissing any perspective outright, but allowing the voice of Scripture to address the viability of each position, even the most unlikely. I share D. A. Carson's assessment that, "Dr. Blomberg's volume is an extraordinary achievement. . . . that is, quite frankly, the best one on the subject" (p. 9).

Blomberg's aim is to establish a comprehensive theology of material possessions by surveying the contributions of *all* major biblical witnesses on the subject. While most recent authors on the subject focus entirely on the New Testament, Blomberg examines the entire corpora of Scripture giving remarkable consideration to the interconnectedness between Old and New Testament perspectives regarding material possessions. He even offers the reader a functional glimpse at the intertestamental writings on the topic. He does not presuppose a certain amount of thematic unity, but allows Scripture to present its own rich, theological suggestions. He does, however, pull together significant implications at the end of each chapter, and summarizes these at the end of the book, drawing conclusions about Scriptural themes and offering practical applications of these themes for believers.

Blomberg scrupulously follows the guidelines of hermeneutical principals as set forth by Klein, Blomberg and Hubbard (*Introduction to Biblical Interpretation*,

1993) paying meticulous attention to historical background. He carefully contextualizes each verse by relating situation-specific mandates to broader, ethical principals. For example, in his treatment of Jesus' sermon on the mount, Blomberg gives social background information which indicates that "give to anyone who asks of you" refers to the Jewish practice of loans without interest, rather than giving money to anyone who begs from you (pp. 129,130). Similarly, he refutes those who would say that Jesus accepts the inevitability of poverty when he said, "The poor you will always have with you." According to Blomberg, those who heard Jesus would have clearly understood this as an invitation to be vigilant in their efforts to take care of the poor among them (p. 142).

My one caveat to Blomberg's survey is in his analysis of Jesus' parables. He suggests that the parables have meaning on two levels–one spiritual and the other material–which, in my opinion, stretches what Jesus intended. Jesus knew that his listeners would easily identify with stories about earning a day's wage, about rich people and poor people, about debt and other financial images. These were issues of daily living. As with his parables about farming and shepherding, Jesus used finances and material possessions merely as a backdrop upon which to paint portraits of spiritual truth. Obviously, financial issues are one of many areas which will be affected by following the precepts put forth in the parables, but most of the parables which mention money or material possessions are not categorically addressing finances–at any level.

Dr. Blomberg incontestably accomplishes his objective: a comprehensive biblical theology of material possessions. As the title suggests, Scripture qualifies neither wealth nor poverty as a virtue. Neither one are prerequisite to righteousness, nor the result of righteous living. Nor are they inherently evil. Blomberg's survey convincingly establishes that God's continuing concern is our dependence upon him for our "daily bread." In the same way, if God's will is to be done on earth as it is in heaven, there must be an intentional interdependence between all of God's children. If you find yourself asking the question, "Is that really possible?" then this book is a must read for you. The answer is clearly laid out in Scripture, and Blomberg has done the work of distilling it for us.   Eric P. Sandberg

Henry J. Cadbury, *The Making of Luke-Acts* (Peabody, MA: Hendrickson, 1999). xx + 385 pp. Paper.

Hendrickson has made the reprinting of enduring classics in biblical scholarship a noteworthy part of its publishing program. This volume is a reprint of the 1927 work by Henry Cadbury, an English scholar whose work on the composition of Luke-Acts is still foundational for the study of these texts.

Cadbury begins with a study of the transmission of Jesus materials in the early church and an assessment of Luke's use of sources (Mark and Q). In a second section, he analyzes the literary forms of the material found in Luke-Acts, including a careful comparison of Luke and Josephus on the use of earlier historical source material. The book concludes with a thorough investigation of the style, social location, theological interests, and purposes of the author in composing Luke-Acts. Thus in a single volume, the reader has access to a landmark work on the source criticism, form criticism, and redaction criticism of Luke-Acts.

The reprint of the original is prefaced with an introduction by Paul Anderson in which Cadbury's enduring contribution to Lucan scholarship is evaluated appreciatively, as is appropriate.   David A. deSilva

Mal Couch, ed., *A Bible Handbook to the Acts of the Apostles* (Grand Rapids, MI: Kregel, 1999). 455 pp, $25.99.

This book seems to "revitalize a sense of urgency and mission" in Bible teachers, missionaries and pastors (p. 7). It presents the theology and a background survey of the Acts of the Apostles. The perspective is avowedly Dispentationalist, and the purpose is to present Acts from a Dispensationalist perspective. The book has three parts. Part one provides an overview of the theology of Acts. Part two focuses on the theology and work of the Holy Spirit in Acts. Part three provides a "Verse-by-Verse Background Guide" to Acts.

The Dispensationalist element shows up throughout the whole work, determining the topics treated in parts one and two. For example, the work goes to great lengths to show how unbiblical "covenant theology" is, and show the "Dispensationalist purposes" of Acts (p. 24). Many topics in part one, such as the ministry of the Holy Spirit, while referring to texts in Acts, are described with references to many other biblical books, especially Paul's letters. On this topic in particular, the book emphasizes that the historical events in Acts are not normative and should not be used in determining theology or praxis for today's Church. This leads to discussions of the nature of speaking in tongues and of all "signs and wonders" by A.D. 70. These phenomena only occurred during the transition between the dispensation of law and the dispensation of the Church. While these topics may be appropriate in some contexts, the question must be asked, Are these issues actually part of the theology of Acts? Does Acts intend to address such issues? This is not to say that all the chapters cover such topics. Chapter seven examines the place of the temple in Acts. Here again, however, the book focuses on what Acts says about the temple in Jerusalem in relation to Dispensationalism, stating that "the supposed abandonment of the temple by the early Church" is an argument against dispensational interpretation (p. 109).

In part three, the book steps through Acts by the chronological divisions, from Chapter 1, "The Wait for the Coming of the Holy Spirit," dated to A.D. 30, which covers Acts 1, to chapter 28, "Paul's Arrival at Rome," dated to A.D. 59. Each chapter begins with a synopsis of the chapter, followed by explanations of items of interest in the chpater. For example, for Acts 20:2, there is a one-and-one-half page description of Greece, followed by a discussion of the individuals named in Acts 20:4, such as Tychicus. Often, items in part three refer back to earlier parts of the book, for exampl on Acts 24:2b, "the Holy Spirit said, " the entry points readers back to the discussion of the personality of the Holy Spirit in part one. Part three will likely be the most valuable section of the books for readers seeking to understand Acts better.

Overall, this book will be disappointing to anyone who is not committed to Dispensational theology, since the book presents Dispensationalism as clearly taught within Acts. The book does refer to various scholars, but generally these are quite dated works, such as Lenski's commentary on Acts, or to various Bible dictionaries. There are occasional references to more recent works, but little evidence of dialogue with recent works on Acts. For instance, there is a discussion of the meaning of Joel 2:28-32 in Acts 2 in which the book lists three possible interpretations, none of which correlate to either the views of M. Rese, or, more relevantly, that of M. Turner (*Power from on High: The Spirit in Israel's Restoration and Witness in Luke-Acts* (Sheffield, England: Sheffield Academic Press, 1996)), for example. Even if one has a Dispensationalist perspective and this reviewer is not seeking to impugn that view, they will likely find this work inadequate for understanding Acts. Any number of recent commentaries on Acts, aimed similarly at pastors and lay people, would be more helpful in understanding the book of Acts, such as those by I. H. Marshall or L. T. Johnson.

Kenneth D. Litwak, Trinity College, Bristol, England

David Crump, *Jesus the Intercessor: Prayer and Christology in Luke-Acts.* Grand Rapids, MI: Baker Book House, 1999. Xviii+295 pp., $29.95. ISBN: 0801022215.

While there are many books on prayer, Crump argues that there has been relatively little scholarly work on prayer within Luke-Acts. While earlier research has focused on Jesus as a "model pray-er," Crump focuses on the christological significance of Jesus' prayer life, what it teaches about his ministry and about his relationship with God. Crump examines the nature of Jesus' prayer life in Luke's Gospel and its role in the presentation of christology in the book of Acts. Jesus' intercessory prayers play an important role in the christology of Luke-Acts. Jesus' intercession, bot in his earthly life and in heave, are at the heart of Jesus' past and present role as savior. Crump examines Luke's editorial notices of Jesus' prayer-life, correlating them with the recorded contents of Jesus' prayers. Next Crump compares Jesus' prayer life to didactive material on prayer in Luke-Acts. This is followed by a comparison of Jesus as the heavenly intercessor in Acts with notions of heavenly intercession in ancient Judaism.

Crump states that "Luke associates the prayers of Jesus with the acquisition of spiritual insight at key locations throughout his gospel (p. 21). Several texts show prayer providing insight to others of Jesus' character: Peter's confession (Luke 9:18-27), the Transfiguration (Luke 9:28-36), the Crucifixion account (Luke 23:32-49) and possibly the trip to Emmaus (Luke 24: 13-35). Crump treats each of these texts in order to show that "Luke presents Jesus primarily, though not exclusively, as an Intercessor" whose prayers for the disciples result in what is necessary for them to be obedient, successful disciples (p. 21). For example, Peter's confession of Jesus as the "Christ of God" came only through Jesus' intercessory prayers. While there may well be an association between Jesus' prayer and the disciples' question in Luke 9:18, is it really valid to infer that Luke intends his readers to understand Jesus' prayer as directed at the disciples correctly answering his question to them about his messianic identity (p. 24)?

Crump connects Luke's language about seeing and hearing in Luke-Acts to Jesus' prayers. Jesus prays that his followers will see and hear him correctly. Jesus' prayer life also plays an important role in the Transfiguration, according to Crump. In the Transfiguration, the praying Jesus is related to the disciples' "reception of a new revelation into the true meaning of Jesus' person and ministry (p. 48).

Crump argues that Jesus in Luke 10:21-24 thanks the Father for hearing and answering his prayers in Luke 9 for the disciples. After reviewing theories regarding the referent of "these things" in Jesus' prayer, Crump argues that "these things" are connected to the mission of the seventy described earlier in Luke 10. The content of "these things" is the identity of Jesus as the "messianic Son of God." This passage also shows that Jesus' role as intercessory mediator was already operative during his earthly mission.

Chapter four focuses on the other two narratives in Luke's gospel which show Jesus' prayers as the means by which an individual received special illumination regarding the person of Jesus. Crump probes how Luke 23:32-49 contributes to Luke's use of prayer for christology. Jesus' prayer in Luke 23:34 is closely connceted with the thief's request of Jesus. Jesus' prayer thus provided the means for revelation to the thief of Jesus' true nature. In Luke 23:44-49, the language of seeing/hearing in the response of the crowd and the centurion "shows itself to be exemplary of the response required to God's revelation (p. 91)." In the prayer-revelation equation used by Luke, perceiving Jesus' true identity leads to salvation. Through his self-disclosure, Jesus' prayers mediate God's salvation. Crump finds a similar connection in the story of the Emmaus Road, Luke 24:13-35. Based on Jewish practices of "breaking bread," Crump asserts that Jesus prayed as he broke bread. This prayer precedes the disciples recognizing Jesus. Through this recognition, they are able to understand the Scriptures (and not the reverse. They receive revelation, not that their prophetic understanding of the messiah needs to be clarified to see "the messiah must be the final, suffering prophet (p. 106)." Once again, Jesus' prayer is seen to play a revelatory role.

Crump examines Luke 22:31-32, which is the only place in Luke-Acts where Jesus makes known to the disciples the contents of his prayer for them and points to its answer in the future. Jesus the pray-er is clearly paradigmatic in Luke 22. Jesus stands against temptation through prayer, while the disciples fail through lack of prayer. Since the disciples after this event needed perseverance, as later disciples do, this text helps show that Jesus' intercession continues on past his death and resurrection. Crump draws from this the suggestion that Jesus' intercession is responsible for the composition of the Church. People are included through Jesus' prayers. One must ask, however, Does Judas' absence in Luke 22:31-32 mean that Jesus did not pray for him? Does Luke 22:3 really show that Jesus' prayers determine the composition of the Church over time?

Turning to Acts, Crump argues that Stephen's vision of the Son of Man in Acts 7:55-56 is the one place in Acts which shows Jesus as the final prophet praying for his people. It shows Jesus as an advocate for Stephen. While this is suggestive, Crump does not provide a substantial enough bridge to get from Jesus as Stephen's advocate to Jesus praying for Stephen. The picture in Acts of Jesus as the final, eschatological Prophet fulfilling the role of heavenly intercessor is consistent, according to Crump, with the idea expressed in many Jewish works from the intertestamental period of human beings who interceded while on earth and now continue that in heaven. Yet, "perhaps Luke's most innovative contribution to NT christology is his presentation of a praying Messiah (p. 235)."

Book Reviews

Overall, Crump's work makes many helpful observations, but his argument, while cautious, is also unconvincing. The arguments are generally based on possible hints in the text, but these are carried forward to assertions that go beyond the evidence. Still, the book raises many important questions and will reward critical readers.

Kenneth Litwak

Jay M Harrington, *The Lukan Passion Narrative. The Markan Material in Luke 22,54-23,25: A Historical Survey: 1891-1997.* Leiden: Brill, 2000. (New Testament Tools and Studies, XXX) xiii+1003pp., $206.

The huge size of this volume says much about both the nature and volume of New Testament scholarship and the industry of its author. Harrington begins with the observation that the volume of scholarship devoted to the question of whether Luke followed a special source or sources in composing his passion narrative has led some to consider that an impasse has been reached. In his introduction Harrington makes no explicit claim to move beyond such an impasse in this history of scholarship on the question, although his own sympathies are with those who reject any special source.

The history that Harrington presents is thorough and comprehensive. Few may wish to read the book in its entirety, but a detailed table of contents and a useful index of authors make it possible for the reader easily to locate discussions and summaries of particular contributors to the debate. The overall structure of the survey is chronological, although Harrington has grouped scholars according to whether or not they support the hypothesis of a special source. This offers more coherence than would be found in a purely chronological account. Harrington offers a synthesis of the evidence for a special source on pages 564-5, and for Lukan redaction of Mark on pages 685-6. He attaches great significance to his observation that some scholars who once advocated Luke's use of a special source changed their position.

One important criterion in assessing a work such as this is the question of whether it represents fairly those whom it surveys. Two observations might be made about some of those whom Harrington names as having changed their minds. First, it seems unfair to cite R E Brown as an important example of someone who has changed his mind. Harrington notes that Brown himself observes that he supported a special source only before he considered the question in detail. Therefore although Brown is an important advocate of Harrington's thesis that Luke drew primarily on Mark, he is not truly representative of those who have come to this position after having defended the opposite view. Second, Harrington observes (correctly) that J B Green makes no further mention of his 1987 defence of a special source (The Death of Jesus) in his subsequent treatment of Luke's theology (*The Theology of Luke*, 1995) and his commentary on Luke (*Luke*, NICNT, 1997), but this is not sufficient grounds on which to infer that therefore he has changed his mind. Indeed, Green confirmed to this reviewer by e-mail that he has not. Harrington may be correct to suggest that a majority of recent scholarship does not argue that Luke drew on a special source independent of Mark, but his argument based on those who are said to have changed their position is overstated. Such observations are important in that they serve as a reminder that there is no such thing as impartial scholarship, but nevertheless this work is an invaluable summary of previous research regardless of whether or not Harrington's conclusions are considered compelling.

Harrington's final section is devoted to the Herod pericope, Luke 23:6-16, one of the most debated sections of the Lukan passion narrative. He notes nine categories in which source-critical opinion on this passage may be arranged and then offers his own exegesis of the passage. Harrington concludes that no appeal to a special source need be made. Rather, Luke composed the Herod pericope on the basis of Markan materials he omitted in earlier parts of his Gospel parallel to Mark 3:6, 6:14-29 and 15:16-20. Therefore, he claims, his working hypothesis that Luke employed Markan materials that he chose to omit elsewhere may now be regarded as a principle. Further conclusions follow, and these are offered in support of his overall conclusion that Luke is guided by Mark throughout his passion narrative.

A bibliography, three appendices (Special LQ Vocabulary and Construction According to J. Weiss; Theories of Lukan Priority; The Relation of the Herod Pericope to the Gospel of Peter) and an index of authors complete the work.

This is an indispensable tool for further study of the Lukan Passion Narrative in particular, and the relationship between the Synoptic Gospels in general. Its price may confine it only to major research libraries, but it deserves to be used widely.

Andrew Gregory, Lincoln College, Oxford

Ruth Hoppin, *Priscilla's Letter: Finding the Author of the Epistle to the Hebrews.* Fort Bragg, CA: Lost Coast Press, 2000. 207 pp. Paper. $19.95.

The theories about the authorship of Hebrews are well-known. Hoppin seeks to provide substantive support for Harnack's suggestion that the author was Priscilla, known to us from Acts. Writing in a lively style, while carrying on a scholarly conversation, Hoppin argues that, when all the possible authors are considered, and those unsuitable are eliminated, Priscilla appears as the best choice for the author.

Hoppin first explores the lack of an introductory statement which names the author and recipients. She states that there are no known examples from the papyri where this prescript is lacking. Hebrews, which she argues is a letter, is the only known exception. Hoppin then argues that while this could be due to accidental loss, this is unlikely. The evidence suggests that the author omitted the prescript intentionally. Hoppin inquires as to why this might be and suggests that this points in the direction of Hebrews being written by a woman. Otherwise, Hebrews would not have been anonymous. Hoppin next (chapter 3) examines the possible personality of the author, seeking to show that the sympathetic and empathetic nature of the letter suggests it was more likely to be from a woman. Looking at the changes in first person pronouns from "we" to "I" and back again, especially in Heb 13:19, Hoppin argues that the most natural way to understand this verse is that "we" is the married couple Priscilla and Aquila, while "I" refers to Priscilla, who requests prayer that she may return to the readers. Because of the affinities with Paul's letters and the mention of Timothy, the author must have come from Paul's inner circle of co-workers. Hoppin argues further that a number of "semi-apologetic pleas for credibility" within Hebrews favor a female author, Priscilla, rather than a male (p. 31). The letter provides "ample evidence for feminine style and outlook (p.33)." Hebrews 11 shows that the author identified with women. The mention at the end of Hebrews 11 of women who "received their dead back by resurrection" refers to women who were aided by Elijah and Elisha. Hoppin suggests, based on the account of these same events in Sirach 48, that a man would have focused on Elijah and Elisha, not the anonymous women of the stories. In contrast to Sirach's roll call "of famous men" in Sirach 44, Hebrews 11 mentions Sarah and Rahab, two women, by name. Hoppin, following Clement of Rome, argues that Heb 11:34 refers probably to Judith.

Hoppin argues in chapter 5 that none of the other individuals offered for the author by scholars are acceptable. She shows why Apollos, Barnabas, Silas and even "the unknown associate of Paul" do not meet the necessary criteria. For example, while Clement of Rome quotes Hebrews, Clement's own style and that of Hebrews are markedly different. The two letters should be similar stylistically if Clement authored both. The same is true for the author of the Epistle of Barnabas. Barnabas, separate from the author of the Epistle of Barnabas, does not qualify as the author either. First, Barnabas was a Levite, well-versed no doubt in temple procedures. The author of Hebrews speaks only of the tabernacle, not the temple, and appears unfamiliar with ceremonial procedures common to both. Moreover, a Jew from Cyprus would probably not be fluent in Greek and skilled in classical rhetoric, as the author of Hebrews is.

Hoppin then examines the association of Priscilla with Rome, where the letter was likely written. Hoppin discusses archaeological evidence for Priscilla's home and well-to-do family. Priscilla would have had the opportunity for education, to meet Paul, and to meet Philo, whose writings the author of Hebrews seems to know and challenge. Hoppin then seeks to reconcile Priscilla as a educated woman in a politically important wealthy family in Rome with her marriage to Aquila, which is perhaps the weak spot of her argument.

Overall, Hoppin has done a fine job of providing a very plausible case that Priscilla wrote Hebrews. My one critique is that Hoppin rarely cites non-biblical primary sources, leaving it as an exercise for the reader to consult all the scholarly works she cites to find out the primary sources she appeals to at various points. This should not detract, however, from the solid argument Hoppin has presented in favor of Harnack's suggestion, making a formidable case that must be dealt with by any who choose an alternate author. Kenneth D. Litwak

Luke Timothy Johnson, *Living Jesus: Learning the Heart of the Gospel*, San Francisco: Harper San Francisco, 1999, ix-210 pp., $22.00.

Luke Timothy Johnson, the Robert W. Woodruff Professor of New Testament at the Candler School of Theology at Emory University and prodigious critic of the Jesus Seminar moves beyond all that in this book. He sees the New Testament as a step-by-step guide to understanding and developing a relationship with the living Jesus. The Jesus presented by the writers of the New Testament is resurrected and alive, not a dead figure of history to be scrutinized. He says, "Jesus is not simply a figure from the past...but a person in the present; not merely a memory that we can analyze and manipulate, but an agent who can confront and instruct us."

Learning Jesus is then not a historical problem needing resolution but a relationship that must be developed. This is accomplished similarly to the way other intimate relationships develop, that is by openness, trust, respect, attentiveness, over time, suffering and faithfulness.

Johnson affirms that the resurrection of Jesus Christ is key to understanding how he still lives. Thus the resurrection is the grounding for the Christian life for it is the resurrection that aroused the disciples to live for Jesus. This implies that there was a sense among them in which Jesus was present. They were not simply relating to a person that they knew in the past.

These ideas are developed through the traditions of the Canon, Creed and Community. The Canon secures continuity with the past and identity for the future and it is to be appreciated for its diversity and not overly harmonized. Mark sees Jesus as the suffering Son of Man. Matthew emphasizes Jesus as the teacher, Luke sees Jesus as the prophet and John emphasizes that Jesus reveals the Father. The Creed articulates how the early witnesses are to be heard. The character of Jesus remains normative for believers. The Gospels, Acts, Epistles and Revelation reveal how Jesus is embodied in community. It is the Community that demonstrates how Jesus continues to be present today.

The author is making a strong, positive statement of what he believes rather than attacking what he is against.   Richard E. Allison

Andreas J. Köstenberger, *Encountering John*, Grand Rapids, MI: Baker, 1999. 277 pp. hb.

This is a winner. "Come on in!" the introductory chapter invites. The format, layout, and the contents quickly engage the reader onto the page and into the book. This volume is one in the Encountering Bible Series, intended by Baker for introductory classes at the college or university level. I would have appreciated this introduction to John during my years as a serious lay Bible student, and will certainly add it to my collection as a pastor.

Köstenberger is Associate Professor of NT and Greek at Southeastern Baptist Theological Seminary. He presents the Gospel of John from a conservative, evangelical viewpoint: high Christology, high view of scripture, and traditional view of John the son of Zebedee as both the beloved disciple and the author of the gospel. Köstenberger acknowledges and briefly addresses other viewpoints.

The structure of this text is "user-friendly." The two-column format, illustrations, subtitles, sidebars, outlines, study questions, and lists, break up the page, add to the ease of reading, and increase interest in the material. Historical considerations, the setting, context, theology, and major themes of John are addressed in Part 1. Parts 2-5 deal with the text in large chunks: the Prologue, the Seven Signs and Mission to the Jews, the Farewell Addresses and Mission to the World, and the Epilogue. Not a verse by verse commentary, the gospel is discussed clearly and concisely in large pericope.

At the end of the textbook are sections on such controversial issues as the history of interpretation, the quest for historical Jesus, the relationships of the Gospel to the Epistles and to Revelation. Köstenberger *provides excurses* on various issues: "the Jews," asides, misunderstandings, and *aporias*. A glossary, tools for study, endnotes, bibliography, and scripture index round out the offering of this volume, which will find wide acceptance as recommended for undergraduate Bible classes, and in my opinion will be valued by conservative Bible teachers, both clergy and lay.   Jean Van Camp

Stanley E. Porter, *The Paul of Acts - Essays in Literary Criticism, Rhetoric and Theology*, Tübingen: Mohr Siebeck, 1999. WUNT 115. Hardcover, ix + 233 pp., DM 148.

The author describes his work not as a monograph but as a series of studies on the Paul of Acts. Thus the literary studies focus on the depiction of Paul as a character in Luke's narrative. Hence, for example, he examines Pauline speeches not in order to see how they fit into the overall pattern of speeches in Acts but in order to explore the character of Paul the speechgiver in Acts. Porter suggests that this work on the Paul of Acts was a natural progression from his work on the Paul of the letters, but he concludes that the difference between the two is not as great as is often posited.

Porter begins with the we-passages, for the question of whether Luke was a companion of Paul affects any understanding of the portrayal of Paul in Acts. Noting that there is no true parallel to the we-passages in ancient literature, Porter argues that they are to be understood not as an indication of the participation of Luke in events narrated but rather as an indication of the use of a continuous and coherent source focussing on Paul and his missionary travels. This source probably originates with someone other than Luke, and Porter finds in it four characteristic theological emphases: an understated depiction of divine guidance which sees Paul as one missionary among others; a Hellenistic world-view which sees the Jews as one nation among many; a characterisation of Paul first not as a brilliant orator but as a man of understated competence; and, second, not as a miracle worker or man of magic. Therefore the we-source is not a major source of much of Luke's theology, but it does allow him to develop his account of the progress of the gospel and to record Paul's travels before bringing him to Rome.

Porter's discussion of Luke's depiction of the relationship between Paul and the Holy Spirit coheres with this conclusion: only once is there a link between Paul and the Holy Spirit in the we-passages, but elsewhere Luke's depiction of a close relationship between Paul and the Holy Spirit is of a piece with his widespread interest in pneumatology.

Porter next turns to the contrast between Luke's depiction of Paul as a rhetorician (who is not recorded as writing letters) and Paul's own testimony to himself as an epistolographer. Porter argues that the summary nature of Paul's speeches in Acts means that it is impossible to analyse them rhetorically as speeches. Therefore he finds no evidence in Acts to consider Paul a rhetorician, anymore than he finds evidence in the letters to consider Paul a rhetorician rather than a letterwriter. The historical Paul may have been a speechmaker, but all that the reader of Acts can analyse rhetorically is the way in which Luke shaped and presented his accounts of Pauline speeches. These speeches Porter considers under the two heads of Missionary and Apologetic speeches.

He finds a number of common traits which distinguish these speeches from others in Acts. This may mean either that they go back to genuine Pauline speeches or that Luke has used them in order to create a Pauline persona. Either way, there is nothing in these speeches that could not come from the Paul of the letters. Thus proposed differences between the natural theology found in Romans 1 and Acts 17 (contra Maddox) are overdrawn.

Porter's discussion of the relationship between Paul and James as seen in Acts 21 is perhaps the most controversial chapter of the book, at least for those who come to Acts with conservative presuppositions. Porter argues that James lures Paul into a trap, and that the Jerusalem church stands passively by as Paul is first attacked by Diaspora Jews and then taken into Roman custody. Thus Paul has been rejected by both Christian and non-Christian Jews by the time he preaches unhindered in Acts.

Just as some scholars will wish to disagree with Porter's assessment of the relationship between James and Paul, so others will disagree with his overall thesis, viz. that there are no irreconcilable differences between the Paul of the letters and the Paul of Acts, and that Acts was written by someone who had close contact with Paul or his beliefs. He notes that the "two-Paul" position of German scholarship has managed to position itself as the consensus view and to push the burden of proof onto those who do not see so great a divide between the Paul of the letters and the Paul of Acts. Yet it is this consensus that Porter seeks to overturn throughout these essays and especially in his final chapter, where he offers a critique of Haenchen and Vielhauer.

Not all will accept Porter's overall traditional conclusions, but this collection offers a significant body of original research which refuses to align itself uncritically with either radical or critical camps of scholars. It opens up new possibilities for interpreting Acts, and it suggests that students of Acts should look forward to Porter's volume on Acts, scheduled (tentatively) to appear in the NIGTC series in 2004.

Andrew Gregory

Peter W. L. Walker, *Jesus and the Holy City: New Testament Perspectives on Jerusalem*. Grand Rapids, Michigan: Eerdmans, 1996. Pp. xiii + 370. $25

This work is a systematic attempt to show that the coming of Christ drastically altered OT expectations of Jerusalem at the very outset of the formation of the Christian movement. This is true, Walker argues, throughout the NT corpus, with the exception of a very few documents. The unexpected conclusion of Christ as center, as opposed to Zion as center, places Jerusalem as a primary focus within the NT Christological argument, both in the historical context of the NT and the current era. The NT reflects a community/communities coming to grips with failed political assumptions for Jerusalem and an embrace of God's new missional purpose for God's people in Christ. Walker intends to develop a "biblical theology" (xiii) of Jerusalem that is hinged on the NT interpretation of Christ's life, death, and resurrection in their historical context as well as later interpretive efforts in the corpus.

The book is divided into two parts: Landscapes of Jerusalem (Part I) and Jesus and the Church (Part II). By far the weightier portion, Part I is subdivided into seven chapters each related to specific NT documents, chosen neither for chronological nor canonical order. Rather, Walker chooses texts considered relevant to the discussion, arranged so that the reader alternates "(roughly) between those documents written before 70 and those which were written subsequently" (xiii). Each document is read with respect to its perceived attitudes toward Jerusalem, the Temple, and, in some cases, the Land. Lack of explicit reference to Jerusalem is therefore compensated by perceptions gained from the interrelation of the three. Walker intends that "these discussions provide confirming evidence as to how they would have approached Jerusalem . . ." (xii). The now rejected status of Jerusalem, how much or little that can be related to the life of Jesus or discernment on the part of the NT author, becomes the focus for Walker in his pursuit of a biblical theology in Part II. The NT confronts what is now an age-old question: Is the OT wrong in its prophetic understanding of the future status of Jerusalem? As a result of Christ, NT reinterpretations of the significance of Jerusalem engage this question, coming to terms with the *new* meaning of what it is *to be* Israel, God's people. It is a Jerusalem "desecrated" (287) that must resign itself to no status in the world; it is God's restoring of God's people in Christ that fulfills OT prophecy, called to missional liberation rather than socio-political glorification (292). A biblical theology of Jerusalem is "therefore illegitimate" (313) without the interpretive contexts of the NT for Christian theology. Continuity in biblical revelation is affirmed as long as one is purposeful in acknowledging the reinterpretive efforts of the NT authors in discerning the ongoing purposes of God combined with the discontinuity of Jerusalem's failed future status as the necessary outcome of God's "economy of salvation" (314).Although at times I find myself in negative reaction to Walker's bold assertions that the NT presents a unified front regarding the "destruction of the formal structures of Judaism" (12), I nonetheless found the book as a whole provocative in its application. Walker rightly calls Christians to an unapologetically Christian attitude of repentance as the framework for an appropriate biblical theology, i.e. a theology that necessitates the interpretive lens of the NT with utmost "humility and self-critique" (316). In addition, Walker has effectively shown a unified perception of a changed Jerusalem within the texts under consideration. Whether or not the specific means of each NT document to explain this change produces a unified theological perspective for modern application is not sufficiently clear, if indeed truly possible. The valuable aspect of this work, however, is its assertion that the Christological debate must be acutely aware of its dependence on the notion of a Jerusalem changed.

C. Jason Borders, Brunel University/London Bible College, England

Marion L. Soards. *1 Corinthians*. NIBC: 7: Peabody MA: Hendrickson, 1999. 390 pages, $11.95 pb.

Marion Soards is NT professor at Louisville Presbyterian and also an ordained minister. His contribution to the New International Biblical Commentary is intended for the non-specialist, although Soards seems to aim for the educated person. Noting this, I would have liked to have seen more interaction with the recent social-scientific and inscriptional studies on Corinth, material which such readers could certainly follow.

This volume offers an introduction followed by a fairly detailed commentary on the text of the NIV. The introduction is altogether brief, and apart from a few quibbles ("Paul" was a Latin, not a Greek, name; Paul did not engage in Hellenistic allegorical exegesis to the extent Soards implies), the main disappointment is the lack of much description of Corinth or the particular problems of the church in that city. We are assured that Paul wrote the letter to correct certain specific problems, but what those problems were and why they had arisen is scarcely addressed.

Commendably, the commentary proper is focused squarely on the biblical text. Each section is followed by Additional Notes, which develop certain critical points or direct the reader to further literature. The commentary is well-written, if a bit conventional in its insights. Some points are explored sufficiently: for example, he concludes that the virgins of chapter 7 are the fiancΘes of the addressees, not the virgin daughters of Christian fathers. On the other hand, the recent debate over the meaning of "headship" in 1 Corinthians and Ephesians is barely mentioned, and the conclusions are vague. He implies that in 1 Cor. 12 enthusiasts were minimizing the humanity of Jesus, but we are left wondering in what way.

The bibliography is extensive for a volume of this nature, Soards interacting most often with the works by Fee, Murphy-O'Connor, Conzelmann, Barrett, Orr and Walther and Nigel Watson. He also takes into account recent journal literature.

Given Soards' pastoral background, there is surprisingly little reflection on contemporary application, but this seems to be due to the nature of the series.

I could imagine giving this volume to an educated layperson or non-Christian. It clearly surpasses the similar offering in the Tyndale Commentary by Leon Morris (1958).   Gary S. Shogren, Seminario ESEPA, San Jose, Costa Rica

Paul Barnett. *The Second Epistle to the Corinthians*. New International Commentary on the New Testament. Grand Rapids: Eerdmans, 1997. 696 pages. hb $45.00.

Paul Barnett's commentary replaces the 1963 NICNT volume by P. E. Hughes. It follows the text of the NIV, with Greek transliterated in the body, but in Greek characters in the footnotes. Barnett was master of Robert Menzies college, and is now the Anglican Bishop of North Sydney in Australia. His field of study is the Roman background of the New Testament. He thus brings both scholarly and pastoral questions to the text, as is evidenced from the chapter called "Pastoral Ministry from Second Corinthians."

While Barnett was unable to use Margaret Thrall's ICC commentary (1994), he interacts extensively with her Cambridge commentaries on 1 and 2 Corinthians (1965), as well as with the 1986 Word commentary by Ralph Martin. The bibliography is fairly thin. Barnett offers superb interaction with Greek and Roman literature (Strabo, Lucian, Epictetus) and rhetorical forms, but very little with the papyri. He includes a nice summary of Paul's relations with Roman Corinth. There is almost no interaction with 1 Clement or any ancient commentary (a strength of Hughes). The lexical background is not as thorough as that given by Martin.

Barnett, like Hughes before him, takes issue with the majority opinion, that 2 Corinthians is a composite of two or more Pauline epistles. He makes good use of his background in Graeco-Roman epistles, arguing from internal evidence that "the letter as we have it is the letter as written by Paul in the first place." He believes that Paul unconsciously followed the genre of an "apologetic letter," such as we have from Demosthenes, a form that was in current use in the 1st century. Thus, the emotional material in 10-13 is not a separate message, but the Peroration, an emotional appeal that drives home the sober arguments of the Exordium.

Paul's opponents were Judaizers from Jerusalem, with a different message of "righteousness" and a boasting of their power and skill. They may have been spun out from the revolutionary foment of Judea and had apocalyptic visions. This resonated with the pneumatic and over-realized theology of some in Corinth. Particularly useful from this standpoint are the "reconciliation" passage in chapter 2, and the social dynamic of "letter-bearing". The eschatological background of the "tabernacle" imagery of chapter 5 is helpful as well.

On the whole better the volume is a reliable update of Hughes. It is readable, accessible, and clear. Nevertheless, apart from the pastoral suggestions, it falls short of the quality of Ralph Martin's Word volume.   Gary S. Shogren

James D. G. Dunn. *The Epistles to the Colossians and to Philemon.* NIGTC. Grand Rapids: Eerdmans, 1996. $32. hb. xviii + 388 pages.

The New International Greek Commentary needs no introduction for serious Bible students, and this volume continues to uphold its fine reputation. Dunn mentions in his introduction that it was a natural move to write on Colossians after doing (groundbreaking) work in Romans and Galatians. Since then, Eerdmans has also brought out his *Theology of Paul.*

This contribution, while fresh and very useful, has a more tentative feel than his Word commentary on Romans. His style is occasionally slangy. There are places, particularly in the introductory matters, where one senses that Dunn has nothing new that he wishes to add to the discussion. In other places, he seems unsure of which exegetical option he should choose. Still, his exegesis is sound and readable and does justice both to the Greek text and the historical background. He makes full use of ancient sources, particularly Philo, the Dead Sea Scrolls, and the pseudepigrapha.

Dunn's theory of authorship is that Colossians represents the final word of Paul, and serves as the borderline between Paul's authentic letter and the post-Pauline Ephesians and Pastoral Epistles. Colossians was written probably from Rome, the Pauline material being reworked by Timothy just before or after his death. This makes for shifting sands at times, since some of the ideas are attributed to Paul, others to Timothy.

Especially important is Dunn's belief that Paul is having to deal with Jewish, as opposed to pagan or gnostic, ideas. He argues that the archaeology of the Lycus Valley shows that the local Judaism was not syncretistic, thus disallowing the idea of some mix of Jewish and pagan thinking. He argues, along the lines of Fred O. Francis, that the Colossian synagogue contained some members with a mystical bent, similar to practices witnessed at Qumran. Thus, the Colossian Error is not a Christian heresy at all, but the Judaism of the synagogue. While Paul had no evidence of Judaizing aggression, as had taken place in Galatia, he had reason to believe that some elements of Judaism (mystical participation in angelic worship, a definite list of rules to live by) might prove attractive to the church.

The work on Philemon follows the viewpoint that Onesimus specifically sought out Paul as Philemon's religious leader, in order to have him intercede for slave with master. This is a useful approach, and Dunn pays very close attention to the nature of slavery, manumission, patronage, and friendship in the first century.

Gary S. Shogren

Jerome D. Quinn and William C. Wacker. *The First and Second Letters to Timothy.* Eerdmans Critical Commentary. Grand Rapids: Eerdmans, 2000. hb, lxxvii + 918 pages. $65.

For the new millennium both Eerdmans and Baker Books have launched new scholarly exegetical commentaries. The Eerdmans Critical Commentary (ECC) on 1 and 2 Timothy turns out to be a gem, although a surprising choice for the inaugural volume. The late Monsignor Quinn was Catholic and the volume bears the *imprimatur*; he dates the Pastoral Epistles after the death of Paul; finally, the series editor is David Noel Freedman of Anchor Bible renown. This series will obviously be more ecumenical than their New International Commentary.

Readers will be familiar with Quinn's full commentary on Titus in the Anchor Bible. In fact, this companion volume was originally intended for that series. Its format is purely Anchor Bible: after the introduction appears an original translation. For each passage there are lexical and critical Notes and then a longer Commentary. Original languages appear in transliteration. Because the Titus volume was intended to preface this one, the introduction is abbreviated and constant reference is made to the AB volume. There is a very full bibliography. Walker spells out the details of his completion to this posthumous work in a heartwarming preface.

Quinn was a wordsmith, and his writing is a pleasure to read. His overall clarity and the absence of footnotes combine to give the text an attractive appearance, even though the lack of signals in the header or margins makes it difficult to locate comments on specific verses.

In this reading of the PE, the three letters were written as an anthology by an admirer of Paul, some time between 80-85. Historically and theologically they lie midway between Paul's epistles and *1 Clement* and Ignatius. The author incorporated Pauline traditions and fragments, and also Jewish Christian liturgy. In fact, most readers will have reservations about Quinn's level of confidence in reconstructing the supposed underlying traditions. He believed that the PE were written to develop and consolidate the church in the second Christian generation. Titus deals with a more primitive form of Jewish house church, and 1 Timothy the more developed Pauline ecclesiastical structure. 2 Timothy is meant to promote faithfulness to sound doctrine.

What is lacking from Quinn's "mirror-reading" is a rationale for the references to specific apostates and particular heresies in the two books. One the one hand, the names of Hymenaeus, Philetus, Alexander, and others are thought to be taken from genuine Pauline tradition (although the fact that they name names is a sign that the letters could not have been written by Paul). On the other hand, their supposed historical authenticity is the main reason the author includes them, since their warnings did not have specific relevance for the church in the 80's. The same problem applies to the positive references to Onesiphorus and to Paul's other co-workers.

On specific points, Quinn's lexical notes are very helpful, drawing extensively from the Apostolic Fathers, Qumran, and the classics (but disappointingly little, considering the nature of the vocabulary of the PE, from the papyri). His exegesis of 1 Tim 2:11-12 apparently could not take the recent book by Köstenburger into account, so its lexical base may already be dated. Thus the epistle does not "permit a wife to teach in the public worship and to boss around her husband" through her teaching. The "women" in 1 Tim 3:11 are "women ministers," similar to deaconesses. Particularly pleasing are Quinn's thoughts on the role of prophetic utterance in the "ordination" of Timothy, and on the nature of the hymnic tradition in 1 Tim 3:16-17. His original translation is worth reading, full of lexical insight. For example: "No question of it. Godliness brings gain, great gain." Some "...have strayed off from the faith and skewered themselves with multiple tortures." Paul was "a man who was formerly a blasphemer and a persecutor and insanely arrogant." Preachers should find the exegesis and pastoral application useful and accessible, more so than in the NIGTC by Knight.

With the ECC offering, and the new ICC volume by I. Howard Marshall, both texts long-awaited, evangelical pastors and teachers will at last be well-served in the Pastoral Epistles.   Gary S. Shogren

Markus Barth and Helmut Blanke. *The Letter to Philemon: A New Translation with Notes and Commentary.* Grand Rapids, MI; Cambridge, UK: Eerdmans, 2000. Pp. xviii, 561, $40.00.

An appropriate memorial to the late Markus Barth (d. 1994), this important commentary offers serious readers important insights into not only the letter to Philemon, but the Greco-Roman environment behind Paul's epistle as well. In particular, the extensive introduction (pp. 1-240), and especially the section on "Social Background" (pp. 1-102), provides the reader with invaluable information regarding the nature of the institution of slavery, and the forms of manumission employed in Roman society. Barth and Blanke, thus, provide invaluable information for the interpretation of several NT passages, including some of the parables of Jesus. The introduction alone makes this commentary an important addition to the library of any serious student of the New Testament.

The "Notes and Comments on Philemon" (pp. 241-498) provide detailed linguistic and historical analysis. The text of the letter is divided into five sections: (1) The Address (vv. 1-3), pp. 243-267; (2) A Christian—A Gift of God (vv. 4-7), pp. 267-306; (3) Intervention for a Slave (vv. 8-14), pp. 306-94; (4) The cost of Brotherhood (vv. 15-20), pp. 394-487; (5) Conclusion (vv. 21-25); pp. 487-98. Numerous excursuses are interspersed within the text, providing the reader with additional linguistic, historical and theological insights. Particularly useful are the excursuses on the legal options for Onesimus's future (pp. 367-8) and the discussion on why Paul does not give a plea for manumission (or, freedom) (pp. 368-9).

Barth and Blanke do not shy away from discussing some of the troubling aspects of Philemon, including the lack of any direct plea for freeing the slave Onesimus. The detailed discussion of various views shows that this issue is far from settled. They also point out that Philemon, far from being the innocent victim, may have been the malefactor whose abuse drove Onesimus away (see especially pp. 139-40). The judgment about Onesimus' character is also far from clear from the text (see pp. 141-50), although for some reason he is described as having been previously useless (v. 11).

The bibliography is extensive, and the authors are well acquainted with not only ancient sources, but also the history interpretation from the patristic period (Tertullian, John Chrysostom, Theodore of Mopsutia), through the Middle Ages (especial citing Thomas Aquinas) and Reformation (citing Calvin and Luther in particular) to the present age (John Knox's and Norman Petersen's work are especially noted). It is, however, surprising that the authors, in spite of their vast reading, have not incorporated more insights from rhetorical criticism. The various sections of the letter are not designated by the appropriate rhetorical terms (exordium, narratio, etc.). Nor is the specific type of rhetoric (judicial, epideictic, deliberative) described. Barth and Blanke may have proceeded in this manner because Philemon is a mixed type of letter, containing elements of an epedeictic (or address of praise or blame) address in vv. 1-4 within the framework of a letter of mediation (see S. Stowers, *Letter Writing in Greco-Roman Antiquity* [Library of Early Christianity; Philadelphia: Westminster Press, 1986], 80, 155. On the other hand, they do note Pliny the Younger's (*Epistulae* 9:21) intercession for an escaped freedman as providing parallel examples to Paul's language (p. 166 n. 114-5).

It should be noted that, occasionally, Barth and Blanke's apparent desire to explore every possible detail of particular verses might cause readers to be overwhelmed. The analysis of Phlm 16 alone is the sixty-four pages long (pp. 410-73). Also, as one should expect in a commentary of this detail and depth, the discussion will occasionally be uneven. An example is found on p. 342, when the authors engage in rather crass psychologizing.

Despite these few caveats, however, Barth and Blanke's commentary is an important contribution to our understanding of Paul's letter to Philemon. In addition, the introduction provides one of the finest analyses of the role of slavery in Roman antiquity available in English. In addition, it provides an important resource for the history of interpretation of Philemon. It is a commentary that the reader should consult carefully and often.

Russell Morton

Frederick J. Murphy, *Fallen is Babylon: The Revelation to John*. The New Testament in Context. Harrisburg, PA: Trinity Press International, 1998. Pp. xx, 472, $30.00.

This commentary, while not providing many new insights into the Book of Revelation, gives the reader a lucid, readable account, summarizing some of the best research in the Apocalypse. Murphy attempts to make the text more transparent to readers to by situating the Apocalypse in its social, religious, and historical context (p. 1). He is highly dependent upon the work of Adela Yarbro Collins, and adopts her analysis of Revelation as consisting of two cycles of recapitulation and five sets of seven visions (see pp. 52-53). Murphy also follows Yarbro Collins's threefold scheme of persecution, judgment, and triumph as key to interpreting the structure of each set of visions.

As a devotee of Yarbro Collins, Murphy adopts a history of religions methodology, recognizing that John both incorporated and transformed mythological themes current in his culture, particularly the combat myth. Where Murphy is especially helpful is in demonstrating that John's use of mythic themes does not vitiate the truth of his vision. Rather, "[m]yths are narratives about another time and place involving supernatural figures, but those narratives interpret everyday existence, expressing profound convictions and feelings about the world that cannot be expressed as well by any other medium" (pp. 22-23).

Murphy's understanding of the date and circumstances of the writing of the Apocalypse are conventional and well documented. Revelation is dated in the mid-90's, toward the end of Domitian's reign. John has been exiled to Patmos "on account of the word of God and the testimony of Jesus" (1:9). His exile is understood as resulting from local persecution rather than imperial policy. Support for this hypothesis is found in Younger Pliny's tenth letter to Trajan, asking advice on how to deal with Christians (see pp. 13-14, 17). Murphy sees this letter, as well as the fact that Revelation only mentions one martyr, Antipas in Pergamum (2:13), as evidence that there was no set imperial policy against Christians at end of the First Century.

While evidence does not exist that Revelation was written in the midst of persecution, John clearly expects it. Indeed, he sees the Roman Empire as demonic and inspired by Satan (see comments on chs. 12, 13, 17). Thus, Christians are called upon to resist. John has confidence that Christians will triumph, however, because reality is contrary to appearances. Whereas Rome appears powerful and Christians weak, Rome, in fact, is inspired by the defeated figure of Satan. Christians, on the other hand, have confidence since their God has already triumphed.

This theme of ultimate, although not visible, triumph, is repeated in chapters 17-20. Chapter 17 describes how the ten kings of the earth will turn against the great Harlot (i.e. Rome), and destroy her. Chapter 18 narrates the instantaneous fall of Babylon (a cipher for Rome), and the mourning of the kings of the earth, the merchants and the sailors of the earth. Yet, it is also a cause for rejoicing for the people of God. John reiterates the theme of the destruction of God's enemies in description of the last battle in Rev. 19:11-21. Finally, the description of the millennium and its aftermath demonstrate God's ultimate victory over evil.

Murphy is weakest when attempting to evaluate John's message for Christians today (pp. 442-444). While appreciating the Seer's call for absolute commitment on the part of Christians, he recognizes that other NT writers had different perspectives on how the believer is to live in society. Murphy also recognizes that believers today live in a very different world than John. Perhaps integrating a canonical approach, similar to Wall's (*Revelation*, New International Bible Commentary [Peabody, Mass.: Hendrickson, 1991), would be helpful here.

The bibliography is short, but provides a good selection of materials in English. It is weakened by not including some of the important commentaries and studies on Revelation in languages other than English. Nevertheless, for students and pastors unfamiliar with this method of interpreting the book of Revelation, Murphy provides a cogent, readable commentary, which may be used with profit.

Russell Morton

W.Randolph Tate. *Biblical Interpretation: An Integrated Approach*. Peabody: Hendrickson, 1997.

The book's jacket is an attractive depiction of a renaissance scholar studying a text. The scholar's cell is within a manorial building suggesting the privileged status of the scholar. It must never be forgotten that the Bible is a gift and that it is an honor to read and study it. The cell is filled with the scholar's "stuff", things which please and inspire? What is your study like? The pose and clothes of the scholar immediately alert the student of this book that hermeneutics is an ancient art. The names come to mind - Paul, Origen, Athanasius, Tertullian, Augustine, Luther, Calvin, Wesley, Schleiermacher, Barth, Brueggeman - all devotees of Scripture, scrupulous, passionate students of the Word. Hermeneutics is a contemplative discipline, practiced alone, prayerfully, but which demands dialogue and discussion with others. Contemporary scholars are connected to a wealth of biblical interpretation and study simply because they are exploring these fabulous texts.

What a wonderful precursor to the exciting world of biblical hermeneutics! Biblical Interpretation is a revised and updated introduction to biblical hermeneutics in which the writer has attempted to integrate contemporary approaches to biblical study into an introductory text without discarding past exegetical methods - and that includes the allegorical method. It is a book which doesn't overload the reader with terminology: neither does it treat the reader like a numbskull. It seeks to deepen the individual reader's engagement with the biblical text, to encourage the reader to explore the multifarious aspects of the biblical text, to read for more and more meaning. This is a text for the seeker: and we are all seekers who study the Bible.

In terms of layout, it is superb! Each chapter features a specific area of study - cultural and historical background, language, genre for example. The writer then concludes each chapter with a summary, a list of key concepts and terms, (which have been printed previously in bold), study questions to be used for discussion, and finally a brief bibliography. The study questions are of immense value since they help the student to make sense of the material just read and to apply what has been read in a study of a particular passage. The footnotes direct the student to further reading on particular hermeneutical issues. The writer also gives an exegesis of a specific text in order to show how the various methodologies can be put into practice.

Besides providing basic coverage of historical criticism, Tate explores literary criticism, reader-response criticism, feminist criticism, deconstruction, *ideologiekritik* and intertextuality. This material is sometimes dense and those unfamiliar with literature and literary criticism may struggle to understand the method. However, Tate does make an effort to analyze and synthesize the basic ideas of the proponents of these hermeneutical methods, again offering a comprehensive bibliography for those interested readers who would like to find out more about these postmodern approaches to the biblical text. The key to these methods is that the reader is a partner with the text and the writer in the construction of meaning. The value of this textbook is that Tate has actually made an attempt to incorporate some of these new approaches to biblical interpretation into a book on hermeneutics.

Finally, Tate examines the gospel of Mark as a case study in which he demonstrates the way an integrated approach to hermeneutics allows the reader to assemble meaning to make sense of the narrative. Tate examines Mark in terms of the structures of the plot, the decisions made by the reader and knowledge of the cultural/historical background of the ancient world.

The world of the text in this view is dynamic, a living organism, presenting itself differently on each reading. This also means that as readers we undergo continual change...As the text discloses itself to us in ever-changing ways, perhaps we gain a vision of God who is not the "unmoved mover", the God of dogma, but the God who is dynamic, always relating to the changing world of humanity.

Tate's is a hearty and enthusiastic welcome to the continuum of hermeneutics.

Dorothy Penny-Larter

Michael Frost, *Seeing God in the Ordinary: A Theology of the Everyday*, Peabody: Henderickson Publishers, 1998, pp. 203, $12.95.

This book is well titled. "Seeing God in the Ordinary" coalesces Frost's purpose and thesis in one phrase. Frost wrote this book to encourage others to be more conscious of the fact that God is in the ordinary aspects of our lives. Using numerous examples that many Christians would consider secular, Frost demonstrates that even the very busy among u, have the time to be deliberate about seeing God--not only in great miraculous acts, but also in the quieter, "ordinary" business of our lives.

Frost begins the first chapter by using Walter Bruggemann's quote about today's "prose-flattened world." Language is so tightly defined that all life has been forced out of words. Christians carry that forcing out of life to the gospel. We are so concerned with wanting to know exactly what the words of the gospel mean that we wind up just going through motions that mean nothing.

Christians also compartmentalize, Frost tells us. Going to church, Bible study, Sunday school are all "good" Christian activities. Yet, watching movies, attending football games, and sunbathing are considered "bad" or even, "profane." This separation, says Frost, is contrary to Jesus' teachings. It reduces the power, "flattens," the truth of the gospel. "Christian" activities may be seen as "better than" others. Why, Frost wonders, do we need to invite God to come to an interview? Why must we invite Him to be a part of the major plans for our lives? Why invite Him as though he were not there with us all along? God's kingdom is already here, Frost reminds us. He then reminds us that Jesus did not teach us to separate--the wheat grew with the weeds.

Having set the basic premise, Frost uses chapters two through six to show us how we too can see God in the ordinary. Being open to awe-inspiring experiences allows us to see Him. These are the times that God compels our attention. Many of Frost's awe-inspiring examples come from nature. Literature and the power of stories provide another avenue Frost strongly recommends we not ignore as a source of God's presence. Not every piece of literature reflects God, but many do. We need to be open to the possibilities. God is in events; He acts in real time and history. Frost warns us that "chance" encounters may well be God's acting in our lives. Frost also warns us against "objectifying" people. If we only interact with others for their utility in our lives, we may have closed ourselves off from seeing God acting in and through them. Keeping ourselves receptive to the possibility of seeing God anywhere we are, whatever we are doing, re-vitalizes our lives.

Frost does make an effort to refute those that may take his crossing of secular/profane with Christian/sacred boundaries too far. He makes clear distinctions between ordinary life activities that we may typically see as "of the world," such as going to or watching movies, reading novels, or listening to secular music, and those acts that are illegal or immoral. He in no way encourages anyone to look for God in the latter type of activities.

In his epilogue, Frost provides practical suggestions about how to be deliberate in one's daily openness to God. Look for God in everything that you do. Look for him in the damp cold, the smile of a friend, or the grace of a baseball player. See him in the writing of a list for the grocery store, in the drive to work, in putting children to bed.

Although a scholarly work, *Seeing the God in the Ordinary* is written in a manner that invites reading by anyone interested in being receptive to God and His presence in their lives. While Frost does use his Australian culture as a source for some of his examples, he explains their significance, thus neutralizing any cultural distance. Lay persons would find the reading easy; pastors or scholars familiar with Celtic spirituality or Brother Lawrence would hear echoes. We must open our eyes to the grace everywhere we are.

Frost offers three excerpts as a prologue. The third, taken from a novel, truly prepares the reader for Frost's arguments. The scene takes place at the deathbed of a young priest. A friend sitting by his side laments that another priest called to perform the last rites might not arrive in time to perform them. With much effort the dying priest says to his friend, "Does it matter? Grace is everywhere...." Katherine A. Simmons

Stephen F. Noll. *Angels of Light, Powers of Darkness: Thinking Biblically about Angels, Satan and Principalities.* Dourners Grove: InterVarsity, 1998. 255pp.

Stephen Noll, professor of biblical studies and academic dean at Trinity Episcopal School for Ministry in Ambridge, Pennsylvania, has written what is quite likely the most helpful single volume in English on the topic of angels and demons. The book began with Noll's 1979 doctoral project at the University of Manchester under the late F.F. Bruce and Barnabas Lindars. His dissertation, "Angelology in the Qumran Texts," prompted him to pursue the topic further from the perspective of biblical theology, and over twenty years of careful research and thought have culminated in this outstanding study. The strengths of this work are numerous and the weaknesses few.

The most significant and most evident benefit is that Noll is thoroughly biblical, both in width and depth of coverage. He investigates every relevant text in the Old and New Testaments, and treats the key scriptures in considerable depth. He brings in numerous references from the apocrypha, pseudepigrapha and Dead Sea Scrolls where these shed light on the canonical texts or the development of angelology. He is able to do this so well in about 250 pages because of the fairly small print type (perhaps a bit too small) and the tightness of his writing. Yet he is not obtuse. While I did wish for greater clarity several times, as with his discussions of the "sons of God" in Genesis 6 (pp. 55-56), "territorial spirits" (p. 149), and Jacob's wrestling with the angel at the Jabbok (pp. 158-159), I was struck with Noll's ability to state his conclusions in a judicious and restrained manner. His restraint is most commendable in view of the sometimes speculative nature of this subject matter and the tendency of popular writers on these themes to fill in and go beyond the canonical materials. While he presents the facts plainly and expresses his conclusions firmly, he refrains from sensationalism. For example, he holds back from proposing a personal guardian angel for each believer (pp. 170-172), yet he believes that "demonization is a possibility for Christians in certain circumstances" (p. 150).

Noll's comprehensiveness makes this the kind of volume that pastors, scholars and other thoughtful Christians will refer to regularly throughout a lifetime of study and service. Every question that arises from the biblical materials, and some from popular speculation, is addressed: Was the Holy Spirit ever an angel? Was Satan ever an angel? Who are the cherubim and seraphim? Why should a woman in Corinth "have authority on her head, because of the angels" (1 Cor. 11:10)? Some readers, eagerly building their collection of popular works on angels and demons, may wish Noll's volume was more "practical," or at least "lighter" reading, with accounts of present day angelic appearances and guidelines for deliverance. It does not seem that Noll would dismiss all such works as foolish or harmful, though some surely are. He would quite likely welcome careful books of this sort. But his task was to produce a more scholarly study, thoroughly grounded in biblical theology, in conversation with the best recent theological minds, for the service of Christ and his church. In this Noll has succeeded admirably.   Robert V. Rakestraw, Bethel Seminary, St. Paul

Luther E. Smith, Jr., *Intimacy and Mission: Intentional Community as Crucible for Radical Discipleship*, Scottdale: Herald Press, 1994, pp. 176, $12.95.

In Acts, we read that the disciples were together and had *everything* in common. They sold their possessions, and no one claimed that any possessions were his or her own. They shared *everything* they had. This description of community makes most Christians nervous, because it conjures up images of cults or Marxist Communism. Many explain it away by saying that this type of communal arrangement was necessary for the First Church to accomplish its mission, and that the disciples had a special dispensation which made this kind of intimacy possible. Are there communities today that are functioning the way we read in Acts? If so, is this level of intimate togetherness for everyone, or just a special few? What is the role of intentional community in the mission of the Church of the 21st century?

Intimacy and Mission by Luther E. Smith, Jr. provides the reader with an insider's view into Christian communities which are operating and active today. Smith's research is thorough, objective and understandable. Pastors, Bible study groups, teachers and individuals will find his work accessible and instructive. Smith's primary thesis is that intentional community can be a "laboratory" for radical discipleship. These "experiments" in Christian living explore a fellowship and mission as radical as the Gospel they proclaim. In a time when alienation and general frustration with the Church as an institution is high, Smith has found that,

> Religious communities symbolize hope. In them members experiment with methods that enable ideals to become reality . . . the instructive potential of religious communities may finally depend on the larger church's readiness to accept and respect them as legitimate expressions of faith in action. (p. 43).

Dr. Smith is associate professor of Church and Community at The Candler School of Theology of Emory University in Atlanta, Georgia. For the purpose of this investigation, Smith chose intentional Christian communities which were committed to the Acts model, including shared property and living space, and a prophetic ministry of social justice. He selected five communities with enough history to discern verifiable patterns of growth and change (a minimum of fifteen years): Church of the Messiah, Koinonia Partners, Patchwork Central, Sojourners and Voice of Calvary. His research was based heavily upon interviews with community members, former members, neighboring residents and civic leaders. He also surveyed their communal documents and covenants. Smith profiles the strengths and weaknesses of each community, their victories and their struggles, as well as the characteristics common to all five. He puts the reader in touch with the pulse of modern communal ministries a single, compact book. *Intimacy and Mission* is an ideal starting place for anyone considering a journey into intentional community, but this is just the tip of its usefulness. The real insight being generated by these communities is not in the answers they yield, but in the questions. Smith challenges the reader with a measuring rod of fundamental discipleship questions, all of which were formed in the crucible of community. This book would open an avenue of significant dialogue for professors and students at theological schools. More importantly, however, it offers a doorway to renewal for the institution of the Church. According to Smith, local congregations would not have to conduct their own communal "experiments in the Gospel," if they will sincerely engage the questions formed there. If the leaders of today's Church are willing to think a bit outside the institutional box, this book will help them "to discern possibilities for radical discipleship in their own lives and churches," (p. 13).   Eric P. Sandberg

Max Turner, *The Holy Spirit and Spiritual Gifts*. Revised edition. Peabody, MA: Hendrickson, 1998. viii + 383 pp., $19.95.

This is an excellent book, and the US edition is an improvement on its earlier British counterpart. Not only are various printing glitches removed (although the footnote on p.136 remains incomplete, and typographical errors also remain) but so too a useful extended contents table is added, as is a bibliography. Not least useful here is a convenient listing of some (but not all) of the author's own articles.

Also worthy of note is the addition of three volumes added to the end of the bibliography, all of which might be considered as systematic rather than biblical theology. This is significant, for Turner's own work is as theologically sophisticated as it is informed by and in dialogue with contemporary New Testament scholarship.

Thus although the book is divided formally into two parts, the first dealing with the development of the doctrine of the Spirit in the New Testament and the second addressing the place of spiritual gifts both then and now, the chapters which form the bridge between the two parts almost warrant a section of their own. Here are introduced lightly and deftly the contributions of figures such as Gabler, Wrede and Schlatter. Having outlined the ongoing implications of their work, Turner, arguing against H Raisanen, seeks to make a case as to why New Testament theology is worthy of study in the secular world of the academy as well as within the confessional world of the seminary.

The case is put briefly, so it is unlikely that Raisanen or his followers would consider Turner's critique to be definitive. Yet what the discussion does succeed in doing is to present sympathetically and cogently (and within the parameters of the historical critical approach to Scripture; Turner, following N T Wright, appeals to critical realism) an argument sometimes assumed rather than articulated by Evangelicals, the most likely readers of this book. The task of New Testament theology thus defended, Turner moves next to demonstrate how he may bring together the voices of the different New Testament witnesses to the Spirit, witnesses whom in part one he dealt with individually.

These witnesses are the usual suspects: Paul, Luke and John. The choice is neither surprising nor unprecedented, but frustrating nevertheless. Certainly these are the three voices that will need to be heard at length in any discussion of a New Testament theology of the Holy Spirit, but surely the relative silence of other contributors will be of as much importance as the contributions of Luke, Paul and John.

What of Matthew, for example with his apparent caution towards charismatics (Mt 7:22) and his Jesus who, unlike the Jesus of Luke and John, appears not to give the Spirit to his disciples precisely because he himself remains with them (Mt 28:19-20, but note Mt 10:20; Cf. Jn 14; Acts 1:8 & 2:33)? Again, there are voices that might be heard from the Apocalypse and from the writer to the Hebrews, just as there appears to be a silence in the letter of James. Or do apparently non-charismatic texts in fact assume the charismatic position of other writers? There would appear to be an imbalance here in Turner's presentation, as in that of other works which have been similarly selective. Perhaps Turner might provide readers of this book with the further benefit of addressing these theological issues in a future work?

Part two of the monograph relates spiritual gifts in the New Testament church to their place in the church of today. Three gifts are focussed on: tongues, healing and prophecy. Turner carefully affirms the contemporary place of all three, and is not afraid graciously but cogently to critique both conservative cessationist and Pentecostal perspectives, as well as some charismatic perspectives, along the way. He is also keen to affirm that the Spirit is at work outside as well as inside the explicitly charismatic and Pentecostal streams of the church. He proposes instead "a via media in spirituality between Pentecostalism and more traditional forms of Christianity".

This is a treatment to be commended as much for its irenic tone as for its substance. Those who are in sympathy with Turner's nuanced charismatic perspective will find here an unparalleled treasure house from which to draw. Those who take other views will find arguments with which they will need to engage.

Readers seeking a detailed and lengthy summary of this book together with a critique from a Pentecostal perspective may be referred to the review article by J C Thomas in *The Journal of Pentecostal Theology* 12 (1998). Turner's response may be found in the same volume.   Andrew Gregory, Oxford

Jon Butler. *Religion in America.* New York: Oxford University Press, 2000, 157 pages.

Butler's work is part of the *Religion in American Life* series being published by Oxford University Press. As the title indicates, this book considers religion, in what would become the United States, during the 17th and 18th centuries. Butler focuses not only on the myriad of Protestant groups that would take root in the New World but also on Catholicism and Judaism and on the religious heritage of Native Americans and the African slaves brought to America during this period.

Butler tells a very readable, fascinating story in his six chapters. He begins with an overview of religious thought and practice in Europe, Africa, and North America ("Worlds Old and New"); portrays the initial complexion of religion in the young colonies ("Religion in the First Colonies"); charts the diversity of religious groups in colonial America ("The Flowering of Religious Diversity"); describes "African and American Indian Religion"; relates the story of the Great Awakening ("Reviving Colonial America"); and considers the effects of the American Revolution on the various religious bodies ("Religion and the American Revolution"). The book concludes with several helpful resources: a chronology, glossary, and suggestions for further reading.

Though he is covering much territory, Butler does so with sufficient detail to give the reader a feel for the "lay of the land." Colorful, engaging stories of numerous individuals and events, insets from primary source materials, and abundant sketches and illustrations provide vistas for understanding religion in this time period. He also considers such interesting issues as the role of women in religion during the colonial period, the apocalyptic themes that were frequently woven into the American self-undertanding, and the development of freedom of religion in America.

I should note that I did find a few factual difficulties. Butler indicates that Christopher Sauer, who published an edition of the Luther Bible in 1743, was "the best-known Dunker in Pennsylvania" (59). He is referring to Christopher Sauer I who, as one influenced by Radical Pietism, remained a separatist throughout his life. His son, Christopher Sauer II, did join the Brethren congregation at Germantown, Pennsylvania, however. In the same paragraph, Butler states that Sauer's Bible was "the first Bible printed in the American colonies." This is also inaccurate since the Puritan John Eliot published a translation of the New Testament in the Massachusett language in 1663, a point that is correctly noted on page 79. It is appropriate to claim for Sauer's Bible that it was the first European language Bible published in America. Butler also holds that Jonathan Edwards held that Christ would come to "usher in a new millennium," (109) that is, he was premillennial. In point of fact, Edwards was an early proponent of postmillennialism. In spite of these minor points, Butler's work provides a very good introduction for anyone wishing to gain an overview of religion during this phase of American history.   Dale Stoffer

John Cassian, *The Conferences*. Ancient Christian Writers 57. Translated and Annotated by Boniface Ramsey, O.P. New York, N.Y: Paulist, 1997.

In the closing years of the fourth century A.D. John Cassian, a young monk originally from the Roman province of Dacia, made two extended visits to Egypt. There, along with his companion Germanus, he made the acquaintance of many of the most prominent desert anchorites. Decades later in Marseilles, he compiled, recorded, and elaborated the wisdom of these holy men in a series of twenty four conferences, or dialogues, which addressed the spectrum of monastic spirituality. The completed work, *The Conferences*, strongly influenced the development of Christian monasticism and spirituality.

A review of the topics addressed by the conferences reveals the reason for the work's enduring influence. Cassian's first conference, with Abba Moses, ostensibly concerns the goal of the monk but offers discussions of matters to which all Christians aspire: inner tranquility, the tension between contemplation and service, the practice of virtues, and the character of love. Subsequent conferences deal with such matters as the cultivation of virtues (e.g. discretion, humility, patience, love, chastity), the practice of disciplines (e.g. prayer, renunciation, fasting), metaphysical speculation (e.g. the nature of the soul, the activities and hierarchies of demonic powers), aspects of Christian living (e.g. the struggle between flesh and spirit, attainment of spiritual knowledge and perfection), and discussions of moral issues (e.g. whether lying or keeping commitments are absolute obligations). The conversational format leads to far-ranging discourses that often have a stream of consciousness flavor, and many times the speakers veer off into topics that may strike the modern reader as obscure and bizarre. Nevertheless, throughout the book the reader encounters profound and practical wisdom on the spiritual life.

The present volume, the first English translation of the entire work, offers a highly readable translation that vividly recreates the conversational ambience of the conferences. Ramsey introduces the text with a succinct overview of Cassian's life and times and then of the *Conferences* themselves. Brief introductions and tables of contents also precede each of the conferences, offering the reader an informed synopsis and reflection of its particular topic and themes. Indexes of scriptural citations and lists of annotations complement these introductions. All are brief and to the point, providing the reader with a thorough understanding of the individual conferences without overshadowing them with commentary. As a result, the reader's focus remains squarely on the words of the abbas, who assume distinct personalities and speak with striking immediacy.

The Conferences is unsurpassed as a compendium of desert spirituality and is therefore an excellent point of entry for those interested in exploring a stream of Christian thought and spirituality that is attracting increasing attention. While Cassian writes with monasticism in mind, the wisdom he conveys speaks to the longing of all Christians who seek the purity of heart to which he aspired. Although a substantial work, it lends itself as well to devotional reading as it does to theological study and will be treasured resource to those who respond to Cassian's invitation to cultivate the inner life.   L. Daniel Hawk

Isaac R. Horst. *A Separate People: An Insider's View of Old Order Mennonite Customs and Traditions.* Scottdale, PA: Herald Press, 2001, 262 pages.

I have always found it fascinating that among the various Old Order groups in North America there is usually at least one spokesman within the fellowship who feels the calling and has the ability to portray the life and witness of that group to a modern audience. This is all the more remarkable because in several Old Order groups, including the Old Order Mennonites, it is rare for a person to receive an education beyond the eighth grade. Isaac R. Horst, an octogenarian among the Old Order Mennonites of Ontario, serves in this book as a guide to familiarize readers with the lifestyle and beliefs of his people.

Much of the content of this book originally appeared in monthly columns that Horst wrote for the *Mennonite Reporter.* He has given it new shape by using the literary devices of a tour guide, a lecturer at an Elderhostel, and finally a wise, old grandpa answering the questions of a granddaughter to provide the reader with an overview of Old Order Mennonite life. His style is folksy and informative. He can, however, be very forthright in advocating the Old Order faith, but he does so with a gentle humility that is quite characteristic of Old Order groups.

The Old Order Mennonites trace their roots back to the Anabaptist movement of the 16th century. For the most part, they are descendants of the Swiss Brethren, the Anabaptist group that would dominate Anabaptist immigration to North America in the 18th century. Following the American Revolution, some of these Swiss Mennonites (they began to identify themselves as Mennonites once they came to America) moved from Pennsylvania to Canada, establishing a new settlement in Waterloo County and other areas. The latter 1800s was the formative period for the Old Order Mennonites, as it would be for other Old Order movements. Progressive forces in the Mennonite Church were advocating the adoption of Sunday Schools, prayer meetings, and revivals. Those who felt that such practices "tolerated and encouraged pride and inflated self-esteem" withdrew from the Mennonite Church to form the Old Order Mennonites (p. 29). Horst's book focuses on one of the largest Old Order Mennonite settlements, that in the northern part of Waterloo County, Canada. Today it would claim around 4000 baptized members and adherents (those under age 18).

Horst's book covers the full range of topics that might be asked by an outsider. Some of these topics are worship practices, education policies, view of women, child rearing philosophy, attitudes toward insurance, Sunday Schools, and foreign missions. A brief overview of a few of these topics will give the reader a glimpse of some of the content of the work. One discussion illustrates the community's willingness to accept some modern innovations. Though having a telephone in the home was initially rejected, in time a slight majority of members came to favor allowing phones in homes, if this change did not disturb the peace of the community. Today there are phones in over half the Old Order Mennonite homes, though it was ruled that phone sets had to be black and that there should be no accessories such as fax, internet, memory, call waiting, etc. Even today, though, some members continue to do without.

The Old Order Mennonites have adopted a view of the Great Commission (Mt. 28:19-20) shared by other Old Order groups: it was fulfilled by the apostles in the first century. This view, used to defend their opposition to foreign missions, is founded on such verses as Colossians 1:23 and Romans 10:18. Horst does note, however, drawing upon an insight by John Howard Yoder in his book *As You Go*, that the Amish and Mennonites have adopted a "migration evangelism" that involves living their faith in the midst of the many cultures throughout the world to which they have migrated.

Horst notes that the influence of the feminist movement in modern culture often leads to questions about their attitude toward women. He is unapologetic about upholding a traditional view of women's roles. He feels that Old Order Mennonite women are generally satisfied with the role of caring for their husband, their children, and their home. He is not bashful in pointing out the problems created by the more "enlightened" concept of women: divorce, wife abuse, neglected children. He is not above admitting that there may be some women in the community "who harbor ill feelings against men in general, and against their husbands in particular," but he feels that the tested and tried counsel of Scripture provides the best counsel for the role of wives and women (p. 115).

Horst has painted a fairly detailed picture of life among the Old Order Mennonites. His book makes an excellent resource for anyone desiring to know more about the Old Order ways. Whatever critique we moderns and postmoderns may have of Old Order life, Horst also provides his own critique of many practices and beliefs that undergird our culture. In answering the most frequently asked questions concerning Old Order life, he raises his own about the culture which we call home. We would do well to learn from both his answers and questions.   Dale Stoffer

Terrence G. Kardong, O. S. B., *Benedict's Rule: A Translation and Commentary.* Collegeville, MN: The Liturgical Press, 1996. $49.95. xviii + 641 pp. Hardcover.

The *Rule of Saint Benedict* stands as a landmark in the history of Christian spirituality, having guided spiritual pilgrims in the monastic Order of Saint Benedict since the early sixth century. In this volume, Father Kardong presents a new translation of the *Rule* (together with the critical edition of the Latin text) and a thoroughgoing verse-by-verse, word-by-word commentary on the Latin text. This detailed commentary lays out the interaction between the *Rule* and the Scriptures that were at the heart of Benedict's monastic vision as well as the church fathers such as Cassian and Pachomius. As Father Kardong's commentary unfolds, the life of the monks living by this *Rule* comes to life. The author's own firsthand experience of Benedictine spirituality comes through in every chapter, as he attends not only to the historical meaning and incarnation of the text, but also to its contribution to the spiritual formation of every Christian.

In short, this commentary stands as a monument to the *Rule*'s richness and depth, the product of the author's decades of research, publication, and, perhaps most important of all, living out this *Rule* as a reliable compass for journeying with God.
                                    David A. deSilva

Beverly M. Kienzle and Pamela J. Walker, eds., *Women Preachers and Prophets Through Two Millennia of Christianity*, Berkeley, CA: University of California Press, 1998, 362 pp., pb, $17.95.

This volume is a collection of essays on the voices of Christian women, in chronological order, by eighteen contributors including the editors. Kienzle is Professor of the Practice in Latin and Romance Languages at Harvard Divinity School and president of the International Medieval Sermon Studies Society. Walker is Assistant Professor of History at Carleton University.

The contributors are: Nicole Bériou, Anne Brenon, Yvonne Chireau, Jacqueline R. deVries, Edith Wilks Dolnikowski, Katherine Ludwig Jansen, Beverly Mayne Kienzle, Karen L. King, Elaine J. Lawless, Linda Lierheimer, Phyllis Mack, Carolyn Muessig, Darleen Pryds, Roberto Rusconi, Judylyn S. Ryan, Karen Jo Torjesen, Peter Vogt, and Pamela J. Walker. The material is presented from an academic, feminist viewpoint of church history.

The essays highlight individuals within groups and movements across church history, and are grouped chronologically by periods: Early Christianity, the Middle Ages, 16th-18th Centuries, and 19th-20th Centuries. The preface, by Lawless, and the afterward, by King, inform the reader what he is going to read and what he has read.

The work focuses on lesser-known women, and is clearly written by academicians for academicians. The documentation is heavy; some essays have nearly as much space devoted to endnotes as to essay. Many of the endnotes are in Latin or French, a tribute to the scholarship of the authors, but a drawback to those of us who are more linguistically challenged. Due to the language barrier, this reviewer had no way of judging if sources were primary or secondary.

The quality of the essays is not consistent. Essays on early church figures are very heavy on assumption and light on substance, because they draw rather vast conclusions from little evidence. Some of the essays are wordy and repetitious, others are more readable. The essays on the Waldensian and Cathar women preachers, by Kienzle and Brenon respectively, and the Ursulines, by Lierheimer, were of overall higher quality. The essay on early Christian *orans* by Torjesen, and that by Rusconi, on women in church art and icons, both feature illustrations.

A recurring theme is the renaming that was necessarily engaged in by many women across the centuries in order that their voices be heard. The inclusion of twentieth century Afro-American syncretic movements does not seem appropriate, given the title of the work.

Academic feminist historians and church historians will want this volume, as would studious pastors with an interest in the topic, and it would be appropriate in university and seminary libraries.   Jean Van Camp

Mary T. Malone, *Women and Christianity; Vol. 1: the First Thousand Years*, Maryknoll, NY: Orbis Books, 2001, 376 pp., pb, $20.

This one-author volume provides a connected chronological account that flows well and is more readable than Kienzle and Walker (reviewed elsewhere in this *Journal*).

Malone is retired from St. Jerome's University, and from the University of Waterloo, where she was chair of the Graduate Department of Religious Studies from 1994-1996. As the title indicates, she documents the activities of women in western Christianity over the first 1000 years. Malone writes from a feminist and Roman Catholic perspective of western Christianity. Although concerned to recover women's activities and voices, Malone's is not a radical feminist treatment.

This book emphasizes the fact that institutional reform was usually detrimental to women. Malone highlights the involvement of women in the evangelism of Europe by means of the royal marriages of Christian princesses to pagan kings, and by egalitarian male-female cooperation in the monastic enterprise.

This volume will be useful to anyone interested in the participation of women in church history, pastors, church libraries, university and seminary classes in church history, or feminist history. Unfortunately, at present Orbis has no information about a forthcoming second volume. Jean Van Camp

Mark A. Noll, *Turning Points: Decisive Moments in the History of Christianity*, 2nd ed., Grand Rapids: Baker Books, 2000, pp. 352, $18.99.

In recent years students of church history have been served by several books which have made the subject easier by reducing the volume of facts to be grasped. Three different illustrations of this trend are A. Kenneth Curtis, et al, *Dates with Destiny: The 100 Most Important Dates in Church History* (1991), Justo L. González's' *Church History: An Essential Guide* (1996), and Mark Shaw's *10 Great Ideas from Church History* (1997). Noll's book continues this trend with its own unique contribution.

The good sales of the original edition (1997) of *Turning Points* justify the excellent reviews the book received from scholars. That a second edition is needed so soon, with the featured change being study questions for each chapter, demonstrates the usefulness of the book for students. My own use of the book as a supplemental text in a church history survey class verifies its appeal to students.

After a stimulating introduction on the usefulness of studying the history of Christianity, Noll devotes twelve chapters to "hinge-points" in the story, where changes in thought or action dramatically affected the direction of the church. His list includes the fall of Jerusalem (A.D. 70), the Council of Nicea (325), the Council of Chalcedon (451), St. Benedict's Monastic Rule (530), the coronation of Charlemagne (800), the schism of the Eastern and Western Churches (1054), the Diet of Worms (1521), the English Act of Supremacy (1534), the founding of the Jesuits (1540), the conversion of the Wesleys (1738), the French Revolution (1789), and the Edinburgh Missionary Conference of 1910. His final chapter sketches out significant twentieth century movements like Pentecostalism, Vatican II, new roles for women, Bible translation, and the survival of the Church under Communism. One could juggle Noll's catalog with selections that reflect a different historical bias, but few can quibble over the significance of the events he emphasized.

The pattern of *Turning Points* has several advantages. First, it helps students and non-specialists to grasp the "big picture" of Christian history. Scholarly texts on church history, especially if they follow a chronological scheme, often overwhelm readers with accounts that are too detailed, and sometimes are overly complex as well.

Secondly, its economy of subjects enables a luxury of understanding. Like a curator of a museum showcases only the most significant artifacts, so Noll's selections assist students to a deeper understanding of representative events. One can absorb the moment and recall its impact. If one gives twelve subjects the attention usually given to fifty (to use a convenient number), it stands to reason that she will have a clearer understanding of those twelve events.

And, finally, *Turning Points* probes connections between decisive events and persons and their contribution to all subsequent church history. Noll is convinced that history matters. "Turning points" cast long shadows. For good or ill, the church today carries the fingerprints of its past, but not in a fatalistic sense. The author believes that the study of the history of Christianity can help shape proper attitudes in contemporary Christians. The historical perspective of the church's mission can clarify purpose in the present moments of decisions (pp. 18-19). Readers of church history are not just custodians of a tradition, they are also change agents in the present and creators of the future. If they have the humility to recognize their fallible humanity in the record of the church's sins, they may also grasp the fact that Christ the Lord is building His church: the real cause that illuminates the church's successes.

The first edition already included many attractive features in each chapter: suggestions for further reading, timely visuals, focused sidebars, and selected prayers and hymns of the period. The second edition includes study questions for each part of the book (pp. 320-336), thanks to the work of Robert H. Lackie. The questions help students and adult study groups to process the ideas that the book raises. They aim both at clearer understandings and more relevant applications of the insights gleaned from the history of christianity.

Noll's intent was to write a book for students and lay persons in the church. He has clearly succeeded, and these readers are grateful.   Luke L. Keefer, Jr.

Eileen Power, *Medieval Women*, edited by M. M. Postan. Cambridge: Cambridge University Press, 1997. 104 pp. $9.95.

Gilbert Dahan, *The Christian Polemic Against the Jews in the Middle Ages*, translated by Jody Gladding. Notre Dame, IN: University of Notre Dame Press, 1998. 130 pp. $10.00.

Somewhere between "Camelot" and the "Dark Ages" lies the true Medieval Period. Scholarship is slowly reclaiming this neglected space. Still, outside of Catholic scholars and history specialists, this age is not well-known by Western readers. These two, slender books are accessible routes into this period of European life.

Brief and introductory books in their approach, they do not overwhelm the reader who is making tentative forays into this subject. Yet the authors probe two vital aspects of the time: the place of women and the church's approach to Jewish people. Plentiful evidence is provided to alleviate ignorance of the period, and interpretations are offered to counter erroneous preconceptions about the culture of the time.

One might wonder why the five popular essays of Power's *Medieval Women* should be republished nearly sixty years after her death, especially when women historians have provided so many works that are more contemporary. There are at least two good responses to that question. First, she was one of the pioneer leaders of social and economic history, with a recognized speciality in women of the medieval period. She earned her academic credentials at Cambridge University and the London School of Economics and subsequently taught at both schools, succeeding academically in a context that was dominatedly male (especially at Cambridge). The outline of her life is nicely sketched by Maxine Berg in the forward. Her life illumines her academic work and would be of interest to anyone interested in feminist studies.

Her scholarly writings accord her a place of prominence in medieval social and economic history. Her research is still basic to those who would work in the period. This collection of essays was published by her husband, M. M. Postan, long after her death, and is primarily directed to a popular audience (pp. xxvii-xxviii). It contains the fruit of her extensive research but with a simplicity of style and a vigor of presentation that captures a common readership. One suspects this is the reason Cambridge University decided to issue it in a Canto edition.

These essays, in the second place, destroy various stereotypes of medieval women. Their real status in the home, workplace, school, and church (especially the nunneries) is contrasted to the inferior place assigned them by the clergy and aristocracy in the early medieval period. Powers notes that the creators of this inferior view of women were the very men who least knew the lot of "the great mass of womenkind" (p. 1). On the other hand, medieval women never occupied the rosy pedestal portrayed by the romantic writers in the "courtly love tradition." It was the real life of medieval women that she wanted to uncover, and that story alone is delightfully informative.

Gilbert Dahan takes a parallel track to Christian relations with Jews in the medieval period to what Powers did with women. He chooses this period because he believes it has much to teach us today about how to dialogue with those who hold to alternate religious views. His introduction addresses head-on the perception of the average reader that the medieval period was among the worst of times in Christian-Jewish relations. He contends that medieval Europe was anything but uniform. Conditions varied widely both in regard to time and place.

Dahan divides these centuries into three periods: the early middle ages when Christianity and Judaism were missionary competitors; the twelfth to the early fourteenth centuries when they had developed solid religious identities; and the end of the age when various crises caused relations between the groups to deteriorate markedly. The author isolates the second period as the setting for his study, because he believes it was best suited to honest dialogue. Both sides were confident of their respective positions but still listening to the other with some admiration short of belief.

Among the diverse literary sources which reflect the Jewish-Christian conflict, the author chooses the dialogue as best suited for his research on the Christian polemic against the Jews. The records reflect various kinds of dialogues, ranging from informal discussions between Jews and Christians in their normal social encounters to staged debates and state-ordered defenses.

There is little surprise that the primary topics became the question of the "true" Israel, the difference in biblical interpretation, and the coming of the messiah. What is of interest, however, are the shifting grounds of the debate and the responses of the Christian world to the Jewish contentions. Dahan illustrates how Christians became aware of the Talmud during the middle period and began to engage it in their polemic. He points to the fact that both church and state issued warnings and prohibitions against ordinary Christians engaging Jews in religious argument as evidence of the strength of the Jewish position. Jews were seen as both better informed and more skillful debaters than their ordinary counterparts. Christian apologists, especially the Dominicans and the Franciscans, were forced to study Hebrew and Arabic in an effort to confront Jews on more even terms.

The book is rich in historical backgrounds and literary sources that bear on the topic. The reader is introduced to many of the key Christian theologians of this period. The only serious question is whether these disputes are as serviceable to contemporary Jewish-Christian dialogue as the author thinks they are. Congeniality depends more upon political and social circumstances than it does formal religious argument. The very best polemic of the medieval period still serves us best today as a negative illustration, rather than a positive model, of how inter-religious dialogue ought to proceed.

Gilbert Dahan really is concerned that Christians and Jews can move toward healing of their troubled relationships over the centuries. The book is very helpful in illustrating one phase of the past. The question is whether his study provides medicine for the healing or merely another diagnosis of the disease.   Luke L. Keefer, Jr.

Paul R. Spickard and Kevin M. Cragg, et al, *A Global History of Christians: How Everyday Believers Experienced Their World.* Grand Rapids: Baker Academic (A division of Baker Book House Co.), 2001, 486 pp., 26.99.

First published in 1994 in the hardback copy which is now out of print, it is available now in paperback. Under the former title, *God's Peoples: A Social History of Christians*, the book was reviewed in the 1996 *Ashland Theological Journal* (pp. 198-199).

The content is the same in both editions. Only the title and form of the book have changed. There is one feature that stands out in the current edition: the cover is vastly improved. The picture of an African American baptismal service is clearly portrayed. The dark cover of the original book all but made the photo indiscernible.

This cover photo underscores the book's purpose to set forth a social history of Christianity, where the focus is upon Christians in their context - their world of culture and experience. As a one volume treatment of the subject, it is an admirable achievement.   Luke L. Keefer, Jr.

Laura Wilson, *Hutterites of Montana.* New Haven: Yale University Press, 2000, 150 pages.

This book deserves to be called unique. Laura Wilson, a professional photographer, has created a stunning portrayal of Hutterite life through the medium of black and white photographs. She weaves into these images a very informative

Book Reviews

narrative concerning Hutterite history, beliefs, and life. The result is a rich tapestry that brings to life one of the most unusual subcultures in North America.

The Hutterites trace their roots back to 1528 when a small group of Anabaptist refugees, seeking sanctuary in Moravia in the present day Czech Republic, pooled all their worldly goods and began what has become a nearly 475 year experience of communalism. The Hutterites flourished during the 1500s, reaching nearly 20,000 under the tolerant protection of the Moravian nobles. During the 1600s and 1700s, however, the ravages of the Turkish invasions and the Catholic Counter-Reformation decimated the Hutterite colonies until only nineteen Hutterites remained in the 1750s. They experienced a renewal when fifty Lutherans joined the movement and when they were invited by Catherine the Great to settle on her vast holdings in the Ukraine in 1770.

Again the Hutterites flourished, only to experience a renewed challenge to their nonresistant, separate way of life in the 1870s when Russia sought to assimilate them and other Germanic settlers into Russian culture. Between 1874 and 1877 the entire Hutterite population came to the United States; four hundred of the approximate one thousand immigrants decided to reestablish their communal life in three colonies in the Dakota Territory. In the United States, the same experience of initial prosperity was followed by the hardship of anti-German sentiment during World War I. Harassed because of their retention of the German language and their nonresistant convictions, many Hutterites moved into southern Canada. Even here the need for large tracts of land for their communes resulted in Canadian laws being passed which severely restricted Hutterite expansion. Since World War II the primary focus of Hutterite growth has again been the United States; they have established many new colonies in Montana, the Dakotas, Minnesota, and Washington.

Today the Hutterites number over 40,000, living in hundreds of colonies on the prairies of North America. Wilson focuses her work on the more conservative Hutterites living in Montana. Over a fourteen year period she was able to win their trust as she respectfully entered into their life for two or three week stays. Hutterites shun many American "necessities": radios, televisions, cars, even photographs. Due to the trust she had gained and her persistence, she was able to obtain permission from the leaders of Hutterite colonies to take black and white photographs of those people who agreed to be her subjects. She says of her photographic documentary, "I tried to take the photographs I needed to tell the story I wanted to tell. I photographed the faces that moved me, not just any faces, but the faces that revealed a story within, including the contradictions" (p. 10). Her work truly succeeds in telling a story that is both hers and that accurately portrays Hutterite life.

I was intrigued by the effect of the exclusive use of black and white photographs of the day to day life of the Hutterites. In contrast to our American culture, which must express itself in as varied and plural "colors" as possible, the Hutterites appear almost monochromatic, stressing the yielding of individualism to the greater good of the community. Indeed, Hutterite society may seem at almost polar opposites to the values of American culture. Yet Wilson's photographs portray people who have personalities revealing strength, variety, and calm assurance of their value and significance. There is enough subtle humor in both image and text to remind the viewer/reader that these people are not somber automatons but find joy and pleasure in their simple, separate ways. Another interesting feature of the work is that none of the photographs has an accompanying caption on the same page as the photograph; all explanations are found on three pages at the end of the book. The effect is to draw the viewer into the story of the image, to force us to engage our right brain, not our left brain.

Wilson's narration of Hutterite life and faith, though brief, gives sufficient detail to answer most questions the reader would have. It likewise provides a textual foundation for being able to understand more thoroughly the life visualized in her photographs. Besides reviewing the history of the Hutterites, Wilson also describes their leadership structure, their religious beliefs, the place of women in their culture, the education of the young, and the strength of their communal tradition.

Though the viewer/reader would want to supplement this work with one of the books in the well chosen list of resources on the Hutterites in the "Suggested Reading" at the end of the book, it certainly deserves a place on the bookshelf or, even better, the coffee table. Wilson's artistic gift makes this pictorial essay a wonderful addition to the slowly increasing literature on the Hutterites.   Dale Stoffer

Avery Brooke, *Healing in the Landscape of Prayer.* Boston: Cowley Publications, 1996.

Avery Brooke is an Episcopal laywoman, a spiritual director, a seminary instructor, and an author. Reading this 115 pages of text feels like one is enjoying a personal conversation with the writer. She wears her learning lightly and shows a remarkable combination of "holy common sense" and spiritual humility. In introducing the book she says, "I am a middle-of-the-road Christian who does a lot of praying and who believes that healing should be seen as a part of the everyday fabric of Christian life— I have written *Healing in the Landscape of Prayer* because I believe healing should be reclaimed to take the central place in the Christian way that it held in the ministry of Jesus and of the early church" (p. xi).

In concluding the book she says,

"While writing this book I found myself almost driven to pray for the church. In learning about healing I have gained a great deal from evangelicals, but they are all too often scorened or ignored by liberals and academicians. On the other hand, many charismatic evangelicals choose to scoren or ignore liberals and academicians. Somewhere in the middle I pray for all sides, not so much that they will change their minds but that they may find in the other what they can admire and thank God for (p. 113).

The book's central, longest chapter contains wise counsel for any who would develop a healing ministry within a congregation. Brooke offers this after chapters which describe her own experience, the history of healing in the church universal, and healing as one element in prayer's larger "landscape." The second half of the book considers inner healing of spirit and psyche (as distinct from what the New Age offers) and the reality of exorcism and deliverance. The work concludes with an excellent annotated bibliography and printed resources for healing services.

This is an ideal place from which to begin exploring Christian healing and how the church can go about it. The book is wisely informed, simply written, devoutly grounded, and delightfully balanced. It can be perused in an evening, but it deserves prayerful pondering.   Jerry Flora

Dallas Willard, *The Divine Conspiracy: Rediscovering Our Hidden Life in God.* San Francisco: Harper, 1998. 428 pp.

Dallas Willard is both a graduate school professor and an ordained Southern Baptist minister. From his position at the University of Southern California he has published widely in philosophy, his teaching field. He is known in Christian circles for two books, *Hearing God* (1999) [originally *In Search of Guidance* 1984] and *The Spirit of the Disciplines* (1998). If the latter was a blockbuster, then his newest work, *The Divine Conspiracy* (1998), is a nuclear explosion on the playground of the churches. Here we have a wide-sweeping, yet penetrating treatment of the Kingdom of God as Jesus conceived it and offered it. For practical purposes, this may be the finest exposition of that topic since the work of George E. Ladd a generation ago (especially *Jesus in the Kingdom*, later retitled *The Presence of the Future*). What Ladd did for evangelical exegesis is now offered more widely in the treatment by Willard.

The Divine Conspiracy is basically an exposition of the Sermon on the Mount. Subtitled *Rediscovering our Hidden Life in God*, the book begins with chapters on "Entering the Eternal Kind of Life Now," "Gospels of Sin Management," and "What Jesus Knew: Our God-Bathed World." Willard's working - even in these titles - suggests that he has tried to think through issues for himself and formulate his conclusions in attractive, relevant phraseology. Aside from Scripture, his chief dialogue partners according to the index are C.S. Lewis and Dietrich Bonhoeffer (with whom he agrees) and Charles Ryrie (with whom he doesn't). The book almost has a feel of a magnum opus, as though all Willard has done in philosophy and religion throughout his career now comes to fruition in this meaty, muscular volume.

This is not the pablum of so much that passes for inspirational Christian writing. This is a training table for followers of Jesus, and - for Willard - that means all believers, period. He will not settle for discipleship as one option for some Christians. It is an all-or-nothing proposition toward which he exegetes, expounds, illustrates, refutes, persuades, and preaches for all he's worth. He finds ammunition in pop songs, philosophers, scientists, poets, devotional writers, news stories, cultural historians, theologians, and hundreds of Scripture texts. The net result is so rich, so concentrated that one cannot digest it in a single reading. Sometimes a chapter can be finished. At other times only a section or just a page. Then one must close the book in order to rest, ponder, and pray. As I read, I often found myself musing, "This is so right! This is so true! This is so wise!"

Richard J. Foster (who terms Willard his mentor) has identified four leading features of *The Divine Conspiracy*: its comprehensive nature, setting out "a Weltanschauung, a worldview"; its accessibility ("so understandable, so readable, so applicable"); its depth ("simply stunning"); and its warmth ("so penetrating an intellect combined with so generous a spirit"). I can easily endorse all of those. On review, shortly after its publication, concluded by saying, "If you read only one book [this year], make it this one." But be warned: Put on your thinking cap. Fasten your seatbelt. Open your heart. And hang on for the ride of your life!   Jerry Flora

Ahmed Ali (translator), *Al-Qur'an: A Contemporary Translation.* 9th edition. Princeton, NJ: Princeton University Press, 2001. 572 pages. $19.95 (paper).

This is an attractive, bi-lingual edition of the Qur'an, the sacred scriptures of Islam. The English version is printed in a bold type that makes it very readable. The Arabic text in parallel columns is painfully small, however, and the bi-lingual Penguin edition is a far better resource for the text in its original language. The translator, a late celebrated Pakistani poet, has produced a fluid and fine translation several levels in literary quality above his competitors. He has, however, striven to take as little poetic license with the text as possible (and pious): that which was obscure in Arabic remains obscure in English (contrast the more periphrastic rendition by Marmaduke Pickthall in *The Meaning of the Glorious Koran: An explanatory translation* [New York: New American Library]). I would have valued more in the way of introduction and explanatory notes.

     In our increasingly global culture, an acquaintance with the sacred traditions of Islam — especially the ways in which those traditions reconfigure the sacred traditions of Jews and Christians — would seem a necessity for Christians entrusted with the Great Commission. This translation, in tandem with a more critical introduction to the Islamic faith, would serve that end admirably.   David A. deSilva

Stephen J. Stein. *Alternative American Religions.* New York: Oxford University Press, 2000, 156 pages.

     This work is part of the Oxford University Press series entitled *Religion in American Life.* It focuses on those movements in American religious history that have at times been labeled as sects or cults. Stein prefers not to use these more negative terms, however, in favor of terms that highlight the fact that these groups are outside the mainstream of religious life: alternative religions, outsider religious groups, or marginal communities. He will also at times refer to these groups with a term developed recently by sociologists: new religious movements (NRMs).

     Stein approaches his material historically, considering NRMs in three American historical periods: the colonial period, the 19th century, and the 20th century. In the introductory chapter, he presents definitions of terms relating to these movements and discusses characteristics that are common to them. His seven chapter headings reveal some of the fascinating and colorful variety found in these alternative religions: Early Dissenters and Popular Religion; Peace Movements in Colonial America; Communitarian Living on the Margins; Apocalyptic Traditions: Watching and Waiting for the End; Healers and Occultists: Women of Spiritual Means; Sectarians in the City; and 20th-Century Sects and Cults. He makes no attempt to be comprehensive in his treatment, but his selection of representative groups does acquaint the reader with the many forms that these groups have taken.

Stein's work is an accurate and fair appraisal of these alternative religions. It is very readable, giving enough detail to acquaint the reader with the main features of each group but not so much as to become laborious. Numerous pictures and illustrations provide visual reinforcement to the text. He also incorporates well chosen first hand accounts to provide "local color" for a number of the groups.

One interesting question that Stein alludes to several times in the book is why America has been the birthplace to so many NRMs. He indicates that several characteristics of American culture have been especially important: an increasingly diverse population, the interaction of countless traditions, individualism, the pioneering spirit, the principle of religious freedom.

This book provides a good, basic introduction to alternative religions in America. It is a good starting place for the reader desiring an overview of these groups. Its bibliography also directs the reader who is looking for a more detailed discussion to excellent resources in the field.   Dale Stoffer

L. de Bois and R. J. van der Spek, *An Introduction to the Ancient World*. New York and London: Routledge, 1997. xx + 321 pp., $70.00 (hardcover)/ $22.99 (paperback).

Karen Rhea Nemet-Nejat, *Daily Life in Ancient Mesopotamia*. London and Westport, CN: Greenwood, 1998. xxii + 346 pp, $49.95.

Daniel C. Snell, *Life in the Ancient Near East, 3100-332 B.C.E.* New Haven and London: Yale University Press, 1997. xvii + 270 pp., hardcover, $30.00.

Piotr Bienkowski and Alan Millard, ed., *Dictionary of the Ancient Near East*. London: British Museum/ Philadelphia: University of Pennsylvania Press, 2000. x + 342 pp., hardcover, $49.95.

The rise in programs on television concerning peoples and locales distant in time and place indicates a welcome realization that the world has a history which might not only be useful to know something about, but might also prove interesting. These volumes indicate a parallel interest in print studies, which are able to provide a more detailed, academic probe into the life and times of ancient peoples than is possible within the scope of a filmed documentary.

The volume by de Bois and van der Spek is the broadest in scope. It is translated from the Dutch original. The classical bent of the two authors is illustrated by the book's content, which covers the ancient Near East in 65 pages, while devoting 81 to Greece and 146 to Rome. The volume begins with a very brief (3.5 pages) introduction which includes a 'diagram' of language families, namely the Semitic and Indo-European. Here a good opportunity for indicating historical development and linguistic interrelationship is lost, since the families are simply listed, with no explicit rationale for their ordering. Egyptian is erroneously included within the Semitic family.

The history of the Near East is given a very cursory glance at a level which might serve for a school textbook. Maps, line drawings, and photographs supplement the text and often provide much more detailed information in their explanatory notes than does the text itself.

Chapters on religion (polytheism, henotheism, monotheism), economy and society (with helpful diagrams illustrating income and expenses of a palace economy and the labor force), and government conclude this section. Even within this brief span one must be wary of infelicities, such as an indication that the laws of Hammurabi were inscribed for public consultation when in fact the populace, as well as the court itself, would have been illiterate. Also problematic is the statement that the prostrate Jehu on the Black Obelisk of Shalmaneser (who could be a royal emissary rather than the king himself) is shown as inferior to the Assyrian overlord because he is smaller. In fact, it is his prostration before the sovereign which indicates his relative status, since both figures are of the same size.

Based on these few observations, I would imagine that the sections discussing Greece and Rome might also need careful evaluating, though the expertise of the authors is noted to be greater in these areas. Not being conversant with these periods, I can only make comment on the section with which I am more familiar. In light of this, the volume will prove interesting to the lay reader, but the need to use a very critical reading which would probably be beyond their expertise suggests that this is not the volume of first choice.

The volume by Nemet-Nejat is a different story. She keeps her attention focused on a smaller geographical area, Mesopotamia, with which she has great familiarity. Her familiarity with the history and sociology of the area is greatly aided by her ability to read and interact with the original texts, so she can check and supplement secondary sources.

The book opens with a 4-page time line running from 12000 to 500 BC giving the archaeological period names with approximate dates, societies and rulers in both northern and southern Mesopotamia, and innovations in culture and technology. This provides a useful overview of history and cultural development. The first three chapters set the stage, discussing the rediscovery of the lost Mesopotamian society and the decipherment of its writing, archaeology and chronology; a very brief general overview of geography and the inhabitants of the area and their languages; and a historical overview. There then follow chapters on: writing, education, and literature; sciences; public and private life; recreation; religion; government; economy. There is a concluding, summary chapter, a helpful 12 page glossary and 3 page bibliography.

The book is well illustrated by black-and-white photographs and drawings. It is written at a level that an educated layperson will find it accessible and fascinating, and scholars will find it a good textbook for classes in ancient Near Eastern civilization. Church, public, college and seminary libraries should have the volume on their shelves.

Snell's volume falls between the two mentioned previously as regards geographical area covered and usefulness. He covers the Near East (Egypt, Israel, Lebanon, Syria, Turkey, Iraq and Iran) from the fourth millennium to the conquest of the area by Alexander in 333 BC. He chooses to arrange his volume chronologically in six chapters ranging from the origin of cities through the Babylonian and Persian periods. In each period he covers aspects of demography, society including its constituent groups, family life, women, work, land and agriculture, animal husbandry, crafts, trade, money, and government and the economy. He has special discussions of Egypt, since much of the relevant information is unavailable since ancient sites are currently occupied, and Israel, which has less available information apart from the Bible, than other areas. Snell also looks a little at the contemporary situations outside the ancient Near East, where there is information. Each chapter starts with a little fictional vignette illustrating and making alive some point of the culture to be discussed in the chapter.

Less depth is provided than in the Nemet-Nejat volume, as is evident from the 132 pages in these chapters compared to double that in hers, though he does have almost 70 pages of notes and 40 pages of bibliography. Illustrations are more limited as well. The two volumes look like they would be a good pair to use together. One could get a more panoramic view of the area through Snell, and then zoom in for a closer and more detailed look through Nemet-Nejat.

As evident from the title, the Bienkowski-Millard volume is a different genre than the previous three, being a reference work. The editors are on the faculty of University of Liverpool, and they are assisted by 11 other contributors from Britain, Germany, Turkey and the US. The geographical area covered includes Mesopotamia, Iran, Anatolia, the Caucasus, the Fertile Crescent, and Arabia, so Egypt is only briefly mentioned. The period covered is from the Lower Paleolithic Period to the fall of Babylon in 539 BC. Articles cover elements of history, religion, society and culture, geography, and language and literature, as well as archaeologists who have excavated and published the various important sites. The volume includes a simple map, a one page chronological chart, a 4 page synoptic king list for Babylonia, Assyria, Elam, Mitanni, Ugarit, and the Hittites, and a subject index. The volume is an excellent one-volume reference work, useful in libraries at all levels, though needing supplementation by such tools as *Reallexikon der Assyriologie und vorderasiatischen Archäologie* in more serious academic settings.

David W. Baker

William W. Hallo, general editor, and J. Lawson Younger, associate editor. *The Context of Scripture*, Volume 2: *Monumental Inscriptions from the Biblical World.* Leiden/Boston: Brill, 2000. Xxvi + 438 pp., hardback, $131.00.

This is the second of three projected volumes which seek to update and replace J.B. Pritchard's *Ancient Near Eastern Texts Relating to the Old Testament*, which has been the standard reference work for the past half-century. The first volume of the series was reviewed in this *Journal* XXX (1998) 105–106. This volume provides an impressive array of texts, (usually) newly translated from Egyptian, Hittite, West Semitic (Moabite, Ammonite, Hebrew, Phoenician, Old and Imperial Aramaic, Philistine, and Nabataean, as well as the dialect of Deir 'Alla), Akkadian, and Sumerian by some 33 scholars from 6 different countries.

The volume commences with an introductory essay on "The Bible and the Monuments" by the general editor. Here he discusses text taxonomy, how texts are categorized in the series. 'Canonical' texts, the title of volume 1, are those which serve as part of the educational curriculum and thus are intended for more than just a single use. Monumental inscriptions, the subject of the present volume, are those intended to 'last for all time as memorials to those kings and other mortals who built or dedicated them, or to the deities to whom they were dedicated' (xxi-xxii). Archival material, presumably the subject of the next volume, is that which is intended for preservation for a shorter time period, being thus more ad hoc and time-oriented.

Egyptian texts include royal inscriptions from the 18th and 19th dynasty and mortuary inscriptions including pyramid and coffin texts, excerpts from the Book of the Dead, some harper songs and grave inscriptions. A bibliography of 5 pages follows the inscriptions. Hittite texts include edicts, annals, treaties and several hieroglyphic Luwian inscriptions, followed by a 4 page bibliography. West Semitic is represented by building and memorial inscriptions in Moabite (Mesha), Ammonite, the dialect of Deir 'Alla, Hebrew (Siloam Tunnel), Old Aramaic (including the Tell Dan inscription in which 'the house of David' is mentioned), Aramaic, Philistine, and Nabataean; votive/dedicatory inscriptions in Hebrew and Aramaic, mortuary isncriptions, seal and stamp impressions, weights, treaties, and various miscellaneous texts like the Gezer calendar. There follows a 14 page bibliography (though the *Encyclopedia of Islam* should probably be listed by the editor H.A.R. Gibb, not W.J. Dumbrell). Akkadian building inscriptions cover the range from the Old Akkadian to the Achaemenid periods. There are also seals, weights, treaties, laws, edicts, boundary stones, royal grants, and an 11 page bibliography. Finally, Sumerian is represented by building, votive, seal and weight inscriptions, laws, and Gudean temple hymns, followed by a 4 page bibliography.

Texts are provided with a brief introduction, bringing out any biblical relevance, and include a bibliography for the text. Footnotes provide help on the translation and other sources which might be of use. The translations are well done, and the editors have done an excellent job. They and the publisher are to be thanked. There are a few slips (e.g. 198, n.* uses a reference system not employed in the volume itself), as might be expected in such a vast enterprise, and a more thorough discussion of the criteria for selection of texts and excerpts would have been useful. Students and teachers will find the work invaluable, and it should be found in any serious academic library.

David W. Baker

C. Marvin Pate, *Communities of the Last Days: The Dead Sea Scrolls, the New Testament and the Story of Israel.* Downers Grove, Illinois: InterVarsity, 2000. Pp. 303. $29.99

In *Communities of the Last Days*, C. M. Pate takes on the dauntingly immense task of comparison of two large bodies of literature, namely, the Dead Sea Scrolls (DSS) and the New Testament (NT). Pate allows the reader to witness the engagement of two communities of the Second Temple period as each attempts to situate itself within the "story of Israel" through its respective claim to be the eschatologically restored/restoring people of Israel (19-20). In Pate's opinion, *Communities of the Last Days* avoids the methodological pitfalls of literary dependence of the NT writings on the DSS (or vice versa) by asserting that the point of comparison is not literary sharing but a reworked, common tradition. According to Pate, "the story of Israel is the metanarrative adapted by the DSS and the NT" (18). This metanarrative is the story of Israel (sin-exile-restoration) retold by each community to redefine the practices, symbols, and beliefs of that story.

Pate attempts to trace this metanarrative in a compare/contrast format, thematically progressing through large portions of the DSS and NT. Throughout, Pate relies heavily on the interpretive perspective of N. T. Wright, especially in Wright's *Jesus and the Victory of God* and *The New Testament and the People of God*. In so doing, Pate not only aligns himself with a gifted scholar/theologian but also inherits the interpretive dangers of an all-encompassing perspective on Second Temple Judaism.

Pate aids the reader in ease of format and thematic progression. Beginning with an analogy of the discovery of the DSS and the sin-exile-restoration motif, Pate introduces the reader to the Deuteronomistic tradition as the dominant Old Testament (OT) perspective on Israel's story within Second Temple Judaism. A concise, although informative, catalog of the various types of literature among the DSS follows, highlighting their common thematic ties of exile-restoration as found in the Deuteronomistic tradition. Pate then continues, in chapter 2, to draw the reader into a discussion of the major arguments for and against the Essene hypothesis, among others, as well as the arguments (dis)associating the DSS from/to the NT corpus. Pate concludes that the best evidence suggests the primacy of the Essene hypothesis as well as an indirect literary linkage, at best, between the DSS and the NT.

Examining the use of pesher in Matthew and the DSS, Pate focuses in chapter 3 on what he considers the central question the literature addresses: Who is the true Israel? The interpretive schema of pesher hermeneutics is applied to that literature which exhibits, according to Pate, the three styles of pesharim (singular, continuous, and thematic) as well as their usage of the four tenets of the Deuteronmistic tradition (disobedience, messenger(s) sent, messenger(s) rejected, and judgment). Pesher, relying on the Deuteronomistic tradition, is, in Pate's view, the "hermeneutic of legitimation" (106) not only for Matthew but also Paul's writings and Hebrews. This is further evidence for each community's concern to redefine the true Israel, in Pate's view.

Continuing the perspective of legitimation expressed by each community represented by the DSS and the NT, Pate addresses the theme of Messianism as is contrasted with the "common interpretation" (112) of Second Temple Judaism. The DSS and NT perspectives on Messianism, in Pate's view, "argue that ethnic Israel is ironically aligned with the enemies of God" in an effort to legitimate themselves as "the genuine people of God," with the understanding that Messianism is nonetheless divergently interpreted within each community (132).

The retelling of Israel's story is no less important in chapter 5; however, Pate here begins to consider those symbols and practices through which the DSS and NT express their legitimating redefinition. Considering the DSS and Luke-Acts in particular, Pate contrasts the DSS and NT with Second Temple Judaism and shows the progressively divergent perspectives between the DSS and NT themselves. Subversion of Israel's story is the *modus operandi*.

Subversion of Israel's story also, perhaps necessarily, becomes subversion of the redefining attempts of competing claims to Israel's story. In this respect, Pate addresses the notion of justification (chapter 6), the "angelic liturgy" (chapter 7), monotheism, covenant, and eschatology (chapter 8), in addition to the notion of eschatological restoration in terms of adherence to halakhah (DSS) or faith in Jesus (Gospel of John) over against the embodiment of wisdom in the Mosaic law (chapter 9). Pate attempts to show that promotion of the story of the new Israel and subversion of the old anticipates the inauguration of the "age to come," which is "synonymous with the kingdom of God" (215). Finally, Pate offers his own theological perspectives (so claimed, 231) regarding the triumph of Christianity over against the failure of the Essenes (Conclusion).

In regard to thematic coherence and the stated objectives in his Introduction, Pate provides an informative and, as is possible in one volume, comprehensive entry into two exciting bodies of literature. The book is understandable, and in most cases, responsibly defensible. Though writing a book that is massive in scope, Pate handles the material in an honest, readable fashion.

Perhaps the areas with most potential for critique involve Pate's own theological bias and his reliance on the works of N. T. Wright. For instance, early on in the book, Pate shows concern for the validity of the canon in relation to the DSS (39). However, Pate is misleading on the manner in which the DSS reflect the canonicity of the OT texts. Pate seems more interested to affirm the canon as it exists today by comparison with the DSS, rather than comment on the controversial issues regarding the status of the OT texts at Qumran as canonical within the DSS writings themselves and for the community/communities that read them (Ulrich 2000, 1:117-120).

Then again, perhaps this is due not so much to theological bias as to methodological presuppositions. Here I refer to Pate's reliance on N. T. Wright. It is no secret that Wright is critiqued on his "tendency to create an artificially unified worldview out of the complex world of first-century Judaism" (Johnson 1999, 210). I would caution the reader toward large claims attributed to Second Temple Judaism, Essenes, and even the NT itself in this book. It is not entirely clear to what extent Pate's work can be considered a sketch of NT or Essene "thought" in light of the increasing tendency toward segmentation of Second Temple Judaism into *Judaisms* of the Second Temple period.

Pate's proclivity toward sweeping claims, modeling the same tendency in Wright, is specifically noticeable in Chapter 5. Pate examines the DSS and Luke-Acts in particular. Reinterpretation of symbol and praxis by each is the topic under consideration, and as a result, the Temple is necessarily discussed. Pate's concern is to show the subversion of the symbol against the "prevailing" interpretation of Second Temple Judaism. So doing, Pate claims that Qumran's reinterpretation of the Temple "included the spiritualization of the whole cultus" (151), based on the opinion of R. A. Horsley in reference to 1QS 5:5-7; 8:4-10; 9:3-6; 4QFlor 1:1-13. This is indeed overstatement, especially in light of the Temple Scroll (11QT). 11QT, as legal literature, is not only an extended treatise on Temple construction but also God's command to build a temple. Pate himself claims 11QT, et al, as a foundational document of the Essene identity and *raison d'etre* (44). Later, in chapter 8, Pate, deferring to S. Lehne, suggests this spiritualization of the Temple and cult is but an interim status for Qumran. One wonders, then, to what extent this interim status was considered replacement/spiritualization of the Jerusalem Temple by the Qumran sect and to what extent the comparison of the DSS and NT becomes more dependent on the claims rather than the evidence.

In conclusion, Pate has, on the whole, offered a thorough introduction to the interpretive worlds of the DSS and NT. Although I differ with some of Pate's interpretive conclusions, *Communities of the Last Days* nonetheless provides the reader

Book Reviews

with an interesting glimpse into the attempts of two bodies of literature to "retell" Israel's story. Pate's work is not without liability, and it would be helpful for the reader to evaluate the interpretive perspective of N. T. Wright so as to see more clearly Wright's permeations (claimed or unclaimed) into Pate's argument. The reader's encounter with the subtleties of Pate's research can be more responsibly considered with an understanding of the larger complexities introduced from the research of Wright.

Bibliography

Johnson, Luke Timothy. "A Historiographical Response to Wright's Jesus." Pages 206-224 in *Jesus and the Restoration of Israel: A Critical Assessment of N. T. Wright's Jesus and the Victory of God*. Edited by C. C. Newman. Downers Grove, Illinois: InterVarsity Press, 1999.

Ulrich, Eugene. "Canon." Pages 117-120 in vol. 1 of *Encyclopedia of the Dead Sea Scrolls*. Edited by L. H. Schiffman and J. C. VanderKam. 2 vols. New York: Oxford University Press, 2000.

C. Jason Borders

Timothy H. Lim, ed., *The Dead Sea Scrolls in their Historical Context*. Edinburgh: T & T Clark, 2000. Pp. x + 309. $49.95 cloth.

The Dead Sea Scrolls in their Historical Context is a compilation of papers presented at the University of Edinburgh Centre for Christian Origins for the conference entitled, "The Dead Sea Scrolls in their Historical Context," held on May 5-6, 1998. Two guiding questions were to be considered by contributors to the conference: 1) "How central or marginal was the community that owned these scrolls?" and 2) "Has our picture of nascent Judaism been skewed as a result of the chance discovery and intensive research into the Dead Sea Scrolls?" (1-2).

To what extent we can classify a normative, Second Temple Judaism is problematic, according to the contributors. In light of the discovery of the Dead Sea Scrolls (DSS), how is one to discern the marginality or centrality of these texts within the larger debate regarding what may be considered "normative" or "common" in Second Temple Judaism? The aim of this book is to situate the DSS "within the context of Judaism in the Second Temple period" (1), understanding the problematic nature of "Judaism" in this historical context.

The articles included in the volume are arranged into four sub-areas: 1) "The Qumran Community, Essenes and other Sects" (5), 2) "The Qumran Biblical Texts and the Masoretic Text" (65), 3) "Sectarian Law and Normative Jewish Law" (121), and 4) "Theology of the Qumran Community, Second Temple Judaism and Early Christianity" (197). Emerging from the book is the sustained attempt to *locate* the DSS texts, which results in the *re-location* and/or *dislocation* of our understanding of "normative" Judaism in the Second Temple period.

Although one article cannot speak for the book as a whole, George Brooke's "E Pluribus Unum: Textual Variety and Definitive Interpretation in the Qumran Scrolls"

(107-119) is an example of the volume's concern to *locate* the DSS. The nuances of Brooke's individual contribution are beyond the scope of this review; however, Brooke shows the Qumran interpretation of biblical texts normative in form and method yet distinctive in content, i.e. the eschatological environment in which the scrolls were written is given expression through God's "singular purpose" (119). For Brooke, what that purpose is does not depend on alteration of method or form of texts but rather on alternate interpretation. Similarly, *The Dead Sea Scrolls in their Historical Context* is a glimpse into an alternate, interpretive agenda of a community relocated in Second Temple Judaism.

On the whole, the book accomplishes its aim. It is no small task to investigate such a wide array of topics and texts and present the findings as a coherent whole. This is not to say that each article anticipates other contributors' findings; however, concern for the marginality and/or centrality of the texts in question within their historical context is apparent.

My criticism of the book concerns the intended audience. The dust cover claims to avoid technical language while not appealing to "popular sensationalism." Although I found several articles to prove themselves true of this description, others require knowledge of not only biblical languages but a range of specialist vocabulary. This is not to say that those articles were not both well-written and defensible. I am simply considering the aim of the book with respect to the intended reader. Since "historiographical issues that are not normally part of the study of other ancient documents" have been raised by "widespread media coverage" of the DSS (2) and their relation to our understanding of Second Temple Judaism, audience then becomes critical if this book is intended to provide a corrective to those who would be influenced by the popular sensationalists.

On a different note, I have been prompted to re-examine the extent I consider the Qumran community *sectarian* as a result of this book. Clearly, differences exist between the Judaism of the DSS and other *Judaisms* of the Second Temple period. Yet, even within the scrolls themselves, differences in interpretation throughout the community's history are evident. Sectarianism as (very simply) *difference* can then become a problematic category. This book makes me wonder to what extent difference, for its own sake, is a helpful category in our understanding of Judaism represented in the DSS and its location within Judaism of the Second Temple period.

This book is an asset in two respects: 1) a valuable reflection of a wide range of current DSS research, and 2) a cohesive unit calling attention to our (lack of) understanding of Second Temple Judaism and its *interpreting* communities. Although a wealth of knowledge, the book's scholarly accessibility could prove a liability to the informed, popular reader.   C. Jason Borders

Al Wolters, *The Copper Scroll: Overview, Text and Translation.* Sheffield: Sheffield Academic Press, 1996. 55 pp. $19.95 (paper).

The *Copper Scroll* (3Q15) is an ancient list of treasures and directions to their hiding places, engraved in Hebrew on a copper roll instead of the more customary vellum or parchment. It is thought by most scholars to represent an authentic list of some portion of the wealth of the Jerusalem Temple (or, less likely, the wealth of the Qumran community), taken into the desert and hidden just a few years prior to the destruction of the Temple in 70 AD. All in all, it represents several tons of lost silver and gold, and the directions in the Copper Scroll are sufficiently cryptic to have prevented archaeologists and treasure seekers from discovering any of the hordes listed.

This slim volume presents an introductory essay on the *Copper Scroll*, originally prepared for publication in the Oxford *Encyclopedia of the Dead Sea Scrolls*, together with a fein bibliography on this scroll, a number of photographs of the actual sections of the *Copper Scroll*, and its Hebrew text and new English translation on facing pages.

David deSilva

Kay Marshall Strom, *A Caregiver's Survival Guide: How To Stay Healthy When Your Loved One Is Sick*, Downers Grove: InterVarsity Press, 2000, pp. 153, $9.99.

"The only true security any of us has comes from God, through the unconditional love found in a personal relationship with Jesus Christ" (138). People who are caring for chronically ill or disabled loved ones often lose their sense of security. With this book, Kay Marshall Strom attempts to help restore some of that security. She shares stories from her 10 years of experience caring for her ill husband as well as from other caregivers as she walks new caregivers through steps that will help them survive new territory. At the same time, she reminds the caregivers that God is with them every step of this new journey.

Caring for a chronically ill or disabled loved one is physically, emotionally, and spiritually draining. Many people focus on the one who is sick or disabled. That person usually receives the flowers, gifts, cards or prayers. Often forgotten is the person or persons with the primary responsibility for providing direct care. Strom had that responsibility. She understands the confusion and sometimes denial that comes with a diagnosis. She understands the changing of roles that is attendant with many debilitating diseases. The book begins at the beginning of the process--recognition that "something" is wrong. Strom and her husband saw several doctors before he was finally diagnosed with a rare degenerative disease. In her case, obtaining a diagnosis in and of itself was a relief although her husband was still denying that he had a problem. Next, she had to deal with the reality of having her husband, lover, best friend being diagnosed with a disease that has no cure, will only get worse and will alter his mental and physical functioning in the process.

> It was two years before a diagnosis was finally made--chorea acanthocytosis, an extremely rare genetic condition. It was another month, several consultations and a whole stack of medical journal articles before the impact of that diagnosis sunk in: profound physical deterioration, increasing dementia, relentless progression, untreatable, incurable, fatal...(15)

In sixteen absorbing chapters, Strom shares how she survived ten years of giving care to her husband, Larry. The reader moves with her through the progression of the disease, her decision to place him in a nursing facility, his death, and the beginning of her healing process. However, as moving as Strom's story is, her story is not the point of the book. Strom uses her story to demonstrate how to negotiate this journey. When "something" seems wrong with your loved one, whether your child, spouse, or sibling--check into the problem. And yes, checking into the problem may take some time. Your loved one may deny that anything is wrong. The first doctor may misdiagnose. When you get a second opinion, it may be a completely different opinion as to what is wrong. Once the diagnosis is definite, neither of you may want to accept it. Your life will be changed. People will want to offer advice, cures, comments intended to help--but do not. How does one handle this well-intended "help" that does not?

Strom provides practical suggestions for successfully maneuvering through the confusion that results when one's life is radically changed, sometimes gradually, sometimes very quickly as they deal with new realities. Roles will probably change. A spouse or parent may seem more like a child. Major decisions need to be made--can you continue to work and care for your loved one? What happens financially if you don't work? Can you live with your decision if you do work? Is your loved one violent? Do you have enough help? Are you taking care of you? How do you take care of you and not appear selfish? How do you handle the feelings of resentment and anger that will surface? What do I look for in a good adult daycare program or nursing facility? If I have to use a nursing facility, do I have to sell my home? Strom answers these questions and many more. And she answers them from a Christian perspective. She continually reminds her readers that we can do all things through Christ. For Strom, staying close to God, finding the blessings in her situation, was what helped her survive.

There are other books that provide some of the information that Strom does. The doctor currently treating my father for his dementia recommended *The 36-Hour Day: A Family Guide to Caring for Persons with Alzheimer Disease, Related Dementing Illnesses, and Memory Loss in Later Life* by Nancy Mace and Peter Rabins. Until I read *A Caregiver's Survival Guide*, I agreed with the excerpts quoted on the cover that extolled its virtues. However, it does not have the personal and Christian perspective that Strom offers. Mace and Rabins can tell me that others also feel helpless, angry, trapped, and resentful. Strom tells me that *she* felt that way, lived through those feelings, and then refers me to scripture that helped her through those feelings. I highly recommend Strom's book for anyone who has a loved one who is seriously ill or disabled whether or not the reader is the primary caregiver. I highly recommend this book for anyone--counselors, pastors, friends, relatives, Christian, non-Christian--who may find themselves trying to support a caregiver. Strom reminds the reader who is a caregiver that he or she is not alone either naturally or spiritually. Non-caregivers will better understand the turmoil the caregiver experiences and will be better prepared to offer true assistance--possibly more often. Strom's testimony is such an effective one that it will encourage Christian readers and perhaps convince non-Christians to become seekers.

Katherine A. Simmons

Book Reviews

Philip Crosby, *The Absolutes of Leadership*. San Francisco: Jossey-Bass, 1996. 144 pp., $16.50.

Finally, a wise and readable text on leadership in under 125 pages. Crosby defines leadership as "deliberately causing people-driven actions in a planned fashion for the purpose of accomplishing the leader's agenda" (p. 2). The author outlines five styles of leadership that readers can use to quickly assess the approach used personally and by their CEO. They are:

The Destructor - disruption without a reason*

The Procrastinator - paralysis due to analysis

The Caretaker - if it ain't broke don't fix it

The Preparer - plan, do, check, act

The Accomplisher - ready, fire, aim

(*The phrases following each leadership description are borrowed from a variety of sources for emphasis.)

Although Crosby clearly believes that the Accomplisher is the most effective leadership style, it would seem from my experience that parts of each of the styles might coalesce into a more integrated approach to leadership. Taking action toward fulfilling the mission and vision of an organization is the compelling purpose for leaders, but finding the proper balance in the leadership styles Crosby purposes becomes the art in leadership.

Crosby lists the *Absolutes of Leadership* as:

- A clear agenda - outline goals and strategies
- A personal philosophy - workable and understandable
- Enduring relationships - these take thought and work
- Worldliness - utilize technology to be informed about and to respect global cultures

(p.3), and then he takes the first half of the book to describe what he means by each of these absolutes.

The second half of the book focuses on leaders and such things as finance, quality, customers, suppliers, employees, and bosses. Crosby reminds us that "the leader is the only one who can make quality happen" (p. 76). The author is a recognized authority on how to define and implement quality in organizations, and this text is well worth reading.

Crosby advocates defining quality performance measures and monitoring them to improve the quality of all the organization does. Non-profit organizations will utilize different performance measures than profit-making organizations, but the process for determining what these measures will be is a very similar one. One person doesn't do this, but a committee of coworkers who "want to give the organization their all" (p. 107).

The wisdom of many years of leadership practice flows easily from Mr. Crosby's words, and younger leaders can learn a lot from the examples and stories woven throughout this short text.   Mary Ellen Drushal, Ashland University

Ross S. Moxley, *Leadership & Spirit: Breathing New Vitality and Energy Into Individuals and Organizations.* San Francisco, CA: Jossey-Bass & Center for Creative Leadership, 2000, 208 pp., $35.00.

Why has it taken so long for authors and consultants to acknowledge the spiritual dimension of leadership development? Since Bolman & Deal wrote *Leading with Soul: An Uncommon Journey of Spirit* in 1995, other authors are putting words to what they have sensed for years.

Pick up any child development text and five areas are always listed that describe a well-balanced individual: social, emotional, spiritual, intellectual, and physical. Luke 10:27-28 describes the same series of developmental areas for those who will inherit eternal life: "love the Lord your God with all your heart (emotional), with all your soul (spiritual), with all your strength (physical), with all your mind (intellectual), and your neighbor as yourself (social)." Leaders must find balance in their lives and practice being who they most deeply are, if they intend to lead individuals and organizations into a vital and dynamic future.

Moxley acknowledges that writing this text caused him to "dig deeply, to consider again my inner life and my outer work" (p. xviii), which is the reflective practice that all leaders should engage in to seek perspective in who they are, what they do, and God's purpose in all that is accomplished. There is a better way to lead people than the traditional top-down, command-and-control, executive-as-leader model. Moxley discusses the problems that traditional leaders have with the use of coercive power, the problems with ego, and the dark side of executives. Moxley provides several "speedbumps" in the way of vignettes or organizations and individuals within them to cause the reader to reflect on what they do. He believes that: "employees want to be involved in the activity of leadership...that they want to find meaning and purpose in what they do... to use all of their energies, to use their whole self, in their work... that they have a need to be seen as individuals, and they want to be involved in community" pp. 11-15).

Leaders who perceive themselves as the executive-as-leader tend to micromanage the task even though they are giving the appearance to others of letting go of the details. This very act subverts the sense of respect and community that exists in the organization. Moxley proposes a partnership model of leadership where leadership is understood as a verb rather than a noun (p. 73). He outlines five requirements for this model to work effectively:

- balance of power
- shared purpose
- shared responsibility and accountability
- respect for the person
- partnering in the nitty-gritty

and then reminds the readers that "In authentic partnerships and communities, individuals flourish. But the importance of relationships and community is also acknowledged and honored (p. 92).

Moxley contrasts the two models of leadership, executive-as-leader and partnership-as-leader and purports that both leaders and followers should examine themselves and determine how best to honor the differences that exist among us.

Book Reviews

We learn from our experiences in leadership and this learning is reflected in the changes leaders make over time in how we lead. Some executive-as-leaders cannot or will not change, because they are comfortable doing the things they know to do. Susan Muto, the Executive Director of The Epiphany Association in Pittsburgh, often reminds us that we are human beings, not human doings. Who we are as leaders is much more important than what we do as leaders.

Moxley reminds us that many of us fall prey to the tyranny of the oughts (you ought to be a researcher, a pastor, or an attorney) when we pay no attention to our true selves and calling. When we follow the oughts instead of the calling, we extend the abuse to our co-workers who become our followers.

All our lives we are taught to trust reality. "If I can touch it, see it, hear it, taste it, smell it, then it is real" (p. 25). But spirit cannot be empirically documented. Self-awareness and self-nurturing are critical components for practicing partnerships-as-leaders, but it is scarey and unsettling to take this inner journey of spirit in leadership.

Wholeness and balance is the reward for taking this life-long journey and the outcome is the ability to develop partnerships and community in organizations who desperately need it. Do not read this book unless you truly desire to change and develop your leadership capabilities from the inside out. Take the road less traveled. Executives-as-leaders abound, even in non-profit organizations, and there is a better way to lead organizations and people.   Mary Ellen Drushal

David S. Young, *Servant Leadership for Church Renewal: Shepherds by the Living Springs*, Scottdale, PA: Herald Press, 1999. 176 p. $12.99.

Churchs and their leadership are thirsty for living waters. Two crucial themes about this reality are Servant Leadership, as a new paradigm of ministry closer to Jesus', and Church Renewal, which is one of the greatest needs of contemporary Christianity. Young meets an actual need by crystallizing a powerful tool for ministry, providing a vital link between these two concepts in *Servant Leadership for Church Renewal: Shepherds by the Living Springs*.

The author introduces the book with a powerful image of sheepdogs, sheep, living waters, and a Shepherd. These convey effectively the very heart of the book's message, and compel the reader to immerse herself into the reading. One of the foundational verses on which Young founded the model of servant leardership for church renewal is Revelation 7,17: "The Lamb in the midst of the throne will be their shepherd, and he will guide them to springs of living water."

The book is arranged in eight very readable and clear chapters, developing the concepts through practical steps to be followed. Young starts with the needed vision for leadership arriving at the goal of faith transformation. Along the way, there are profound and operative insights that have to do with pillar issues for Church renewal, such as, the leaders' spiritual formation, carrying and sustaining the vision, empowering leaders, funding servant structures, serving and being served, and team building and functioning.

The author unfolds essential themes with a solid theology, helpful use of images, along with a holistic conception of the three journeys needed both for personal and corporate spiritual growth (ch. 2). These paths are the upward journey to God as the source and reason of life, the inward journey to self-understanding by identifying the strengths and needs, and the outward journey of outreach to the community.

A remarkable virtue of Young is his down-to-earth approach expressed by giving not only a biblically based method to church renewal, but also by addressing the organization of this enterprise, and making us aware of, and giving advice for hardships that a leader is surely going to face. Moreover, the book has contributive resources such as reference notes, a recommended bibliography for each chapter, and worksheets (like "developing a team," "assessment of needs," "envisioning a plan of renewal," or "implementing a plan of renewal").

I unreservedly recommend the book for Seminary students, pastors and lay leaders of churches. I also believe that what Young proposes is applicable for the congregations of the Brethren Church in Argentina, most of them being small churches with an urgent need of church renewal lead by a servant leader who shepherds God's people to living waters.

The book is remarkably free from errors though with a small exception on p. 53 where the reference should be Revelations 7,9-17 instead of 7.9-19.

Young's book is a very valuable resource for today's leadership. Hence it is worth being read and thoroughly used. Servant leaders are those who by listening to God's voice are able to lead the church to the very source of life and empowerment, that is, to the powerful renewing living springs of the Holy Spirit. The Lamb of God was transformed in the Shepherd. Let us become the kind of servants who understand the nature of our call. Marcela A. Rivero

Paul S. Fiddes, 1999. *Freedom and Limit: A Dialogue between Literature and Christian Doctrine*. Macon, Georgia: Mercer University Press.

For any student of theology and lover of literature this is a "must read". It is a compelling study of the interaction and interrelationships between theology and literature and the various ways in which writers have explored theological concepts. It is also an example of the ways in which a theologian may interpret literature through the lens of the Christian faith and how the study of literature can enrich the study of theology. It is a study of literature in light of theological discourse, the interpretation of literature through the eyes of the Christian. By necessity it is an examination of literary symbols and metaphors, values and beliefs, which have their origins in the story of Christ and the way in which writers of secular literature have appropriated these to invest them with further meaning for the reader.

As a student of English Literature I have been amazed at how often a poet, playwright or novelist has been able to capture a theological idea, explore it from a highly personal perspective and present it as testimony to the activity of God in the secular world and in their lives. How often is the sacred world made manifest in the secular world of literature and ideas? How alert are Christians to the possibilities for developing and nurturing the spiritual life through the reading and study of literature? Literature invites the reader to participate in lives other than our own which expands our range of consciousness, extends our experience of God, changes our perspective and which can lead us to God.

For example, the story of Jesus makes particular experience and feelings possible because the story shapes the reader's imagination, invites the reader's participation in the realm of the imagination, and thereby enables the reader to speak a language inherently of God. The story points the reader to "a divine story-teller who is the God of the future, who is always free to do new things and bring new reality into being"(20). As a result, the story structures the lives of the readers/believers, but presents challenges, possibilities, opportunities for the future. As the reader reaches out in the imagination towards a new world it is only because God is reaching out toward humanity and in partnership that new world can be realized. In a sense it is a form of incarnation, an invitation to participate in divine imagination which leaves room for human originality. "So even the fulfilment of divine purpose in the incarnate Christ has the character of promise, of beginning as well as end" (46).

Fiddes spends an entire chapter discussing the structure of the Christian story. It takes a U-shaped form encompassing fall from perfection to alienation and return to perfection again. After exploring the story of Christ as the prototypical narrative form, Shakespeare provides the literary paradigm, because he is the writer who most imitates this structure, occupying and exploring the boundaries between comedy and tragedy, healing and curse, alienation and restoration. The happy endings of the comedies suggest aspects of the new world to come; the tragedies end with wasted lives which we regret. "Each overlaps with the other, bearing witness to the Great Story of the God who includes both pain and bliss in his own life" (82).

Following this protracted introduction comes a masterly analysis of the work of William Blake whose poetry criticized the dominance of human reason over imagination, the rule of law over the spirit, the imagination, passion. For Blake law is stifling because it imposes a false sense of guilt. The cross is not a punishment for the ancient sin of Adam finally inflicted by a legalistic God, but the redeeming power of sympathy and compassion here and now. Humanity is held prisoner by the hegemony of rational law; the release of humankind into new life is assured by the power of imagination, which cannot be fully tamed, least of all by the God of the Deists, with His mathematical and technical skills.

D.H.Lawrence was greatly concerned with the disintegration of human personality as a result of cultural stress. The exploration of relationships is a particular focus of Lawrence for it is in relationships that broken human personality can be restored to perfection. As a writer he was in search of the wholeness or integrity of the self and he suggested that "Jesus loved mankind for what it might be, free and limitless" (147), which is the search Lawrence undertakes in his writing. Love in all manner of manifestations is a particular emphasis of Lawrence, because love is the locus for the denial of the self in favor of the lover and the encouragement of the lover to be fully her/himself. For Lawrence, "love means a sharing of experience and hence a participation in the suffering of another" (149) which opens up the participants in a relationship to the possibilities God has for them and the world. Omniscience then, according to Lawrence, is God's knowledge of possibilities, but these have to be realized by human beings.

Fiddes' studies of Iris Murdoch and William Golding are particularly interesting. In Murdoch's reality art is the representation of revelation, grace, salvation and imago dei; relationships are the place where the self can be put to death and human suffering confronted as the means by which the self can indeed die. For Murdoch, "God is present in the world in a mode of weakness and suffering", and "It is because God really participates in the human experience of pain and death that he is not dead - ie irrelevant - to the world" (193). God is not absent but hidden for the sake of human freedom. It is suffering which is a form of revelation and the individual's free participation in the suffering of Christ which is the means of revelation.

The characters created by William Golding find God in the heart of darkness. Primitive landscapes seem to require primeval behavior, where the brutal human nature clashes with the cultural norms and values of civilization. For Golding, the human fall into sin is not a fall into freedom as might be expected, because the life in sin is limited by a sense of guilt. But Golding suggests the necessity for a dalliance with this sinfulness in order to fully recognize the enemy. Besides it is this guilt which provides the possibility of forgiveness, for conscience is the first recollection of the presence of grace, the first reminder of divinity dwelling amongst humankind and participating in each individual life.

How then to define freedom and limit after this stunning read. Simple. Freedom can best be described as spiritual vision, the unleashing of imagination, a daily journey of daily revelations, a life spent in pilgrimage searching for and enjoying the presence of God in every aspect of the human existence, the exploration of possibilities, rising to the challenge of being an individual called by God. We are only limited by the pull of the flesh.   Dorothy Penny-Larter

James Sire, *Habits of the Mind*, Downers Grove, IL: InterVarsity Press, 2000. 224 pp.

What is an intellectual? Is it proper for a Christian to also be an intellectual? Can the intellectual life be a Christian calling? Are there certain moral responsibilities for the so-called Christian intellectual? James Sire, former editor of InterVarsity Press and author of the well-circulated book on worldviews, *The Universe Next Door*, has written a new book, *Habits of the Mind*, focusing on the nature of the intellectual life for the Christian. He defines an intellectual as

> one who loves ideas, is dedicated to clarifying them, developing them, criticizing them, turning them over and over, seeing their implications, stacking them atop one another, arranging them, sitting silent while new ideas pop up and old ones seem to rearrange themselves, playing with them, punning with their terminology, laughing at them, watching them clash, picking up the pieces, starting over, judging them, withholding judgement about them, changing them, bringing them into contact with their counterparts in other systems of thought, inviting them to dine and have a ball but also suiting them for service in workaday life.

And for the Christian it is all this "to the glory of God."

The person chosen by Sire to model the Christian intellectual life is John Henry Newman of whom Sire says, "I know of no Christian thinker - scholar, cleric, or

Book Reviews

both, as Newman was - who has given us such a vivid picture of the 'perfection' toward which all Christians should aspire to the limit of their ability." In consecutive chapters Sire describes how Newman is an intellectual and how Newman views the intellect. Sire uses numerous lengthy quotes from Newman which demonstrate the value of the intellect, of holiness, and of certainty in order to provide a vision of the perfected intellect for the purpose of bringing order to knowledge. This section is insightful regarding Newman but the quotes are quite extensive and take a high level of concentration to follow. The section concludes with Newman's valuable warnings of the dangers of the intellect. Sire's next chapter focuses on how thinking feels. This chapter attempts to clarify his earlier definition of the intellectual, but adds little to the rest of the book.

The middle of the book develops the relationship between knowledge and morality, a topic that most Christians have little understanding of and which was the section this reviewer considered Sire's best and most valuable. For Sire the moral intellectual life for the Christian in inseparable from the practical life of the Christian. One must think through the truth and actively live it out to be a Christian intellectual. He states "we only know what we act on" and "we only believe what we obey." His section on the intellectual virtues of constancy, patience, perseverance, courage, and humility encourages the reader to understand how good thought is manifested in virtuous actions. For example, he tells the reader that if beliefs are false it may take courage to reassess or abandon the beliefs or it may take courage to speak forth a new discovery into a generation where the ideas may be viewed as "heretical." This theme of thought and action knits together much of what Sire has to say in this book.

Sire provides practical ways to improve one's intellectual thinking through such means as the use of solitude and silence, through what he calls lateral thinking, and through removing the barriers to intensive thinking which he describes. He even makes reference to meditative thinking as prescribed by Martine Heidegger. Continuing the theme of improving thinking, the following chapter focuses on improving thinking through reading (a chapter that could be valuable in itself if published separately as a tract). Mark Hamilton, Ashland University

Jeffrey Schultz and John G. West, Jr., eds. *The C.S. Lewis Readers' Encyclopedia*, Zondervan Publishing House, 1998, 464 pp.

This massive effort is an exhaustive guide to the life and writings of C.S. Lewis, including descriptions of all of Lewis' works, brief biographies of everyone he wrote about or knew well (I particularly enjoyed the updates on David and Douglas Gresham), and summaries of seemingly all of the ideas or concepts found anywhere in Lewis' writings. The editors have gathered contributed materials from a great variety of writers from very diverse backgrounds with expertise on Lewis and the topics related to Lewis, and placed them in a one-volume encyclopedia.

The fifty-seven page biography by John Bremer at the front of the book is quite detailed and impressive. Bremer includes material that this writer did not know about Lewis even after reading several full-length biographies on Lewis. Bremer provides solid information on Lewis' life but the focus is on Lewis's literary career and how Lewis' works were received in his lifetime.

The alphabetized encyclopedia covers everything in Lewis' writing from *The Abolition of Man* to Yeats and from angels to women. The book is not easily read from cover to cover because of its encyclopedic structure, nevertheless, because of the amount of fascinating material in it and the depth of many of the topics covered, I found myself doing just that, reading through topic after topic in consecutive order. Many of the subjects covered are like reading independent articles on Lewis. For example there are nine full pages describing the letters of Lewis, three pages on Literary Criticism and Theory, and two pages on *The Screwtape Letters*. There are also numerous column or page length topical summaries of Lewis' view on such subjects as imagination, fantasy, satire, education, heaven, or hell. There are short paragraphs summarizing the multitude of Lewis' brief articles, such as "Myth Becomes Fact" or "Is Theism Important? A Reply." Charts listing all of Lewis' book dedicatees, all of the plays and films about Lewis, and charts on the versions of the Chronicles of Narnia are also included. The reader can discover what Lewis meant by chronological snobbery, Blimpophobia, or the Anthoposophy of Rudolf Steiner that was embraced by Lewis' close friend Owen Barfield. One can examine the list of books from a 1962 article where Lewis posted the ten books that most influenced his philosophy of life.

This encyclopedia is packed with scholarly information, yet is also surprisingly readable. It has become a great resource for my lectures and college courses on Lewis. Any person who wants to engage Lewis in further study, who wants further information on a subject Lewis speaks about or who wants to know where in Lewis' primary works to find his comments on various topics, then this text is an invaluable tool. It is an excellent compliment to the *Quotable Lewis*, edited by Wayne Martindale and Jerry Root in 1989, where Lewis is directly quoted on various topics in alphabetized order.

Mark Hamilton

Book Notes
Brief reviews by the editor

John W. Miller, *The Origins of the Bible: Rethinking Canon History*. Theological Inquiries. New York/ Mahwah: Paulist, 1994. 250 pp., paperback, $18.95.

Canon, the extent and content of Scripture, is an important and vexing problem, as evidenced by disagreements between folks like Marcion, Luther, the Mormons, and the Taliban. Miller holds that the reform movement under Ezra and Nehemiah was key for the canonization of the Hebrew scriptures. The book concludes with an annotated bibliography. For college and seminary libraries.

Duane Christensen, *Bible 101: God's Story in Human History*. N. Richland Hills, TX: D & F Scott Publishing, 1998. xv + 248 pp., paperback, $19.95.

This is a textbook introducing the Word of God as it became canon in the Bible, its transmission history, and its authority. Aimed toward laity or entry level

Book Reviews

classes, it uses some excellent pedagological approaches particularly aimed at engaging the reader in critical thought. Church, college and seminary libraries will find this volume of use.

Albert H. Baylis, *From Creation to the Cross: Understanding the First Half of the Bible.* Grand Rapids: Zondervan, 1996. 392 pp., hardcover, $24.99.

A quick run through the OT with useful timelines, maps, interaction questions, and suggested readings for each section. Coming from a conservative position, it at least acknowledges some critical issues (e.g. the date of the Exodus and Daniel) while virtually ignoring others (e.g. the authorship of the Pentateuch and of Isaiah). Useful for an introductory college or seminary level course. This volume would find a place in church, college and seminary libraries.

Henry J. Flanders, Jr., Robert W. Crapps, David A. Smith, *People of the Covenant: An Introduction to the Hebrew Bible,* 4th ed. New York/Oxford: Oxford University Press, 1996. 562 pp., hardcover, $59.95.

A beginning level introduction to the OT and its study from a 'moderate' Southern Baptist perspective. Following chapters on interpretation and history-geography, the books proceeds chronologically. A critically 'mainline' approach as regards such matters as Pentateuchal authorship (espousing the Documentary Hypothesis) and a late date Daniel, it would be very useful text for an introductory college level course if accompanied by careful teacher input, as is true for every textbook choice. The price makes it somewhat prohibitive, however. The volume should be in college and seminary libraries.

Larry R. Helyer, *Yesterday, Today and Forever: The Continuing Relevance of the Old Testament.* Salem, WI: Sheffield Publishing Company, 1996. xii + 459 pp., paperback, $23.95.

An interesting elementary introduction united by following several motifs such as the plan of salvation, faith and politics, faith and ethics, and faith and the future through the OT. While looking at content and context, this volume is more theological and applicational than most of its genre. It should serve its purpose well, and would be appropriate from college and seminary libraries. It is unfortunate, however, that so many conservative institutions such as publishers, and even colleges, see no ethical problem in adopting the name of already established and respected endeavors.

Victor H. Matthews and James C. Moyer, *The Old Testament: Text and Context.* Peabody, MA: Hendrickson, 1997. ix + 308 pp., hardcover, $29.95.

A well-conceived, though very brief, elementary introduction to the OT, a chronological survey of the material follows an introduction to tools of bibliography and method. They follow the uniting themes of covenant, universalism, wisdom and remnant. Strong on ancient Near Eastern context, the authors provide helps such as study questions and a glossary. Colleges and seminaries should have the volume in their libraries.

Watson E. Mills, Richard F. Wilson, ed., *Pentateuch/Torah*. Mercer Commentary on the Bible Vol. 1. Macon, GA: Mercer University Press, 1998. lviii + 226 pp., $19.95.

This volume, from a moderate Baptist press, brings together 10 articles on the Pentateuch from the *Mercer Dictionary of the Bible* (1997) and commentaries from the *Mercer Commentary on the Bible* (1994). It shows a mainline critical approach to Scripture, and would serve as a good student introduction to that particular perspective. The commentary lacks depth, due to its nature and audience, so readers will be quickly moved to more in depth studies. For college and seminary libraries.

C. Houtman, *Der Pentateuch: Die Geschichte seiner Erforschung neben einer Auswertung*. Biblical Exegesis and Theology 9. Kampen: Kok Pharos, 1994. xxii + 472 pp., paperback.

A very useful, detailed discussion of the question of Pentateuchal authorship and interpretation from the time of Christ up to the time of writing. The volume provides a needed update to H–J Kraus, *Geschichte der historisch-kritischen Erforschung des Alten Testaments*. All specialized biblical studies libraries need to have this book .

Duane L. Christensen, *Bible 101: The Torah: A Study Guide*. N. Richland Hills, TX: D & F Scott Publishing, 1998. xxii + 105 pp., paperback, $15.95.

This guide is one of six comprising a two-semester, undergraduate introduction to Bible course. It includes actual syllabus components, an introduction to inductive Bible study, and a survey of each of the Pentateuchal books. Considerable attention is given to literary structure, chiastic structures in particular. Study questions are scatted throughout, and some, called 'concept checks' are answered in the back. Good for personal, church, college and seminary libraries.

M. Vervenne and J. Lust, ed., *Deuteronomy and Deuteronomic Literature: Festschrift C.H.W. Brekelmans*. BETL 133. Leuven: University Press/ Peeters, 1997. xi + 637 pp., paperback, $97.00.

A volume in honor of a retired professor from the Catholic University in Leuven, the volume brings together 28 leading scholars writing in English, German. Spanish and French. The volume is divided into sections on Deuteronomy, the Deuteronomistic History, Pentateuchal composition and the deuteronomic traditions, and miscellaneous topics unrelated to the volume title. For academic and specialist libraries.

Book Reviews

Mark J. Boda, *Praying the Tradition: The Origin and Use of Tradition in Nehemiah 9.* BZAW 277. Berlin/New York: Walter de Gruyter, 1999. xiii + 284 pp., hardcover, 176 DM (approx. $85.00).

This Oxford University PhD thesis explores the important issue of how biblical texts employ earlier material, or intertextuality. Among other things, he finds his research to indicate that the author used an already completed Pentateuch similar to our own text. This is not a complete study of the chapter since it does not fully address literary concerns such as structure and the relationship of the chapter with the book as a whole, but it does help in understanding the text. For academic and specialist libraries due to its use of untranslated Hebrew.

Anneke Kaai and Eugene H. Peterson, *The Psalms: An Artist's Impression.* Downers Grove: InterVarsity, 1999. 55 pp., hardcover, $19.99.

A visual feast of 25 mainly abstract paintings, each of which are accompanied by the sections from Psalms which inspired them, taken from Peterson's translation, *The Message.* They are also accompanied by brief individual discussions of each work. The book serves as a welcome reminder that exegesis of a text need not only be text-bound. A good volume for one's coffee table, church and even public library.

Mark E. Cohen, *The Cultic Calendars of the Ancient Near East.* Bethesda, MD: CDL Press, 1993. Xxiii + 504 pp., hardcover, $37.50.

The historical study of the OT soon comes across problems with the calendric systems of Israel and the ancient Near East. Cohen here explores the cultic calendar, that is the timing of various religious festivals and other periodic observances. He divides the study chronologically (3rd millennium, early 2nd millennium, and second and first millennia BC), with a concluding chapter on festival themes. The volume is somewhat mistitled, since Egypt and the Hittites are not covered, but texts from Sumer, Akkad, Mari, Elam, Alalakh, Ugarit, and Israel (the Gezer Calendar being the sole representative) are studied. For academic and specialist libraries.

John H. Walvoord, *Prophecy in the New Millennium: A Fresh Look at Future Events.* Grand Rapids: Kregel, 2001. 176 pp., paperback, $10.99.

This volume shows that the old dispensationalism is unchanged for the new millennium. Written by a doyen of this hermeneutical approach, the former president of Dallas Theological Seminary, it is a very popular level overview using no secondary sources. Providing no hermeneutical justification for the approach, nor adequate indication that there are alternative hermeneutical views, one wonders if speaking *ex cathedra* is not solely a Catholic doctrine. For college and seminary libraries.

John J. McDermott, *What are they Saying about the Formation of Israel?* Mahwah, NJ: Paulist, 1998. iv + 115 pp., paperback, $10.95.

Addressing one of the most controversial historical issues facing OT scholarship, McDermott discusses available evidence and notes the 3 'classical' models of conquest, peaceful infiltration, and social revolution and himself suggests that Israel developed from a gradual Canaanite resettlement. He states that the discovery of future texts could lead to modification of this view, which is ironic since an already discovered text, the Bible, itself suggests that his approach needs modification. For seminary and specialist libraries.

Elizabeth Achtemeier, *Preaching Hard Texts of the Old Testament.* Peabody: Hendrickson, 1998. ix + 192 pp., paperback, $14.95.

Some texts from both Testaments are hard to preach for various reasons, including their presentation of God which makes us uncomfortable. While this might be our problem rather than that of Scripture, it is still difficult to know how to handle some texts. While not attempting to be exhaustive, Achtemeier looks at 32 passages from the aspects of 'plumbing the text' (exegesis) and 'forming the sermon' (interpretation and application). Useful in providing examples of interpretation, the volume will find a place in seminary libraries.

William Horbury, ed., *Hebrew Study from Ezra to Ben-Yehuda.* Edinburgh: T&T Clark, 1999. xiv + 337 pp., hardcover, $69.95.

A useful series of studies of the history of the study and preservation of Hebrew from the Persian period through the modern period. Written by 22 scholars who teach in Britain, the Netherlands and Germany, the volume should find a place in specialist OT and Semitics libraries.

Jacob Neusner and William S. Green, ed., *Dictionary of Judaism in the Biblical Period: 450 B.C.E. to 600 C.E..* Peabody, MA: Hendrickson, 1999. xxvi +693 pp. hardcover, $59.95

An unmodified reprint of the 2 volume work with the same title published in 1996 by MacMillan. Lacking any updating, and still lacking any bibliographic resources, libraries with the first edition need not purchase this. It is a useful, popular level reference volume which should at least in some form be in college and seminary libraries.

R. Samuel Thorpe, *A Handbook for Basic Biblical Exegesis.* Lanham MD/ Oxford: University Press of America, 1999. ix + 85 pp., paperback, $17.50.

A basic outline of exegesis with steps to cover for translation, textual analysis, linguistic, historical and literary analysis, theological interpretation, and application. Each step has examples and is accompanied by a bibliography. Appendices touch on English Bible translations, ancient texts and versions, examples of the Hebrew, Greek and English of selections from Numbers and Luke, a summary of the steps, a useful sample exegetical paper, and a complete bibliography. While students will find the volume useful, they will probably find that G. Fee, *NT Exegesis* and D. Stuart, *OT Exegesis* are more so, and cheaper.

Stanley E. Porter and Richard S. Hess, *Translating the Bible: Problems and Prospects*. Journal for the Study of the New Testament Supplement Series 173. Sheffield: Sheffield Academic Press, 1999. 336 pp., hardcover, $85.00.

13 articles by 11 scholars teaching in Britain, Canada, and the US. The three sections include: theory and method, discussing the Contemporary English Version, the responsibility of the translator toward reader or author (literal vs dynamic approaches), the LXX translational traditions today, and inspiration and translation; OT, with one translator's personal reflections, and discussions on Joshua and Judges 1–5; NT, looking at translation in the process of exegesis, the relevance of literary foregrounding for translation and interpretation, verbal tense and aspect, Philemon, and the differences between original and canonical texts. For academic and specialist libraries.

J. S. LaFontaine, *Speak of the Devil: Tales of Satanic Abuse in Contemporary England*. Cambridge/New York: Cambridge University Press, 1998. xi + 224 pp., hardback/paper, $64.95/15.95.

Unfortunately, the topic of sexual and ritual abuse is too important to ignore, as has been the approach by many in the past. This British social anthropologist sets out to explore the topic, following a topic raised by her previous report on ritual abuse in Britain. Linking ritual abuse to witchcraft such as that alleged at Salem allows her too easily to counter the former by association with the latter. Her blanket denial of organized ritual abuse seems to ignore available evidence. For academic libraries and those with specific interest in pastoral care issues.

Richard Abanes, *American Militias: Rebellion, Racism & Religion*. Downers Grove: InterVarsity, 1996. x + 296 pp., paperback, np.

Although unfortunately out of print due to the tardiness of this note, this volume is all too relevant in the light of recent terrorist activities undertaken by religious fringe elements. Here is the necessary reminder that bigotry is not just elsewhere, but is right in our own heartland. The volume deserves a place in church and academic libraries.

Walter A. Elwell and J. D. Weaver, *Bible Interpreters of the 20th Century: A Selection of Evangelical Voices*. Grand Rapids: Baker Book House, 1999. 447 pp., paperback, $24.99.

35 Caucasian (except for 1), male (except for 1) biblical interpreters are provided with a biography, their scholarly development, an evaluation of their contributions, and a bibliography of primary sources. Of possible use as a reference volume, its actual audience is not clear. For seminary libraries.

Gil Alexander–Moegerle, *James Dobson's War on America*. Amherst, NY: Prometheus, 1997. 306 pp., hardcover, $29.00.

Written by a co-founder with Dobson of Focus on the Family, this volumes seeks to critique some of his theologically and politically conservative beliefs and practices. While well-founded critique of any leader is necessary and can be valuable, one must also ask whether a study by a former, apparently disgruntled, employee might be swayed in ways a more neutral critic might avoid. After careful evaluation, the volume could find a place in church and academic collections.

C. Dennis McKinsey, *Biblical Errancy: A Reference Guide*. Amherst, NY: Prometheus Books, 2000. 852 pp., hardcover, $135.00.

A curious book intended to provide ammunition against those who believe in scripture. Arranged alphabetically by topic from abortion to works, passages which are deemed most problematic are marked. This is a good example of why a basic understanding of hermeneutics and exegetical method can spare one a lot of grief. Not suitable for many libraries, unless as a resource for apologetics courses, and then the price far outweighs its marginal usefulness.

Nicholas Wolterstorff, *John Locke and the Ethics of Belief*. Cambridge Studies in Religion and Critical Thought. New York/ Cambridge: Cambridge University Press, 1996. xxi + 248 pp., hardcover and paperback, $59.95/ 19.95.

Wolterstorff, one of the world's leading philosophers who is also an evangelical, studies the thought of one of the leading Enlightenment philosophers. Locke argues against belief based on tradition but rather belief based on reason. Wolterstorff discusses the debate between Locke and Hume, comparing their approaches to that of Descartes. For academic and specialist libraries.

D. G. Hart and R. Albert Mohler, Jr., *Theological Education in the Evangelical Tradition*. Grand Rapids: Baker Book House, 1996. 320 pp., paperback, $24.99.

This book well reflects its title. In 5 parts by 18 authors, the volume looks at the breadth of the evangelical movement (Baptist, early Methodist Episcopal, Holiness, and Presbyterian and Methodist traditions) as it relates to theological education, spiritual formation and theological education, women and theological education, church–academy relations (particularly looking at England, the Netherlands and Canada), and theological education's future. There is also a 7 page bibliographic essay. For seminary and specialist libraries.

Book Reviews

Dennis D. Martin, translator, *Carthusian Spirituality: The Writings of Hugh of Balma and Guigo de Ponte*. The Classics of Western Spirituality. New York/Mahwah: Paulist Press, 1997. xxiv + 356 pp., paperback, $23.00.

The Carthusians rose in the 11th century and especially flourished three centuries later, immediately following the writing of these two authors. The book begins with a 66 page introduction and closes with almost a hundred pages of notes and bibliography. Hugh's own words could summarize the aim of the volume: "This book aims to attend to how the soul might aspire with all her heart to union with the Bridegroom" (119). Part of an extensive series from across the Protestant, Catholic, Orthodox, Jewish, and other traditions, this volume should be in specialist libraries.